Praise for *The Smartest Places on Earth*

"An absolutely fascinating tour of cities in the United States and Europe that were once traditional centers of manufacturing which are now re-inventing themselves as hubs of innovation. If you want to understand how economies at the local level can transform themselves, this is the book to read."—**Liaquat Ahamed, author of *Lords of Finance***

"Van Agtmael and Bakker paint an exciting picture of the future based on progress made possible by cooperative processes they call 'brainsharing.' Citing unheralded developments in specific places and specific industries, this extraordinarily well researched book challenges the conventional view of a developed world in relative decline. The authors make a compelling case for the role of connectors, who bring together a diverse collection of players required for collaborative success. This compellingly argued and lucidly written book is a must read for anyone who cares about the future of the planet."
—**David F. Swensen, Chief Investment Officer, Yale University**

"A lively, lucid story of innovation and transformation powered by brainpower and business, academe, and regional governments working together . . . the smartest book on one of the most important and promising trends in the American and global economy."
—**Strobe Talbott, President, Brookings Institution**

"In every chapter of economic history, unexpected places have cultivated the dynamism that transforms society at large. Antoine van Agtmael and Fred Bakker describe how the next generation of emerging hotspots are located in unlikely places, as industry connects with the energy of universities and academic medical centers to transform rustbelts into 'brainbelts.' This scouting report will interest students of the future taking shape today."—**Richard Brodhead, President, Duke University**

"This eye-opening account of innovation in unlikely places will raise the spirits of anyone discouraged by the gurus who keep telling us the future belongs not to the established democracies of the capitalist world, but to emerging powers mostly in Asia. No, van Agtmael and Bakker tell us, the 'smartest places on earth' may be in little-heralded cities in the United States and northern Europe, where business people, scientists and creative managers are inventing smart new products and ingenious new ways to manufacture them. They tell us that many of the old economies of the developed world 'are entering a revolutionary new phase' because 'the global competitive advantage is shifting from cheap to smart.' I found

their arguments, and the facts they have gathered to support them, both intriguing and convincing. And their book is fun to read."
—**Robert G. Kaiser, former Managing Editor of the** *Washington Post* **and author**

"This book upends conventional wisdom about how the global economy works and which places are primed to thrive and prosper. Van Agtmael and Bakker capture the complex market dynamics that are revaluing the formidable assets of U.S. and European older industrial cities: advanced industries and networks of universities, companies and governments that collaborate to compete. These are refreshing insights that build on real world experience and evidence rather than antiquated group think."
—**Bruce Katz, Brookings Institution Centennial Scholar, coauthor of** *The Metropolitan Revolution*

"The authors offer a compelling and insightful look at how companies and communities are turning ashes into silicon valleys."
—**Harold L. Sirkin, Senior Partner, The Boston Consulting Group (BCG)**

"The riveting story of how failing rustbelts in the United States and Northern Europe have transformed themselves into emerging brainbelts through the triumph of collaboration and ingenuity to become promising models of bottom-up innovation."
—**Hilda Ochoa-Brillembourg, Founder and Chairman, Strategic Investment Group**

"Antoine van Agtmael and Fred Bakker have written a serious book that anyone with an interest in business, technology, innovation, or the future of the world economy should read. It looks at the trends that are redefining the way the world works but have not yet been fully appreciated or understood—but that will drive future growth and the creation of new opportunities. Given van Agtmael's exceptional record as an investor and major trend spotter throughout his career, his views and insights deserve special attention."
—**David Rothkopf, CEO and editor of the FP Group**

"Van Agtmael and Bakker take us on a joy ride to understand the importance of smart people forming bonds of trust in far-flung places. Welcome to the new world of manufacturing, where freedom to innovate trumps cheap labor, putting the US and Europe back at the center of the global economy."
—**Jessica Einhorn, former Dean, School of Advanced International Studies at Johns Hopkins University**

THE
SMARTEST
PLACES ON EARTH

THE
SMARTEST
PLACES ON EARTH

*Why Rustbelts Are the Emerging
Hotspots of Global Innovation*

● ●

ANTOINE VAN AGTMAEL
and FRED BAKKER

PUBLICAFFAIRS
New York

Published in the United States by PublicAffairs™, a Member of the Perseus Books Group

Printed in the United States of America.

PublicAffairs books are available at special discounts for bulk purchases in the United States by corporations, institutions, and other organizations. For more information, please contact the Special Markets Department at the Perseus Books Group, 2300 Chestnut Street, Suite 200, Philadelphia, PA 19103, call (800) 810-4145, ext. 5000, or e-mail special.markets@perseusbooks.com.

Library of Congress Cataloging-in-Publication Data

Names: Agtmael, Antoine W. van, author. | Bakker, Alfred, author.
Title: The smartest places on earth : why rustbelts are the emerging
   hotspots of global innovation / Antoine van Agtmael and Fred Bakker.
Description: First edition. | New York : PublicAffairs, [2016] | Includes
   bibliographical references and index.
Identifiers: LCCN 2015036396| ISBN 9781610394352 (hardcover) | ISBN
   9781610394369 (ebook)
Subjects: LCSH: Technological innovations—United States. |
   Academic-industrial collaboration—United States. | Research,
   Industrial—United States. | Industries—United States. | Industrial
   Location—United States. | Entrepreneurship—United States.
Classification: LCC HC110.T4 .A645 2016 | DDC 338/.0640973—dc23
LC record available at http://lccn.loc.gov/2015036396

First Edition

10 9 8 7 6 5 4 3 2 1

For my granddaughter Victoria, who will grow up
in the world that is the subject of this book
—A. v. A.

For Frances, Sam, and Jim
—F. B.

CONTENTS

WELCOME TO THE BRAINBELT

The People, Places, and Practices
That Are Turning Globalization on Its Head

The central idea of this book—that the revitalization of former rustbelt areas is bringing new competitiveness to the United States and Europe—developed for each of the authors from two very different starting points.

For Antoine, the thinking was sparked by comments like those he heard in conversation with David Ku, the chief financial officer of Mediatek, a leading designer of chipsets for smartphones and other products, based in Taiwan. It was the spring of 2012, and Antoine, newly free from the responsibilities of managing the multibillion-dollar investment firm he founded and built, had been traveling through Asia, discussing with senior business executives and political leaders the challenges they saw to the competitive advantage they had held for the past many years in the global marketplace. Ku, who has experience in the global financial industry in addition to his career in high-tech manufacturing, was showing Antoine around the Mediatek facility in Hsinchu City, when Antoine asked him about the global market. "You know," Ku said, "We are facing much stronger American competition again." Antoine asked him to elaborate. What kind of competition? From whom? Ku, who earned his MBA from the University of Illinois and understands the American market, immediately mentioned Qualcomm, the tech giant based in San Diego, as a particular threat. "Their R&D is so advanced, so far ahead of ours," Ku explained. Antoine saw that Ku was genuinely concerned about the situation. "They can easily squeeze us," said Ku and then changed the subject. Antoine, who coined the term "emerging markets" in 1981 when he was at the International Finance Corporation (IFC), the private-sector-oriented affiliate of the World Bank, and had spent much of his career focused on Asia, had not heard an Asian businessperson complain about being squeezed by American competitors for at least two decades. Was Mediatek an anomaly? Or was this an early signal of an important trend? Could it be that developed countries had created an advantage in design and manufacturing that worried the low-cost producers in Asia?

For Fred, thinking along these lines was also inspired by travels. Recently retired from his position as editor in chief of *Het Financieele Dagblad,* the major financial newspaper in Holland, Fred was journeying through Mexico, Indonesia, South Korea, and Turkey (the MIST countries), talking with businesspeople, politicians, researchers, and entrepreneurs about their views on where global business was headed. He heard several comments that were similar to those made to Antoine by David Ku. The low-cost labor advantage that companies in the MIST countries had leveraged for the past couple of decades to gain economic growth was losing power, Fred was told. Making things cheap to gain an edge over high-cost Western companies just wasn't cutting it anymore. The days of the low-cost advantage were essentially over.

In addition, Fred saw that the way companies were working was changing. When in 2011 the city of Eindhoven, Holland, was selected as the smartest region in the world by the Intelligent Community Forum (ICF), an American think tank that makes the award annually, Fred was reminded of a conversation he had had with Gerard Kleisterlee, the former CEO of Philips, some years earlier. Kleisterlee had explained how the electronics giant had transformed its once-thriving research lab in Eindhoven—whose reputation rivaled that of Bell Labs in the United States—into an open-innovation campus, where researchers from different institutions and companies could collaborate. Certainly, this kind of activity must have contributed to Eindhoven's recognition as a center of innovation, one of the smartest places on earth?

These comments and observations contradicted the Western conventional wisdom that had prevailed for some time. Just a few years earlier, at a conference in the Netherlands, for example, Rem Koolhaas, the renowned architect and astute observer of global business, had provoked his audience by showing a map of the world, redrawn with a shrunken United States at the global margin and the emerging countries dominating the center. At the time, financial analysts were often heard lamenting that Europe would soon become the "museum of the world."

Travels completed for the time being, Antoine returned to the Washington, DC, area where he lives, and Fred went home to Amsterdam. But, in our separate ways, intrigued by what we had heard and observed, we began to explore these ideas further. Was it possible that a new form of manufacturing, this time based on sophisticated R&D, was having some kind of renaissance in the developed countries? Could it be true that cheap labor was no longer the advantage for the developing countries it had once been? Was there a new spurt in the processes of innovation and product development?

To learn more, Fred went on further travels, primarily in Europe, and what most captured his interest was what he heard from chief technology officers about process. Increasingly, they said, they were working in collaboration with multiple partners, often universities and even government agencies, because their companies could no longer bear the cost of research alone and because they needed specific expertise they did not have, or did not want to establish, in house. Antoine hit the road again, too, visiting research labs and factories, primarily in the United States (after a long career spent traveling in Asia and Latin America), and became intrigued by the changes he saw, particularly the reinvented role of research in product creation, as well as the use of advanced production methods such as robotics and 3D printing.

In January 2013, while we were developing these ideas separately, we were introduced by a mutual friend, and a Skype chat led to a meeting and several days of conversation. Although we both believed (and still do) that the global economy's center of gravity was shifting toward emerging markets, we also agreed that competitiveness from companies in the United States and Europe was on the rise again after many years of being on the defensive. Exactly how or why, we weren't completely sure, but we had a theory: after several decades of a near-obsession with making things as cheap as possible, the next decades would focus on making things as smart as possible. Smart innovation, rather than cheap labor, would be the key competitive edge, and leading tech companies such as Apple and Google offered proof.

Our thinking continued to evolve. Fred wrote an essay analyzing what he had learned about Eindhoven. Antoine shared the article with Bruce Katz, of the Metropolitan Policy Program of the Brookings Institution, and Bruce decided to visit Eindhoven with Fred to see what was going on. He was impressed but not completely surprised. He suggested that Eindhoven had unique features, such as the revolutionary developments in the supply chain, but that similar places existed in the United States, such as Albany, New York, and Akron, Ohio, and many others.

The evidence accumulated. General Electric had sited a new production facility in the United States rather than in a low-cost labor location, which is what the company would have done a decade earlier.[1] And this was not any factory; it was for the production of next-generation aircraft engines, a central element of GE's business. This was a compelling model, proof that major American companies were bringing some of their most important manufacturing operations back to the United States. What struck us in particular was the exact location of the new facility: a town called Batesville, Mississippi. Why there? According to Jeffrey Immelt, CEO of GE, the reason was that Batesville was right next door to Mississippi State University, whose researchers had amassed tremendous knowledge of new materials of the kind that would be needed in the creation of the next generation of superlight, ultraquiet, extremely fuel-efficient aircraft engines. And that's exactly what happened. The iconic global corporation worked closely with the little-known educational institution, with results so positive that Immelt vowed to locate more GE production sites within spitting distance of other hotbeds of cutting-edge research.

If GE, one of the most professionally managed corporations in the world, was bringing research, development, and manufacturing activities to the hinterlands of the United States, we had to take notice. Neither Batesville nor Eindhoven was likely to make any list of the world's most successful innovation hubs, which has long been topped by the amazing concentrations of brainpower in Silicon Valley, California, and Cambridge, Massachusetts. Nor would they yet be mentioned in the same breath as advanced manufacturing centers such as Stuttgart, Germany. But we sensed they might eventually make the list—sooner rather than later—and that they were bellwethers of a hugely important phenomenon that was arising in similar cities and regions of the United States and Europe: areas that, in the United States, we call rustbelts, former industrial citadels that had been hit hard by offshoring, suffered decline, but were now coming back stronger than ever. Although the term "rustbelt" is not a familiar one to Europeans, the profile of the regions there was similar. These areas had been transforming themselves from also-rans into centers of innovation and smart manufacturing that we called "brainbelts."

We knew we needed to test our theory, and to do that, we needed more data. We decided to do more fieldwork, this time together, and started with a trip to Albany, in the Hudson Valley of New York, and Akron, Ohio. What we witnessed there filled us with excitement. We saw groups working in collaboration, new technologies and manufacturing methods being employed, and smart, value-added products being created. Cities and whole regions were being revitalized by the activities.

That trip turned into a two-year journey through the United States and Europe in which we visited ten locations. In Europe we went to Dresden, Germany; Eindhoven, the Netherlands; Lund-Malmö, Sweden; Oulu, Finland; and Zurich, Switzerland. With the help of Bruce Katz and his Brookings colleagues, we put five regions in the United States on our itinerary: in addition to Akron and Albany, we traveled to Minneapolis, Minnesota; Portland, Oregon; and Raleigh-Durham, North Carolina. We also conducted interviews with leaders in many other areas, participated in numerous conversations with people in various disciplines and positions around the world, and did our due research diligence—reading, reviewing material, and digging into the relevant data.

We realized there are many other examples of new, university-centered brain hubs, some of them former "rustbelts," whereas others were not anchored in an industrial past. Some are already well known, some others only just emerging. In the United States, Austin, Texas (information technology [IT] and biotechnology), was the most promising example of a new brainbelt that does not have an industrial history. Its high-tech area, Silicon Hills, started in the 1990s around the University of Texas, and companies such as IBM, Dell, and Oracle and now has at least fifteen incubators.[2] Other examples of brainbelts are Houston (energy) in Texas; Palm Bay (aerospace) and Gainesville (life science) in Florida; and Boulder (aerospace and life science) in Colorado. In Europe, we also see the phenomenon in Cambridge, United Kingdom; Stockholm and Göteborg, Sweden; Berlin and the Munich-Stuttgart region in Germany; Paris, Grenoble, and Toulouse in France; and Graz in Austria. Outside the United States and Europe are Seoul in South Korea; Singapore; Hsinchu in Taiwan; and Tel Aviv in Israel.

The discovery and creation process was an amazing experience for us, an economist and a journalist traveling the world, trying to understand what was going on, gradually accumulating evidence and steadily sharpening our thesis. We visited universities and community colleges, big corporations and tiny start-ups, laboratories and production facilities. We talked with senior executives in suits and start-up founders in jeans, researchers in cleanrooms and tinkerers in lofts, administrators of science parks and government officials in statehouse offices. They all told us about a process of innovation and the creation of products that involved collegial collaboration, open exchange of information, partnerships between the worlds of business and academia, multidisciplinary initiatives, and ecosystems composed of

Brainbelts

Country	Region	Name/Place	Focus	Universities, Research Institutes, Hospitals
United States **Well-known**				
California	West	Silicon Valley	IT, bioscience, electric car, next-gen bendable and wearable electronic devices	Stanford, University of California, Caltech
Massachusetts	East	Cambridge (and Route 128)	Bioscience, robotics	MIT, Harvard
Texas	South	Austin (Silicon Hills)	Computers, new materials, bioscience	University of Texas
Focus of this book				
North Carolina	Southeast	Durham-Raleigh-Chapel Hill (Research Triangle Park)	Bioscience, new materials, energy (LED)	Duke, UNC, NC State
New York	East	Albany (Hudson Tech Valley)	Semiconductors	SUNY, RPI
Ohio	Midwest	Akron	New materials, polymers	University of Akron, Kent State
Minnesota	Midwest	Minneapolis-St. Paul	Medical devices/bioscience	University of Minnesota
Oregon	West	Portland (Silicon Forest)	Bioscience	OHSU

Country	Region	Name/Place	Focus	Universities, Research Institutes, Hospitals
Others				
Pennsylvania	East	Pittsburgh	Robotics, IT	Carnegie Mellon
New York	East	Rochester	Photonics (link with Albany)	University of Rochester, SUNY
New York	East	Buffalo (Buffalo Billion, Riverbend)	Battery technology, clean energy	University of Buffalo, SUNY
New York	East	New York (Silicon Alley)/ New Jersey	IT, digital media, telecom, biotech	Cornell
Ohio	Midwest	Columbus	Bioscience, agribusiness	Ohio State University, Battelle Memorial Institute
Ohio	Midwest	Dayton	Aerospace, RFI, new materials, sensors	University of Dayton, National Air & Space Intelligence Center, Kettering
Michigan	Midwest	Ann Arbor	Bioscience, electronics, engineering	University of Michigan
Michigan	Midwest	Detroit-Oakland County (Automation Alley)	Automation, automotives	Wayne State University
Illinois	Midwest	Chicago (Golden Corridor)	Materials, IT, engineering, biotech	Northern Illinois University
Kansas	Midwest	Wichita	Aerospace, heavy machinery	Wichita State University
Missouri	Midwest	St. Louis (Cortex, Missouri Research Park)	Bioscience, ag-tech	Washington University, University of Missouri

Country	Region	Name/Place	Focus	Universities, Research Institutes, Hospitals
Minnesota	Midwest	Rochester	Life science	Mayo Clinic, University of Minnesota
Indiana	Midwest	Indianapolis	Biotech	Indiana Biosciences Research Institute
Washington	West	Seattle	Aerospace, automotives, IT, retail, biotech	University of Washington
Idaho	West	Boise (Boise Valley)	IT, engineering	University of Idaho, Idaho State University
No rustbelt background				
Utah	West	Salt Lake City-Ogden-Provo (Silicon Slopes)	IT, life science, automotives	Brigham Young University
Colorado	West	Boulder-Denver (Denver Tech Center)	Aerospace, life sciences, energy	University of Colorado, NREL's National Wind Technology Center, National Oceanic and Atmospheric Administration (NOAA)
Arizona	West	Tucson (Optics Valley)	IT, optics, aerospace, bio-science	University of Arizona
California	West	San Diego and Tech Coast	Defense, biotechnology, nanotechnology, wireless	University of California
California	West	Los Angeles metro	Bioscience, aeronautics, entertainment, defense	UCLA

Country	Region	Name/Place	Focus	Universities, Research Institutes, Hospitals
Texas	South	Houston	Energy, bioscience	Rice, University of Houston, Texas Southern, Texas Medical Center
South Carolina	South	Greenville	Automotives	
Florida	South	Palm Bay	Avionics	
	South	Gainesville	Life science	University of Florida, Shands Hospital, Veterans Affairs Medical Center
Alabama	South	Huntsville (Cummings Research Park)	Aerospace	University of Alabama, Huntsville Hospital system, NASA Space Flight Center
Mississippi	South	Batesville	Aerospace	Mississippi State University
Tennessee	South	Knoxville	Composite materials and process technology	Oak Ridge National Laboratory, University of Tennessee
DC region	East	Washington (Dulles Technology Corridor)	Defense, homeland security, biotech	Johns Hopkins, University of Maryland, George Washington University
Canada and Mexico				
Canada		Waterloo-Kitchener	Wireless, bioscience	University of Waterloo, Wilfrid Laurier

Country	Region	Name/Place	Focus	Universities, Research Institutes, Hospitals
Canada		Ontario	Aerospace	University of Toronto, Ryerson University, York University, Centennial College
Mexico		Monterrey	Biotechnology, mechatronics, nanotechnology	Monterrey Institute of Technology
Northern Europe In book				
Netherlands		Eindhoven (High Tech Campus)	Semiconductors, new materials	Technical University
Sweden		Lund-Malmö (Ideon)	Life science, new materials	Lund University
Finland		Oulu (Technopolis)	Medical instruments, wireless	Oulu University
Germany		Dresden (Silicon Saxony)	Semiconductors	Max Planck
Switzerland		Zurich	Life science	Technical University
Others				
United Kingdom		Cambridge (Silicon Fen)	Bioscience, engineering	Cambridge University
United Kingdom		Oxford (Science Park)	Bioscience, IT, clean tech	Oxford University
Germany		Munich-Karlsruhe-Stuttgart-Heidelberg (Isar Valley)	Automotives, robotics, bioscience	Fraunhofer, Stuttgart University, Heidelberg University, Karlsruhe Institute of Technology
Germany		Berlin (Silicon Allee)	IT	TU Berlin (Technical University), Humboldt University, Free University

Country	Region	Name/Place	Focus	Universities, Research Institutes, Hospitals
Germany		Aachen (E.ON Research Center)	Clean energy	Technical University of Aachen
Germany		Kaiserslautern (Silicon Woods)	IT	University of Kaiserslautern
Netherlands		Delft (Technopolis Innovation Park)	Cleantech, 3D printing, IT	Delft University
Netherlands		Enschede (Kennispark Twente)	New materials	University of Twente, Saxion
Netherlands		Wageningen	Agri-bio	Wageningen University
Netherlands		Heerlen (Avantis European Science and Biomedicine Park)	New materials	Zuyd University of Applied Sciences
Netherlands		Leiden (Bio Science Park)	Bioscience	University of Leiden
Sweden		Stockholm (Kista)	IT, robotics	Stockholm University
Denmark		Copenhagen (Science City)	Bioscience, clean tech	University of Copenhagen, Metropolitan University College
France		Grenoble (Giant Campus)	Nanotech, bioscience, clean tech	Grenoble Institute of Technology, Inria
France		Toulouse (Aerospace Valley)	Aerospace, agri-bio	University of Toulouse, University of Bordeaux
Israel		Tel Aviv (Silicon Wadi, Kiryat Atidim Hi-tech Zone)	IT, bioscience, plant bioscience	Tel Aviv University

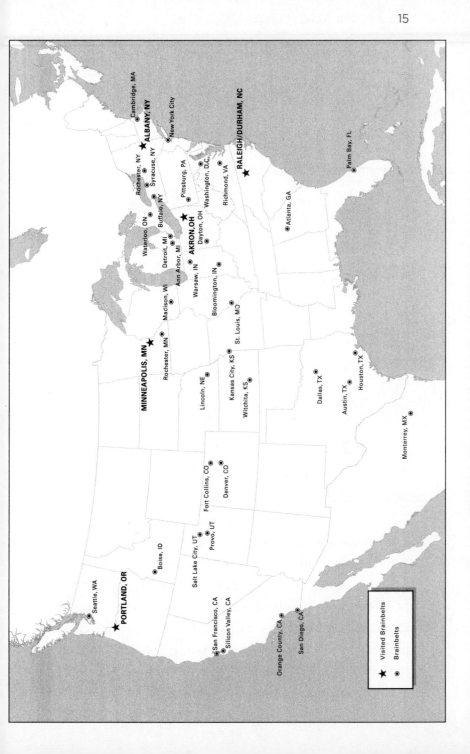

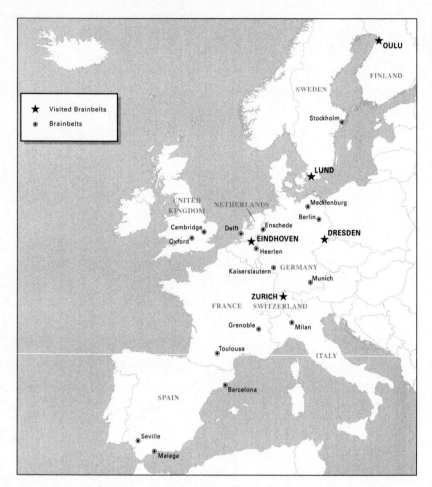

an array of important players, all working closely together. The much-storied model of innovation—featuring the solo genius or the brilliant pair of geeks in a garage—was no longer relevant in an era when new product development is expensive, multidisciplinary, and complex. And the brainbelt approach went far beyond the joint ventures and occasional project-based engagements we had seen before. We began to refer to it as the "sharing of brainpower."

With each visit, it became clearer that we were indeed witnessing a whole new phenomenon in which the sharing of brainpower was taking place in very unlikely places that were becoming hotspots of innovation. Most of these were cities and regions that had been ravaged by the outsourcing of the 1980s and 1990s and had formulated a new approach and kindled a new ambition. By sharing brainpower, they were achieving exactly what their Asian and MIST competitors were worried about: creating smart, complex products that delivered value far greater than products that could be created using the outdated, low-cost model.

But there was more to it than sharing brainpower through collaborative partnerships. There was the actual making of things. What we were seeing in such places as Batesville and Eindhoven was not, however, what journalists sometimes like to call a "return" to traditional manufacturing, but its reinvention. For some time, R&D had taken a backseat in the corporate enterprise, with disastrous consequences. But R&D got a new lease on life and got even smarter than before, when companies integrated it with manufacturing. Then, when low-cost sensors became available, it was possible to reintegrate all of the elements—information technology, data analytics, wireless communications, new production methods, new materials, and new discoveries. This created a new branch of the economy, which soon flourished. Companies in these brainbelts had no intention of firing up the old equipment and hiring back laid-off workers to run the assembly lines. No way. These facilities were radically different, like the GE plant in Batesville: smart, clean, flexible, and operated by processes that integrated electronics and mechanics. The people engaged in the facilities worked in teams of specialists and professionals, some with advanced-skills training, some with PhDs, and, yes, some retrained former line workers. And the products that emerged were innovative, connected, customized, and of high quality—as complex as a jet engine or as seemingly simple as an athletic shoe. This was by no means your father's manufacturing—things fashioned by the repetitive interplay of hand and machine—but rather smart manufacturing: very clever things created by the creative interaction of skilled workers and professionals with smart technologies.

So it was this combination of sharing brainpower and smart manufacturing that was turning global competitiveness on its head and making people like David Ku shake their heads with concern. *Cheap was giving way to smart.* And there was no immediate response for the low-cost producers in the emerging economies because it is the "old" economies, such as those of North America and Northern Europe, that have the necessary elements in place to create brainbelts: research facilities with deep, specialist knowledge; educational institutions; governmental support for basic research; appealing work and living environments; capital; and, most important, the atmosphere of trust and the freedom of thinking that stimulates unorthodox ideas and accepts failure as a necessary part of innovation—different from the hierarchical, regimented thinking so prevalent in many Asian and MIST economies.

Which is not to say that the sharing of brainpower and the development of brainbelts looks exactly the same in the United States as it does in Europe. Indeed, there are fundamental differences that pertain to infrastructure, history, and culture. The United States is a world power with a huge defense budget, some of which is allocated to R&D activities through agencies such as the Defense Advanced Research Projects Agency (DARPA) and the National Aeronautics and Space Administration (NASA). Many innovations—including the Internet, drones, and the self-driving car—originated in DARPA and NASA initiatives. What's more, the National Institutes of Health (NIH) has a major impact on fundamental health research through its funding of projects.

Much innovation in the United States is also driven by start-up companies, funded by venture capitalists and operating as privately held concerns until they are big and successful enough to make a public offering or are purchased by a larger, established leader in their market.

In Europe, there is no common defense budget. Some countries, such as France and Sweden, conduct research on fighter aircraft and naval vessels. But the market is fragmented and the national budgets, as a percentage of the country's gross domestic product (GDP), are much smaller than that of the United States. Europe lives under the security umbrella of the United States, so high-tech innovation does not receive massive support from the military. Neither is there a coordinated, European Union–wide health research budget. Nor is the level of start-up activity as significant in Europe as it is in the United States, although that is slowly changing. Instead, innovation in Europe has been stimulated through national research institutes—including the Fraunhofer in Germany, the Netherlands Organisation for Applied Scientific Research (TNO), and the Swiss Federal Laboratories for Materials Science and Technology (EMPA) in Switzerland—as well as funding agencies like Sweden's innovation agency, VINNOVA, and the Finnish Funding Agency for Technology and Innovation (Tekes), which is an organization of the Finnish Ministry of Employment and the Economy. These are little known in the United States. In an era of collaboration, Europe leverages this fragmentation in a creative way, however, by requiring the cofunding of projects. Both situations have their advantages and disadvantages, which affect how former rustbelts make their transformations to brainbelts.

Our thinking, therefore, is influenced by some of these fundamental differences. Antoine grew up in the Netherlands but has lived primarily in the United States since 1968, while Fred has lived in Holland his whole life, although he has traveled extensively around the world. The result of our own sharing of brainpower is this book, which tells the story of our journey and presents the results of our research. We also make the argument that these brainbelts can serve as models for other areas, offering principles and practices that can be adapted to the particular character and assets of cities and regions that want to gain a global advantage. Beyond that, as the model becomes better understood and the processes more defined, it will take less time for an area in decline to regenerate itself and become an innovative player in its markets and industries.

So, our message is an extremely positive one: the economies of the United States and Northern Europe are regaining their competitive edge. Not only are they reinventing manufacturing, creating new jobs, and revitalizing regions, they are—and this is perhaps most important of all—developing new products and technologies that will transform just about every aspect of our daily lives: vehicles and transportation, homes and cities, farming and food production, medical devices and health care. Everyday products such as shoes and clothing will be made competitively again in the West, and these products will not only fit, look, and feel better and be more versatile and sustainable but will cost no more to make, nor be more expensive to buy.

Ultimately, this new paradigm will do more than revitalize Western enterprise. Yes, for a time, the sharing of brainpower, combined with smart manufacturing, will shift the competitive advantage back to the developed world, and developing economies will struggle to close the innovation gap. But, in the longer run, it will bring benefits for the entire world by making smart products that help address challenges that affect us all.

With this new approach to creating smart products, then, Europe need not end up as a museum, the United States will not be pushed to the margin of the world map, and the creation of innovative twenty-first-century products need not be a zero-sum game. While Silicon Valley and Cambridge and the other established innovation centers will surely continue to thrive, the list of the smartest places on earth will look very different in the years to come.

Welcome to the brainbelt.

Chapter One

SHARING BRAINPOWER AND SMART MANUFACTURING

How a Rustbelt Becomes a Brainbelt

In the 1960s we had a space race. Today it is a robot race.

—DANISH TECHNOLOGICAL INSTITUTE

Despite all that we had heard and read about brainbelt areas such as Batesville and Eindhoven and many others, when we set off on our journey we confess that we still had the rustbelt stereotype in our minds. We expected to find crumbling industrial sites, to drive through dilapidated neighborhoods, to meet with people struggling hard to keep their heads above water, and to miss the enjoyment of a good glass of wine or a memorable meal.

What we discovered—about smart manufacturing and its technologies, sharing brainpower and the products being created in the brainbelts, as well as local cuisine—quickly blew those images out of our heads, even though the transformations are far from complete and have often created losers and gaping disparities in the process. A single conversation with Luis Proenza, for example, might have been enough to change our thinking (although we had many more like it). Proenza was then president of the University of Akron and had been instrumental in revitalizing the city, indeed, the whole region of Northeast Ohio, turning it into a center of excellence in the field of new materials. We met him and his group of international colleagues for dinner at a trendy restaurant in the renovated downtown area. Akron, Ohio, long the center of the global tire industry, had slipped into decline as tire production went offshore. But Proenza was brimming with enthusiasm for the region, its people and organizations, and the work they were doing, and he had a glowing vision of its future. He proudly told us that the 1,000 start-ups in the area employed more people now than the four big tire companies had in the region's manufacturing heyday.

In Sweden, we visited Lund and the nearby city of Malmö, which had taken a serious blow in the mid-1980s when the major shipyard in the area went bankrupt, another victim of the low-cost advantage of manufacturers in Asia and elsewhere. In response, local politicians, entrepreneurs, and Lund University came together to create Ideon, Scandinavia's first technology park, in Lund. Ericsson brought its research group to the park, as did many pharmaceutical companies. Today, the leaders of the cities of Malmö and Lund meet regularly, and Lund University is the engine that drives the corporate spin-offs that create cutting-edge products for the life-sciences industries.

In North Carolina, we visited the Research Triangle Park (RTP)—surrounded by the three university cities of

Durham, Raleigh, and Chapel Hill—the first park of its kind in the United States. In its early days, the RTP had been a roaring success, attracting 170 companies and creating employment for over 40,000 people. But they operated in ways that were customary at the time—in isolated buildings hidden among trees, guarding their ideas, working in secrecy, keeping disciplines separated. As the emerging economies zoomed forward, the inevitable happened, and the RTP lost some of its cachet. What we found in 2013, however, was evidence that the new brainbelt model was spreading its wings right next door to the RTP. In Durham, Duke University had set up an incubator in the renovated buildings of the old Lucky Strike factory. In Raleigh, North Carolina State University's Centennial Campus had become a whole new type of research campus where promising start-ups, big companies such as the Swedish-Swiss ABB and German Mann, have labs and offices right on campus, working jointly with university researchers on projects around new materials, clean energy, and smart grids. We could see young entrepreneurs everywhere.

What Sharing Brainpower Looks Like

The brainbelts of course look to leaders such as Apple and Google, Stanford University and the Massachusetts Institute of Technology (MIT), and the iconic innovation zones of Silicon Valley and Cambridge for inspiration and models, but each one develops in its own distinct ways. From our two years of research, we learned that every brainbelt—including those we visited and the many others we did not travel to—share a number of characteristics. In particular, they:

- Take on *complex, multidisciplinary, and expensive challenges* that could not be handled by any single player (an individual or organization) alone. The lone, iconic innovator is an outdated concept.

- Are driven by a *connector*, an individual or group with vision, relationships, and energy that is largely responsible for establishing and building the ecosystem.

- Operate in a *collaborative ecosystem* of contributors, with research universities at their center and typically composed of start-ups, established companies with a thriving research function, local government authorities, and community colleges or similar vocational institutions. Health-care institutions, such as teaching hospitals, are often a part of the ecosystem, as well.

- *Focus* on one, or just a few, particular disciplines or activities.

- Are *open to sharing knowledge* and expertise. To facilitate openness, the organizations are *de-siloed*. The walls between academia and industry and public governance have been taken down. The sharp separations between academic disciplines, such as chemistry, physics, mathematics, and biology, have been removed.

- Contain *physical centers*, such as incubators and start-up spaces, often within modernized factory or warehouse complexes, that house and encourage collaborative efforts.

- Foster an *environment that acts as a magnet* for talent. The area offers not only an existing talent pool in universities, research institutes, and start-ups but also non-work attractions and benefits, such as affordable housing, a variety of cafés and restaurants, good schools, and recreational activities.

- Have *capital* available. There is sufficient money available for investment in start-ups and spin-offs, as well as for facilities and incubators.

- Have an *understanding* and *acknowledgment of threat*. Unlike the days when corporate researchers did not worry much about outside competitive forces, people in brainbelts recognize that the region has been hit before and could be threatened again. This leads to a strong sense of identity, regional pride, and activities of continuous improvement.

Ecosystem: A Network of Organizations and Individuals, Linked by a Connector

A brainbelt is more than a collection of entities conveniently co-located in an appealing region. Each brainbelt is a tightly woven, collaborative ecosystem of contributors, typically composed of research universities, community colleges, local government authorities, established companies with a thriving research function, and start-ups, usually supported by a variety of supporters and suppliers, including venture capitalists, lawyers, design firms, and others. These different types of entities establish their own unique identity as they share knowledge, interact, form a community, grow, and improve.

Besides a major research university, a brainbelt ecosystem usually includes a major corporation, a global player, such as Intel in Portland, Oregon. Big companies bring a special and necessary ingredient to the brainbelt because they feel the cold wind of global competition more keenly than start-ups, and certainly more so than regional, technical, and educational institutions. Therefore, they understand that regional collaboration is often crucial to gaining a competitive advantage. Furthermore, researchers in big private-sector companies, like Intel, know viscerally that conducting research for its own sake is no longer tenable and their development efforts must lead to marketable products. They can no longer sequester themselves, as they once did, in the safety of well-funded R&D enclaves, devoting their careers to fascinating lines of inquiry that don't create value for the company. The bottom line is top of mind for them, and R&D budgets are not what they used to be. These companies understand that corporate R&D, with its internal bureaucracy and hierarchy, is often stymied in developing unorthodox ideas, and thus the necessity arises to partner with outsiders that lack the capital and global organization to bring new products to market but also have fewer disciplinary barriers and bureaucratic complications. A company like Intel can offer its superfast computing in analyzing the new knowledge created by university researchers, who, in turn, are able to give them access to unique, massive data sets.

As a result, these big companies, ones that in earlier times might have worked in glorious isolation, come to feel a genuine connection with the brainbelt area. They invest in its facilities and people, which further strengthens both the company and the region. For example, Intel's Portland campuses comprise the company's "largest and most comprehensive site in the world—a global center of semiconductor research and manufacturing and the anchor of Oregon's economy. The company has nearly 17,500 employees in Oregon, making it the state's largest private employer."[1] During our tour, we saw firsthand how important the presence of global players is to all the brainbelts we visited.

The big company, however, is just one player in the brainbelt ecosystem. There is always a *connector*—usually an individual but sometimes an organization—with vision, relationships, determination, clout, diplomatic skills, convincing power, and energy who is largely responsible for catalyzing the sharing of brainpower among multiple entities. The style of that connector influences the way a brainbelt will develop. Sometimes the individual connector is an entrepreneur, sometimes a scientist, sometimes a local politician or administrator. Whatever background connectors may have, they have a vision for the region and the ability to take heroic action to realize it.

In Zurich, for example, the connector was Michael Collasius, CEO of the Swiss branch of the German company Qiagen Instruments.[2] There were several companies in Zurich working in the field of laboratory equipment, but they did not collaborate extensively and no one of them alone could conduct the research needed to distinguish the area as a leader in the lab-equipment field. That changed when forensic researchers—major clients of the lab-equipment producers—wanted better, faster, and cheaper ways to do their work on DNA. In 2003, Collasius convinced the companies to join forces to create a research institution called ToolPoint. Today, more than thirty companies, all focused on some aspect of the creation of lab equipment (although not direct competitors), are part of the ToolPoint ecosystem. "Trust between all the participants is high," Hans Noser, director of ToolPoint told us, "which is promoted by their proximity."[3]

So, when big companies reach out, connectors bring groups together, and companies join forces in new initiatives, a community begins to develop. People start to feel a sense of identity and pride in the brainbelt. In various ways, they define a set of values and establish rules, some explicit and some tacit. Members of the brainbelt live by them in the knowledge that they can only succeed together.

Intriguingly, the strength of community often derives in part from an acknowledgment of threat. Unlike the days when corporate researchers did not worry much about outside competitive forces, people in brainbelts recognize that the region has been hit before and could be threatened again. Residents of Akron, Eindhoven, Portland, and elsewhere remember the good old days and also the troubled ones that followed. As things improve, the brainbelt comes to see itself as resilient and more able to take on new challenges as they arise.

Collaboration: Diverse Players Share Brainpower to Address Complex Challenges

The members of a brainbelt form connected ecosystems for a very particular reason: to take on complex and often expensive challenges that demand a multidisciplinary approach and cannot be handled by any single player alone. This requires a form of intensive collaboration that goes well beyond the kind of joint ventures and project partnerships we have seen in the past. These collaborations bring together people and organizations from the academic and business worlds—big companies and start-ups—with participation from government agencies as well as other players, such as philanthropists, venture capitalists, law firms, design studios, cultural institutions, incubators, public-private trade and industry organizations, and others.

This depth of collaboration between academia and commercial enterprises, in particular, is a relatively new phenomenon. Traditionally, academics and business did not mix. There were some important exceptions—most notably Bell Labs, NASA, and the US Department of Defense collaboration with industry in aerospace—but, as a rule, academics disdained entrepreneurs, and businesspeople distrusted anything that smacked of public-private partnerships.

Then, in the 1970s, that began to change. In Europe, Charles Weissmann, a professor at the Swiss Federal Institute of Technology in Zurich, founded Biogen, which became the first successful European biotech company. Now based in Cambridge, Massachusetts, it is the world's third-largest biotechnology company. In the United States, Genentech was founded by Herbert Boyer, a biochemist, with Robert A. Swanson, a venture capitalist, to pursue work in the field of recombinant DNA technology. These firms and others presented a new model to the academic world: serious researchers with the instincts and drive of the entrepreneur creating for-profit companies driven by research and focused on the creation of breakthrough products.

Jealous of the dominance of East Coast manufacturing and finance, researchers and entrepreneurs in the West had long been eying an opportunity to make their own mark. Their breakthrough came when researchers at Stanford (with its dean of engineering, Frederick Terman, serving as connector, starting in the 1950s) teamed up with scientists-entrepreneurs to develop the transistor, the integrated circuit, the microprocessor, the PC, the inkjet printer, and the precursor of the Internet.[4] Local entrepreneur Ralph Vaerst and journalist Don Hoefler coined the term "Silicon Valley" in 1971, to describe the area stretching between San Francisco and San Jose. There, where orchards once flourished, semiconductors made of silicon and lots of related, research-based industries became dominant, along with leading venture capital (VC) firms that backed many of the early start-ups.

The success of Silicon Valley demonstrated that patents generated by government-sponsored research should not stay on the shelf (as they often did) but that close collaboration between the government, universities, and entrepreneurs would stimulate the commercialization of unorthodox ideas as long as the required incentives were in place. This notion became the guiding principle behind the Bayh-Dole

Act of 1980, which allowed researchers and universities to benefit financially from research undertaken under government grants and would allow the Silicon Valley model to spread like wildfire all over the United States.

It took some time for the new models from Switzerland and Silicon Valley to take hold. Scientific research continued to be seen as sacrosanct and commercial application as a violation of the holy separation of science and commerce. But as new scientific insights, such as the mapping of the human genome, presented new opportunities for commercial applications, the application of academic research accelerated. Gradually, it became an accepted option for engineers, computer scientists, biologists, chemists, or physicists to start companies, and they usually did so by focusing on a specific activity related to their research, such as a new technology, drug, or material.

In Europe, regulatory changes forced the acceptance of such collaborative efforts. In 1991, for example, the Swiss government created a shock wave with a new law that required state universities, including the Federal Institute of Technology, to apply their research to the development of commercial products. Researchers had little choice but to seek new sources of funds, and contract work with commercial companies became a major source. It was the beginning of a trend, as other national governments in Europe cut the budgets of state-funded educational institutions.

Within large companies, the move for collaboration—with academics and with other business organizations, particularly start-ups—has been accelerated by corporate chief technology officers (CTOs) in companies as different as

Shell, Philips, ASML, Fokker, DSM (State Coal Mines), and Xerox. Leaders in these companies told us that cooperation with universities and start-ups, especially in the early stages of product development, is now standard practice—indeed, a no-brainer—for them and their companies. DSM, based in Heerlen in the southern Netherlands, for example, is a leader in the development of new materials. Marcel Wubbolts, chief technology officer of DSM, told us that his company had long been seeking to develop an energy source that did not rely on fossil fuels. "It is too complicated and too expensive to develop a second-generation biofuel on your own," Wubbolts said.[5] DSM partnered with the small American company POET and in early 2014 opened the first biofuel plant (using corn waste rather than corn) in Emmetsburg, Iowa, a town better known at the time for its gambling casino than for technology development.[6]

There is another important reason that companies cite for the move toward collaboration with outside partners: to keep abreast of what is happening in their industry and in adjacent fields of activity. There is so much research and innovation going on in so many places, it is impossible for any single organization to be aware of every development that might be relevant, including those developments that might pose a competitive threat. With the proliferation of start-ups and tiny companies working under the radar, the threat of a new technology emerging that could make a company's own research obsolete is ever-present. Pharmaceutical companies, in particular, see this kind of industrial reconnaissance through collaboration as essential. That's why Medtronic, Novartis, and Roche have established offices in science parks in Lund, Oulu, and Zurich (and of course have a major presence in Cambridge, too), where they can keep an eye on dozens of potential partners or competitors with the aim of investing in start-ups that do not have sufficient resources to test a new medicine. This, in turn, gives them access to the smaller company's knowledge and expertise beyond the specific project itself.

Focus and Openness: And the Necessity of Trust

The sharing of brainpower among a diverse set of players in a brainbelt ecosystem is most effective when the entities have the right mix of focus and openness. Focus means they concentrate their energies on a particular discipline or activity. Openness means they are open to sharing their knowledge and expertise with others.

Sharing is not known as a typical organizational behavior. What would compel an individual or a company that has focused its energies and resources on creating new knowledge to share it openly with others? One reason is obvious: necessity. There is no other way to pursue the kind of big, complex projects that characterize brainbelt initiatives. Mutual dependency demands that collaborators open up to each other. Another reason is less obvious: when a company is sharply focused, its commercial activities don't significantly overlap with those of its partners, so sharing knowledge is less likely to create a competitive threat.

In Portland, for example, an academic institution— the state-funded Oregon Health & Science University

(OHSU)—entered into a collaborative research project with a decidedly for-profit entity, the chip maker Intel, which has a major presence in the Portland area. The purpose of the initiative was to analyze a vast amount of cancer-related patient data that OHSU had gathered from around the world. The university did not have the capacity to manage "big data" at this scale and had no interest in developing it. Big data is the term for massive and complex collections of data, typically generated from many different sources and often in real time, that cannot be analyzed by the human brain or through traditional data-processing applications but require instead enormous processing power, high-level analytics, and sophisticated algorithms to yield proprietary and practicable insights. Intel did not have the kind of supercomputer power typically applied to the management of big data in medical research, but it could link computers together to manage OHSU's data in smaller batches, which was sufficient for the needs of the research.

In this extraordinary partnership, Oregon Health & Science University entrusted Intel with its huge store of patient data. In return, Intel allowed OHSU into its inner computing sanctum. The two were eager to work together because both parties needed the other's expertise, but there was virtually no risk they would end up competing. Added to those practical considerations were the sense of pride and identity in the Portland brainbelt and an understanding of the values and rules that prevailed. The collaboration, therefore, was based on commercial necessity and mutual trust. Both parties were so committed to working together and so unconcerned about potential violations that the project began before the formal contract was even finalized—almost unheard of in a big technology deal.

The importance of sharing brainpower and the necessity of openness has, as you can imagine, forced a change in structure and working relationships in business and academic organizations. The two had similar characteristics that got in the way of collaboration and innovation. They were typically hierarchical in nature, operated with organizational silos, and fiercely protected their intellectual property. In brainbelts, we found that entities—like OHSU and Intel—that have focused missions are very open to sharing their knowledge with other focused partners and collaborators. And they will do so at a very early stage of product development, when, traditionally, they would have kept the doors to the laboratory tightly shut.

Not only has the evolution of the innovation process changed the attitudes that business and academic entities have toward one other, it has caused a shift in how academics work together within their own institutions. As Shirley Ann Jackson, a Bell Labs veteran and now president of Rensselaer Polytechnic Institute, put it to us: "Cutting-edge research is now completely interdisciplinary. The major new discoveries are *between* the academic disciplines." So the sharp separations between academic disciplines—such as chemistry, physics, biology, mathematics, and engineering—are crumbling, and as new knowledge is gained, organizational silos are, as Jackson put it, "dying a slow, natural death."[7] As the walls crumble, collaboration blossoms still more luxuriantly.

Environment:
Attracting People and Catalyzing Ideas

A brainbelt is more than an ecosystem of disparate entities that have developed collaboration skills and mutual trust: it also features a distinct environment, one that acts as a magnet for talented people and focused businesses, and that supports their collaborative initiatives.

These environments feature physical elements that bring people together in appealing ways. Science parks, start-up incubators, shared-working facilities, and offices in renovated factory complexes are all there, sometimes grouped together in innovation districts. Such environments attract a young, mobile, and diverse talent pool of graduate students, entrepreneurs, engineers, corporate researchers, venture capitalists, designers, and others. Beyond the work environment itself, people choose a brainbelt area because of the availability of affordable homes and nonwork attractions and benefits, from cafés and restaurants to good schools and recreational activities. They have many informal opportunities to meet, interact, and stimulate each other's thinking.

Once word gets out about a brainbelt environment, it may start to take off. The number of start-ups increases. Large companies create spin-offs. More business plans are filed with potential investors. The global players who are in the area invest anew in talent and facilities and even open new units and initiate new endeavors, attracted by the availability of talent and the relatively low cost of operating in a former rustbelt, when compared to doing business in Silicon Valley or Boston. Forgotten downtown areas are developed or improved. New shops and businesses open. The tax base increases. Local services are bolstered or added. As companies achieve success and some enterprises are sold, new wealth is created, some of which is reinvested in the area. As collaboration develops and trust grows, local players begin to understand they are involved in something special.

Leaders, role models, and local heroes emerge. Entrepreneurs and researchers stay in the area and take on new roles, as mentors, coaches, investors, advisers, board members, partners, and teachers. They may invest in training programs, establish professional associations, and become the spokespeople and lobbyists for the interests of the brainbelt. They champion incubators and establish science parks. In Zurich, for example, the Technopark opened its doors in 1993 and is now home to more than three hundred start-ups employing more than 2,000 people. Lesley Spiegel, who spent five years as CEO of the Technopark, told us she spends most of her time now coaching entrepreneurs. The young people have plenty of enthusiasm, she said, but little management know-how. "I interact at any stage of their business, to suggest better ways of attracting people and approaching funders."[8]

Awakening Beauties: From Dormancy to Collaboration and Focus

We think of successful brainbelts—including all the ones we visited—as "awakening beauties." That's because, like the fairy-tale Sleeping Beauty, they have lain dormant for a long time—doomed to a state of inertia by the evil witches of policy or (lack of) leadership or faulty analysis—and have been given up for lost by entrepreneurs and investors. But, just because they lie inert does not mean they have lost everything. They still have their fine qualities. There is still energy, skill, knowledge, talent, and potential there.

Then something happens to bring the sleeper awake. In the fairy tale, it's a prince's kiss. In sleeping rustbelts, it's a bit more complicated. Beauties typically awake when an individual or a group reaches a tipping point of frustration or, often, when a new player arrives on the scene. Although people have long been aware of their area's dormancy, they have done little, just wishing and hoping that *something will happen*, perhaps in the form of a government bailout or the discovery of some unknown resource. At last, when it becomes clear that no solution is going to appear from out of the blue, a connector resolves to take matters into his or her own hands, and when that happens, people are ready to respond. The connector brings people together—politicians, entrepreneurs, scientists, executives—to identify strengths and resources, find common ground, and collectively set ambitious goals.

Gradually, as we have described, the different players learn to collaborate and sharpen the focus of their activities. The style and nature of their collaboration gives each brainbelt a distinct profile. They build on what they already have—the dormant expertise—and then expand and extend it. In Akron, Lund, and Eindhoven, for example, there was already tremendous knowledge about materials; in Albany, Dresden, and Eindhoven it was chips and sensors;

biotechnology and bio pharma are the main attractions in Zurich, Dresden, Raleigh, and, to a more limited extent, Portland; medical devices dominate in Minneapolis, Oulu, and Portland.

Collaborations develop, and as time goes by and early goals are achieved, the members of the brainbelt become more self-aware and work to define themselves and their qualities. Gradually, as collaboration becomes ubiquitous and the players deepen their knowledge of others in the brainbelt, they build trust in one another and confidence in their ability to take on even more complex and difficult innovation challenges.

The beauty is now not simply awake but more fully alive than it was before the evil witch invoked the curse. The awakening beauty develops new capabilities, particularly the ability to adapt to new circumstances and to refocus its energy on new areas of activity. Three of the regions we visited were early starters in exploring new concepts of sharing brainpower. In Lund, it was the Ideon science park that was the birthplace of Ericsson's handheld phones in the 1980s. When Ericsson lost its market position, Lund lost its focus. But the area did not lapse into a period of dormancy, as it had earlier. Instead, it adapted. A $300 million investment in a new particle accelerator will refocus on new materials and pharmaceuticals. A similar development took place in Oulu, Finland, where Nokia was also the victim of Apple's and Samsung's success with their smartphones. But entrepreneurs and local politicians built on their wireless expertise and focused on wearable medical devices.

Awakened beauties remember their dormant times and are far more aware of the risks that can befall them. They become highly adept at avoiding evil spells.

How Smart Manufacturing and Smartfactories Work

The brainbelt model not only involves a new process for generating ideas, it revolutionizes how those ideas are realized as products and technologies. New manufacturing methodologies—particularly robotics, 3D printing, and the Internet of Things, all described below—enable the creation of a whole new generation of smart products. Unlike the low-cost, just-in-time factories of the past several decades, smart manufacturing focuses on customization, localization, complexity, and quality.

In traditional manufacturing, the focus was on the productivity of individual workers, whereas in smart manufacturing, the emphasis is on sharing brainpower among members of teams.

As the following table details, the "smartfactory" looks and operates very differently from traditional factories, in many ways: equipment, organization, processes, metrics, and mindset. The smartfactory is highly automated and often small. System operators, designers, and researchers work side by side. The factory no longer operates only during standard business hours but rather 24/7. Customer orders, raw materials, supplier parts, production, delivery, and maintenance are all part of the same information system. Advanced materials are widely used, and scrap and waste have virtually

Traditional Manufacturing	Smart Manufacturing
Mechanization	Automation and connectivity
Worker productivity	Teams adding value
Efficiency	Learning
Outsourcing	Sharing brainpower
Rigid hierarchy	Flat organization
Power from job position	Authority from knowledge
Regimentation	Creativity
Rule following	Questioning
Command and control	Commitment and influence

disappeared. Close monitoring of every part of the process (nearly) eliminates defects. Customers care more about custom fit, high quality, speedy delivery, and innovative design than they do about low cost, so production is in custom-designed batches rather than huge volumes. The smartfactory is compact and clean enough to be located downtown in innovation districts of brainbelts where the technicians and engineers who operate them like to live.

The smartfactory of the future will be transformed with three key technologies: robotics, 3D printing, and the Internet of Things. Next-generation robotics—smart, versatile, mobile, and cheap—will make automation affordable to start-ups and smaller enterprises and will offer an unprecedented level of customization to consumers. The use of 3D printing will reinvent how we produce components (with an ever-increasing range of materials) and will dramatically reduce waste while allowing unprecedented creativity. The Internet of Things will create a system in which machines, components, products, producers, suppliers, customers, and just about everybody and everything else can communicate with one another. The purpose will not be to create endless chatter and useless information but to shorten the time from order to production, drive defects to zero, reduce downtime to nothing, and take waste out of every system.

In every brainbelt and innovation zone we visited, we caught glimpses of the new way of making things: smart, fast, cheap, customized, creative, complex, amazing.

Robotics: Automation Obliterates the Labor Cost Advantage

When we met with Scott Eckert, president of Rethink Robotics,[9] at his research lab in Boston,[10] for example, he introduced us to Baxter, one of his employees. Baxter looks rather like an ordinary human, at five feet ten inches and 165 pounds, with the requisite eyes, arms, and a brain of sorts. He is pushed around a room easily and responds to commands. He is not a human, of course, but a humanoid robot, functioning in the world with the aid of three cameras, sonar, multiple sensors, and other technologies. Baxter can "see" and "feel" his environment. He can find things even when their location changes. He can grab, hold, lift, and move objects. He works as an assistant to real people and is a skilled multitasker because one arm can do a completely different job from the other.

Baxter is not only versatile but also cheap to buy and operate. With a purchase price of $22,000 and a work capacity of 6,500 hours, Baxter gets "paid" about $3 an hour. This kind

Rodney Brooks, founder of Rethink Robotics, with Sawyer and Baxter.
Credit: Rethink Robotics

of labor cost advantage makes Baxter and his ilk extremely appealing to smaller companies that, until now, could only dream of using robots in making things. Such companies simply couldn't afford the six-figure price tags or the massive infrastructure such robots required. In terms of mobility, innovation, and cost, Eckert compares traditional industrial robots to mainframe computers and Baxter to a PC.

Designed by former MIT professor Rodney Brooks, a robotics pioneer who is sometimes called the "bad boy of robotics," Baxter exemplifies the smart robot designed for the smartfactory.[11] A dozen or so companies in the United States, Japan, Germany, and South Korea make such humanoid robots, but until recently they were mostly for research or military applications.[12] Now that they're taking their place on factory floors, these user-friendly robots are transforming the notion of what a factory is.

Robots and automation are key to smart manufacturing. As the price of robots comes down and wages rise in developing economies, it makes less sense to produce goods halfway around the world when you can make them close to the consumer for the same price. When we asked Phil Knight, founder and chairman of Nike, whether shoes could be made by robots in high-wage countries, he said, emphatically, yes. "In fact, Olympic shoes are mostly made that way already. I can see the day when anyone can have their feet measured with 3D equipment and shoes are then made entirely to order, avoiding the problems people have with shoes that don't fit quite right."[13] The same may be true for garments, from underwear to outerwear.

Baxter illustrates just how much more versatile, cheaper, easier to use, and smarter this generation of humanoid robots is compared to its forebears. Combining artificial intelligence, sensors, and big data analytics with cheap computing power, these smart robots can keep learning instead of repeating the same task over and over again—they can learn, and their "brains" can expand in capacity. Robotics experts estimate that robots currently perform only 10 percent of the industrial work of which the latest generations are capable,[14] so the potential remains huge.

However, it will take time to realize that potential. Innovations like the humanoid robot require the development of common standards and operating systems as well as the creation of specialized components. Still, even with these challenges, automation is becoming the new normal, and brainbelt entities are leading the way in its development.

3D Printing: Creating Almost Anything in Additive Layers

The second essential element of "smartfacturing" is additive manufacturing, also called 3D printing. Today, 3D printers are at work in research labs, start-ups, outer space, operating rooms, museums, and schools—and are now becoming more and more a factor in manufacturing.

In traditional manufacturing, objects are created in a variety of ways that include injection molding, machining, laser cutting, and welding. The 3D printer deposits layer after layer of material to construct three-dimensional shapes in a single solid piece without joints or weak points. A digital design template (CAD file) instructs the printer about the exact shape of each layer in order to form the final object.[15]

We saw 3D printers at work in an old warehouse in Youngstown, Ohio,[16] that houses America Makes—formerly called the National Additive Manufacturing Innovation Institute (NAMII)—the first of fifteen such institutions announced during President Obama's 2013 State of the Union address.[17] Kevin Collier, manager of the Innovation Factory at America Makes and a former employee of 3D Systems, gave us a tour of the facility. He described the extensive progress made in moving from rapid prototyping to real manufacturing during the previous four years. "Each day, the number of applications and types of processes grows, the speed improves," he said. Chronic problems, such as warping and how to work with two different materials, are being resolved. Automotive and aircraft makers are using 3D printing for making prototypes and also for shaping the composite materials that are becoming ubiquitous. In medicine, 3D printers are building knees, hips, and replacement parts for people with battlefield injuries. "The progress keeps accelerating," Collier says.[18]

When we visited Chapel Hill in North Carolina, venture capitalist Steve Nelson, managing partner of Wakefield Group, intrigued us when he partially lifted the veil on a remarkable new device, a 3D printer that would take on the entire production process, from fashioning prototypes in the lab to turning out whole products on the factory floor. One of the inventors of the system, Joseph DeSimone, personifies the breakdown of academic silos and sharing of brainpower between academia and business. DeSimone is professor of chemistry at the University of North Carolina and professor of chemical engineering at North Carolina State University and has over 350 patents to his name. He is also an entrepreneur who cofounded several companies and took a leave of absence from his academic positions to become CEO of a new company, Carbon3D. Its new system will be dramatically faster than previous models—eventually as much as 1,000 times faster—and can fabricate to extremely tight tolerances. It can be used in the "microfabrication" of products such as stents that can be custom designed for a particular patient's anatomy and that can dissolve over time, for vaccine and drug delivery systems, and for high-precision turbine blades. "Our process allows anyone to produce commercial quality parts at game-changing speeds," DeSimone said.[19]

We believe that 3D printing will create a highly efficient manufacturing model that saves energy while eliminating flaws and waste. Most important in the long run is that 3D printing holds tremendous potential for unleashing creativity and imagination that will lead to products we can't yet imagine.

The Internet of Things: Connecting Everything, Everywhere

The third smart manufacturing component is the Internet of Things. According to statistics from the World Bank, 25 billion "things"—as compared to about 5 billion people—are, in 2015, using the Internet, increasing the necessity of wireless machine-to-machine communication. Embedding sensors in machines and constantly analyzing the data they produce reduces unplanned downtime and warns when maintenance is due. In the future, it may even allow for fixing machines before they break. In a TED talk he gave in 2013, Marco Annunziata, chief economist at GE, called the Industrial Internet "a marriage between minds and machines that is as powerful as the Industrial Revolution. . . . It makes machines not intelligent but brilliant."[20]

Recognizing this revolution, Intel, Cisco, IBM, AT&T, and GE announced the formation of the nonprofit Industrial Internet Consortium (IIC) in March 2014, an open-membership group aimed at setting common standards so that information can flow freely between machines. Projects like these show that at least some key, technology-savvy American companies are taking the Industrial Internet seriously.

Siemens does, too, with Siemens Industry Sector North America CEO Helmuth Ludwig claiming that "the future of smart manufacturing is today. There is nothing less than a paradigm shift in industry: real and digital manufacturing are converging. New technologies are bringing the once-separate worlds of product design and planning, production engineering and execution, and services together in exciting ways."[21]

Siemens isn't just acknowledging the future—it's already applying these principles. At a 108,000-square-foot smart manufacturing facility in Amberg, Germany, Siemens builds 950 different types of Simatic control devices (with 50,000 annual product variations) from over 1.6 billion components made with 10,000 materials from 250 suppliers—with only fifteen defects per million. Touch screens are strategically located in the plant to allow the machine operators to check everything down to the production line and individual part.[22]

To see how the Industrial Internet works within a factory, we visited GE's brand-new industrial battery factory in Hudson Valley's Schenectady that is ironically surrounded by old buildings that once housed GE's old lamp and generator factories—truly a rustbelt-to-brainbelt transformation. In this $170 million facility, GE employs its version of the Industrial Internet in the form of an advanced system of connected sensors that records and tracks every parameter of the production processes—ranging from contaminants and resource source to temperature and machine number—so that any potential inconsistency can be digitally traced to its source and corrected. Presented with a completely clean slate, GE has built this state-of-the-art information system right into the new machinery to help identify exactly where errors occur or efficiencies can be achieved. It also helps to reduce unplanned downtime to zero and to fix machines before they break. GE's factory vividly illustrates the ever-increasing role of digital technologies in traditional manufacturing.[23]

So, these three elements—robots, 3D printing, and the Industrial Internet—come together to support products and technologies developed through the sharing of brainpower in smartfactories of the kind that exist or are being developed in brainbelts throughout the United States and Western Europe.

And that brings us to the result of all this "brainsharing" and smart manufacturing activity: the products and technologies they produce. As we'll see in the following chapters, these are concentrated in three areas: chips and sensors, new materials, and life sciences (including biotechnology and medical devices). These are brainbelt activities because they are endeavors that could not be pursued by a single player with anywhere near the speed, efficiency, or creativity of a brainsharing endeavor, if they could be developed at all.

But fortunately they *are* being developed, in unexpected places like Akron and Eindhoven, Lund, and Dresden, and, yes, even in the former rustbelt, often snowbound, towns of upstate New York.

Chapter Two

CONNECTORS CREATING COMMUNITIES

Hives of Innovation in Chips and Sensors

In our travels to the former rustbelt regions throughout the United States and Europe, our research uncovered strong similarities among brainbelts—the history, types of players involved, connectors, methods of sharing brainpower, and the use of advanced manufacturing technologies—as well as distinctions. Each brainbelt is focused on one or two well-defined economic activities, even though they all involve specialized technical research and high complexity, require multidisciplinary collaboration, and share costs that are often too high for any single party to bear. In Akron and Eindhoven, for example, the major focus is on polymers. In Minneapolis and Oulu, it's life sciences. In Albany and Dresden (and also Eindhoven), chips and sensors. What makes brainbelts different from industrial clusters—which consist essentially of a group of related businesses and their suppliers proximately located in a particular area—is that *universities* are an essential part of the mix and that the entities in a brainbelt are not only connected but are also highly collaborative. Their knowledge is so specialized and their research so focused that they do not feel threatened by others and, as a result, feel free to form close partnerships and engage in open collaborations that make all the participants stronger and more competitive. They are secure enough in their positions to sometimes compete with one another in separate areas where their respective expertise does not overlap.

To create this unique combination of focus and openness, whatever the industry, the fundamental factors are the same, as we'll see, but come into play somewhat differently. In this chapter, we'll look at the following elements: the role of the connector, the importance of the physical environment, the power of legacy, the transformation of supply chains into value chains, and the way that strong community is built to push forward the creation of breakthroughs in the field of chips and sensors.

A Quintessential Brainbelt Challenge: The Rise of the Internet of Things

Today, smartphones connect several billion people and put an exploding amount of information at our fingertips, but this is nothing compared to the impact on our lives of the Internet of Things, which could connect hundreds of billions of machines, devices, and other things to one other, and enable instantaneous analysis of the massive stream of big data they produce. Cities, homes, transportation systems, communications networks, manufacturing facilities, and public utilities—imagine a world in which virtually every device can be connected through the Internet to every other device, sharing information in real time. The implications for our health, productivity, food security, education, and indeed, happiness are immense. For example, the self-driving car may help solve gridlock in crowded metropolitan areas and reduce accidents causing injury and death. Tiny sensors in our bodies could help monitor and manage our health. And smart energy grids could enable us to tap into alternative sources of power with phenomenal efficiency and reliability. The positive potential of the Internet of Things is almost unimaginable. (There are also, of course, major issues related to security and privacy.)

Realizing these potential benefits hinges first and foremost on the computing power and storage capacity of sensors embedded in all those gadgets and the chips used to connect them and process the enormous quantities of data gathered. They must become ever smaller, ever more powerful, and ever cheaper to produce. That is the quest of technology innovators worldwide, not only in the well-known centers of innovation but also in three brainbelt areas that we visited: Albany, New York, at the center of the Hudson Tech Valley; Dresden, Germany; and Eindhoven, the Netherlands.

These under-the-radar, chip-focused areas are competing in the latest phase of the decades-long quest for tinier, more powerful chips by concentrating their efforts on two fundamental issues. First, how to create larger silicon wafers (the thin slice of semiconductor material from which chips are fabricated) that yield a greater number of chips per wafer, thus cutting cost. And, second, how to shrink the distance between the microscopic electric wires (circuits) in each chip, so that smaller chips can pack even greater processing power. These challenges require the sharing of brainpower in design and development and smart manufacturing methods in production.

In Albany, the focus is on designing the next generation of large silicon wafers, 450 millimeters in diameter, through the use of nanotechnology, which is the manipulation of matter at the scale of atoms and molecules. In the Dresden brainbelt, the manufacturing processes themselves take center stage. In Eindhoven, the sharing of brainpower is applied to both the design of chips and the development of manufacturing processes, particularly a new method that employs extreme ultraviolet lithography (EUVL) to more reliably create chips of ever-higher precision.

All three brainbelts are examples of "awakening beauties," areas that have been brought out of a period of dormancy through a fortunate combination of the factors common to all brainbelts.

Albany: The Essential Role of the Connector in Bringing Brains Together

The Albany area would not have become a brainbelt without the engagement of Alain Kaloyeros, head of the $20 billion SUNY Poly's NanoTech Complex, the short name for SUNY Polytechnic Institute's Colleges of Nanoscale Science and Engineering (CNSE), part of the State University of New York system. He was raised in Lebanon, where, as a young

Alain Kaloyeros, president of the SUNY Polytechnic Institute. Credit: SUNY Polytechnic Institute

man, he fought as a Christian militiaman in the Lebanese civil war. After narrowly escaping death several times in the strife-torn labyrinthine streets of Beirut, he abandoned the life of an urban guerrilla and turned to academia. In 1987, he earned his PhD in experimental condensed matter physics from the University of Illinois, and he quickly proved his mettle as a physicist. Although he has heavy-duty scientific credentials, he is neither the prototypical tech nerd from MIT or Stanford nor an entrepreneurial boy wonder from Silicon Valley, but brings the all-important skill of the connector in fostering the renaissance of a rustbelt region, a skill whose importance we will see time and again throughout the book.

It's important to understand, however, that a brainbelt connector takes the role of a "social" connector one step further. The social connector is typically part of several different social groups and helps to bring diverse people into contact with each other. Usually those people are already interested in making connections beyond their current circles. Connectors in brainbelts, by contrast, do not merely have the interest and communications skills to make introductions and then go on their way. They also have the vision to persuade others to embrace something that is beyond their radar screen and embrace that vision as their own. They motivate people to connect, work to find common ground and establish new relationships outside of their comfort zone, and then build these relationships into lasting communities. Beyond that, they may have hard going at first because the people and groups they want to connect are not interested in doing so, or are even hostile to the connector's efforts.

How did Kaloyeros take on this essential and difficult role? In 1988, he was recruited by Governor Mario Cuomo of New York to come to Albany to head up the CNSE. Cuomo and a small circle of like-minded policy makers in New York state had become convinced they needed to find a long-term solution to problems stemming from New York's declining rustbelt industries. With support from IBM and participation of the State University of New York, they focused on chip making. But they needed a strong leader and articulate spokesperson to push forward the effort, someone with academic chops and entrepreneurial drive. An exhaustive search led to Kaloyeros.

When we first saw SUNY Poly's NanoTech Complex on that visit to Albany in 2013, we both had the same thought: this is the kind of advanced research campus one might expect to find in Asia—at the Hsinchu Technology Park outside Taipei, for example—not on the outskirts of one

The clean room at SUNY Poly College of Nanoscale Science and Engineering's NanoTech Complex. Credit: Peter van Agtmael/Magnum

of America's supposedly struggling cities, Albany. What we found at the NanoTech Complex was a modernistic concatenation of glass- and metal-skinned structures, housing offices and labs, connected by glass walkways.

Then we met Kaloyeros, and we were similarly impressed by his engaging manner and quick mind. One moment he might be talking cars—he drives a Ferrari F458 Spider, a $250,000 car that can hit 60 miles per hour in barely three seconds—and the next he would speed-shift into a discussion of the intricacies of the next generation of semiconductors. We saw that he was a compelling booster for the Albany brainbelt, with a simple pitch: it's time to challenge Asia as chip-maker-to-the-world. We could also understand he had the academic and business credentials to convince the world's top semiconductor firms to bring their cutting-edge research initiatives to Albany.

What we didn't get right away was why a world-class physicist with countless opportunities would choose Albany. Yes, there was the matter of compensation, but it was more than a rich offer that attracted Kaloyeros. As he explained to us, he could have found a rewarding position in any number of industrial monoliths or academic institutions. But in Albany he saw a unique opportunity to do something much more challenging and meaningful. He could engage in the most exciting industry of the day, build a critical mass of science and engineering expertise, and awaken a sleeping beauty that might one day rival the current meccas of chip making and would alter the competitive landscape that had been dominated by Asian chip makers for so long.

Kaloyeros knew the process would not be as simple as bringing a few people together for a meeting or two. He would have to overcome deep industry skepticism about the feasibility of pulling together the various players into a focused effort and work with them to collaborate in a process of open innovation that would sustain itself for years.

Fortunately, both the governor of New York and IBM, which had its headquarters nearby, knew the region was in a precarious situation and needed to confront reality. The state government, the state university system, and the companies in the area felt very keenly the threat of competition from abroad and from other regions in the United States. The university leadership at SUNY Albany was eager to keep pace with the state of the art in advanced manufacturing technology but had learned the hard way that it could not compete with top research universities like MIT by chasing one government or industry grant after another. At the same time, IBM, then a leading in-house semiconductor manufacturer with facilities in East Fishkill, New York, was coming to the realization that its innovation process, which it called the "Kremlin model"—closed, autocratic, siloed—was obsolete and would not deliver the kind of breakthrough innovations the company needed to stay in the forefront. No single company, even one that was massive and replete with talent, could make the multibillion-dollar investments required to keep a step ahead of the entire industry.

Kaloyeros saw, therefore, that the players all needed something they didn't have but could gain through the sharing of brainpower. SUNY's Center for Global Advanced Manufacturing, for example, relied heavily on industry for funding of its research facilities, and the companies depended on the academics for basic research, but the relationships were project based, were not well focused on a collective goal, and were not particularly open, in that knowledge gained was not necessarily shared beyond the project participants.

What was needed, Kaloyeros decided, was a new brainsharing environment, and the best way to establish that was with a facility that would serve as an incubator, an innovation hub. That was the impetus behind the creation of what he calls the "800-pound gorilla," SUNY Poly's NanoTech Complex, which had so impressed us.

There, industry researchers could work side by side with members of the SUNY faculty and their graduate students. Kaloyeros believes that by owning and operating the research facility, industrial companies are encouraged to keep innovating. And as long as they keep doing so, the university will benefit from the collaboration, through contracts, increased attractiveness to talent, and the creation of start-ups and spin-offs, as well as the securing of patents and the like. "In the end," Kaloyeros told us, "we believe that those who build the infrastructure will get the fruits of advances in technology."[1]

Kaloyeros knew he would have to do more than convince enough of the existing players to locate to the center. He would also have to attract new ones. He became the driving force in creating the Global 450 Consortium (G450C), persuading industry leaders from all over the world—Intel and IBM, Nikon in Japan, Samsung in South Korea, TSMC in Taiwan, and GlobalFoundries (GF), among others—to locate their next-generation research activities in the Albany area. The research activities on the 450-millimeter wafer are carried out at the NanoTech Complex, but GlobalFoundries manufactures semiconductors in Malta. Samsung and TSMS conduct research and have manufacturing facilities outside Seoul and Taipei. During a follow-up visit to Albany in August 2015, we were given an opportunity to enter the cleanroom and see a dozen engineers hard at work testing the world's first 450-millimeter machine in operation. Achieving this took more than a decade, amazing perseverance, creative thinking, and solid arguments.[2]

Kaloyeros made a strong case to these proud competitors for setting up the G450 consortium. His first argument for collaborating in an unprecedented manner was that it would increase effectiveness. The brainsharing process is much more effective than the traditional fragmented and unfocused process the companies and universities had been following, with its projects and initiatives a poorly integrated patchwork of efforts.

Second, he stressed the important structural advantages to the approach of sharing brainpower. Only under the mantle of a university effort can companies that are competitors within an industry pool their resources and share information without having to worry about antitrust scrutiny from the federal government. As part of a collaborative effort, they can jointly spend billions of dollars on state-of-the-art equipment and processes that are too expensive for individual companies to purchase and not be in danger of accusations of collusion or price fixing. By doing so, they create an open platform whose research benefits everyone, with the individual participants still able to apply the research to create their own proprietary products.

Third, Kaloyeros promised that the participants in the Global 450 Consortium would be able to take on far bigger challenges with far greater chances of success and the possibility of dazzling rewards. Today, at SUNY Poly's Nano-Tech Complex, 3,500 industry scientists and engineers, together with faculty and graduate students, are working day and night in a $30–$40 billion effort to solve the problems associated with the creation of the next-generation 450-millimeter silicon wafers, including the use of EUVL technology. Nikon of Japan, ASML of Holland, and lens maker Zeiss and laser expert Trumpf, both headquartered in Germany, are all key players in the work.[3]

SUNY Polytechnic also serves as an incubator of local start-ups and spin-offs cooperating with the group Eastern

New York Angels (ENYA), which has already invested between $50,000 and $250,000 in each of nine start-ups with the $3.9 million it has raised in two rounds of financing. One example is Bess Technologies, a start-up that is developing more efficient lithium-ion batteries for electric cars and consumer electronics with higher storage capacity and faster charging.[4]

Kaloyeros believes that these efforts have made the semiconductor industry into a model for other American industries that want to be at the cutting edge of complex technology innovation. "People used to say that all roads to Albany go through IBM," he said, "but they now say that all roads to IBM go through Albany." And he does not mean Albany, the seat of state government, but rather Albany, home of SUNY Poly's NanoTech Complex.

The Environment as Talent Magnet: The Expansion to a Regional Center

The Albany brainbelt extends beyond the city itself: the success of the NanoTech Complex is just one example of collaborative innovation taking place among the state, academia, and corporations in what has become known as the Hudson Tech Valley.

Shirley Ann Jackson, president of Rensselaer Polytechnic Institute, a major academic research center twenty minutes' drive from Albany, agrees that the NanoTech Complex has successfully promoted nanotechnology, brought back semiconductor companies, and created jobs throughout the area. Just as important, she says, the work of the experts at the center has catalyzed a whole new wave of research that will move the industry beyond silicon-based semiconductors. The researchers at Rensselaer, she said, "are trying to think beyond 2020" by finding ways to marry nanotechnology with biotechnology to overcome the limitations of silicon production altogether.[5]

The influence of SUNY Poly's NanoTech Complex extends beyond research into manufacturing, as well. We drove 20 miles north of the academic research labs of Rensselaer on Interstate 87 to the town of Malta where GlobalFoundries, the world's second-largest independent semiconductor foundry,[6] has committed $10 billion to the creation of an advanced manufacturing facility, known in the industry as a "fab." Mike Russo, director of government relations for GlobalFoundries, told us the plant was the biggest greenfield construction project begun in the United States after the Great Recession and will be one of the most modern and automated plants in the world. The first stage of the facility became operational in 2012, and as of 2015, about 3,200 employees are working there. The facility runs 24/7, and technicians, wearing white coveralls and blue glasses, constantly monitor the equipment. Over half the employees are chemical, electrical, and mechanical engineers, who hail from all over the world. The annual payroll is $350 million, with a salary average of about $90,000.

By establishing its new Malta facility, GlobalFoundries—which operates older, less-advanced plants in Singapore and Dresden, Germany, and took over IBM's semiconductor manufacturing plants and intellectual property in October 2014—is now technologically[7] in the same league as the biggest manufacturers in the semiconductor industry, such as TSMC and Samsung, even though GlobalFoundries is smaller in size.

The second stage of the fab was under construction during our visit in August 2014, with 5,000 construction workers laboring on any given day. The entire site can accommodate as many as four fabs, but the timing of construction of stages three and four will depend on how fast the market grows and how well the Malta infrastructure and environment can support additional expansion—through tax incentives and the availability of a plentiful supply of energy.

Not only will GlobalFoundries have a major presence in the brainbelt, many of the company's major suppliers have moved in, too, including Applied Materials, Tokyo Electron, and ASML. Mike Russo is convinced that eventually a whole new supply chain will form here as production increases. Another manufacturer, the German-Austrian M+W Group, has built $1.4 billion worth of high-tech plants in New York state and has moved its US headquarters from Austin, Texas, to the Hudson Tech Valley.

So, jumpstarted by the collaboration between the state of New York, its university system, and IBM, the Hudson Tech Valley has become a thriving brainbelt. And, as is characteristic of all brainbelts, many kinds of businesses in the region are benefiting, not just those involved in technology innovation. When we ate dinner at a restaurant in nearby Saratoga Springs, our waiter commented that the influx of jobs from the investment GlobalFoundries has made in the fab has sparked a revival of the city's downtown area. Employees from China, Europe, and India have brought new

Watervliet Arsenal machine rebuild shop, 1845.
Credit: Library of Congress, Prints & Photographs Division, HAER,
Reproduction number: HAER NY,1-WAVL,1/14--10

life to the streets and shops of this picturesque town, which has long been famous for its racetrack and summer arts festivals but now is known as the home of one of the most advanced manufacturing facilities in the world.

Just across the Hudson River from Rensselaer is the historic town of Watervliet, New York, where brainbelt town start-ups are thriving. Watervliet is a quintessential rustbelt town. In the nineteenth century, it housed a federal arsenal that turned out cannons and ammunition for use in the War of 1812 and the Civil War, and it continues to produce armaments for the military. Watervliet is still the home of Bennett Laboratories, a major research center for the US Army.

Today, Watervliet has become the preferred venue for new companies that are springing up around the semiconductor initiative and have ties to SUNY Poly's NanoTech Complex. With the presence of twenty smaller high-tech companies—including Cleveland Polymer Technologies, Solid Sealing Technology, and Vistek Lithography—the Watervliet area is becoming a high-technology manufacturing zone.

Our visit to the Albany region was an eye-opener. We had begun to get a sense of the brainbelt. We had felt the intensity and witnessed the skills of the connector who had begun it all. We understood that, at least in this case, a physical facility was necessary to anchor the effort. We learned how a single initiative like the "800-pound gorilla" facility can then become a magnet to attract others and a catalyst for research and development that broadens the original focus of the activity. And we saw how a brainbelt like Albany can become a model for other areas and other industries. Clearly, Jeffrey Immelt knew what he was doing when he selected an obscure town in Mississippi for GE's futuristic aircraft engine plant. A brand-new form of manufacturing, we saw, is making its entry into the United States, in unlikely places and exciting ways.

Dresden: Leveraging a Legacy

Would the same be true in Europe? We had already visited Eindhoven, but we needed more evidence to determine whether rustbelts were transforming into brainbelts in a wide variety of communities. As we arrived in Dresden by plane, we found it hard to imagine that this picturesque capital city of the state of Saxony, in eastern Germany, had been a leading scientific, industrial hub in the 1930s, known for its excellence and innovation in automotive, aircraft, and lens manufacturing.

It had also been an important cultural center for centuries. Indeed, Johann Sebastian Bach's great desire was to be in residence at the Dresden Court rather than in the dreary nearby city of Leipzig. It was equally amazing to ponder how Dresden is once again becoming an industrial powerhouse, a brainbelt every bit as significant in the world of chips and sensors as the Hudson Tech Valley region. Like Albany and Eindhoven, its turnaround benefited from a politician's having to deal with a crumbling manufacturing sector and a new eagerness of academia and businesses with something to prove.

Today, Dresden, and its Saxony surrounds, has become a high-tech center. GlobalFoundries,[8] the manufacturing leader we first met in Albany, has a significant part of its chip production located in Dresden, as does Infineon.[9] And, around these two companies, a collaborative ecosystem has sprung up, composed of more than 2,000 high-tech companies employing 51,000 people.

How did this happen? This is the question we posed to Bettina Vossberg, who manages the High Tech Startbahn,[10] an incubator at the Technical University of Dresden, the largest university of its kind in Germany. She provided a bit of instructive history. The state of Saxony in East Germany—which is home to such cities as Leipzig, Dresden, and Jena—had been the country's premier industrial and research center before World War II. When the area came under Communist rule after World War II, most of the entrepreneurs left the region and settled in the states of

In 1946, streetcars run through the ruins left from
Dresden's bombing by Allied forces the year before.
Credit: Getty Images/William Vandivert

Bavaria and Baden-Württemberg, in West Germany. The
departure of so much talent led to an industrial decline in
Saxony and a concomitant Wirtschaftswunder (economic
miracle) in the west.

Dresden and Saxony went into a period of dormancy for
several decades, until after the fall of the Berlin Wall in 1989
and the election of Christian Democrat Kurt Biedenkopf as
prime minister in 1990. In his three terms in office, a period
of twelve years, Biedenkopf played the key role of connector, helping the region return to its science-and-industry origins. Attracted by Biedenkopf's vision that Dresden could

Dresden Christmas Market, the oldest and most popular of Germany's Christmas markets. Credit: Getty Images/Matthias Haker Photography

once again play a major role in technology innovation, a host of scientific institutes set up shop there, including the Max Planck Institute for basic research,[11] the Fraunhofer Institute for applied research,[12] the Helmholtz Association, with its scientific focus on studying twenty-first-century challenges,[13] and the Leibniz Institute, which continues to fund the best research coming out of former East German think tanks.[14] That made for a significant amount of brainpower.

But, as we've seen, brainbelts are not built on brainpower alone. Saxony needed the presence of a large, established company. During the Communist era, Zentrum Mikroelektronik Dresden (ZMD), a major player in semiconductors—employing 3,000 people—played that role. But the company was controlled by the army, had no market focus, and when the Berlin Wall fell, lost its funding and went bankrupt. ZMD was broken into pieces, one of which remained in Dresden and now produces analog-digital chips for the automotive industry. The other merged into X-FAB, a third-party producer of chips.

As Dresden came to life, it got the anchor company it needed. In 1994, Infineon, a spin-off of Siemens, invested more than €3 billion in Dresden-based facilities and cleanrooms for the production of large silicon wafers and intelligent chips. The company focused on the development of software that made chips and sensors smarter with highly desirable applications for cars, credit cards, and windmills. In the global automotive industry, Infineon is now the leader in the field, with a 25 percent share of the market. Infineon has become a force to be reckoned with in the automotive supply chain, competing with Bosch, also based in Germany, and Japan's Denso.

As we learned in Albany, once a player is established and the ecosystem starts to flourish, important players are eventually attracted to the area. Although it took years and plenty of tough negotiations, US-based AMD was finally enticed to settle in the region in 1996. After achieving tremendous growth in Dresden, AMD sold its chip manufacturing unit to the Emirate of Abu Dhabi, which continued the business under the name GlobalFoundries (GF). Today, GlobalFoundries manufactures chips for technology companies such as AMD, Broadcom, Qualcomm, and STMicroelectronics, from its fabs in Dresden and Singapore as well as the Hudson Tech Valley. In Dresden, the company invested $10 billion, making it the largest chip manufacturer in Europe.

Gerd Teege, head of GF's design center in Dresden, explained to us the production challenges they face in making silicon wafers larger and, at the same time, the chips themselves smaller. Two components are essential: the silicon material and the photomask that determines where light will shine through from a light source onto the silicon, thus creating the pattern of circuits. To provide these elements, GlobalFoundries and Japan's Toppan Photomasks (TPI) jointly created the Advanced Mask Technology Center (AMTC),[15] staffed by researchers who collaborate in the technological development of new masks and share their research with both parent companies. The facility is located a stone's throw from GF. The German company Siltronic,[16] the world's third-largest silicon wafer producer, has long had a presence in the town of Freiberg, southwest of Dresden, and also has a branch in Portland, Oregon. In 2004, Siltronic opened a plant in Freiher, Saxony, for the production of large 300-millimeter wafers. Today, AMTC and Siltronic are important players in the innovation ecosystem of the Dresden brainbelt.

As these key companies flourished, start-ups began popping up. Many of them were founded by former employees of the mostly defunct ZMD. DAS,[17] for example, specializes in purifying the air in cleanrooms. Another start-up, HAP,[18] specializes in robotizing chip production. The software firm AIS[19] writes code that is needed to realize the world of the Internet of Things. The architectural concern DERU[20] focuses on the design and construction of cleanrooms.

Creating a Balance:
The Development of Silicon Saxony

As all this positive activity progressed, something very interesting happened. Although a brainbelt needs an established firm of substantial size, it also needs to maintain a balance between the influence of the big player and the contribution of the smaller and supporting ones. Once Infineon and GlobalFoundries settled into the region and began to grow in size and influence, the smaller companies, all privately owned, felt the need to join forces to create a kind of counterweight to the big chip manufacturers.

A leader was needed, a connector skilled in sharing brainpower. The entrepreneurs turned to Gitta Haupold, a physicist who had been employed at ZMD. Since leaving the company in the early 1990s, Haupold had been coaching start-up entrepreneurs. She immediately understood the need for an organization to bring together the start-ups and represent their interests. She accepted the role and, in 1998, founded the organization Silicon Saxony, borrowing the name from a journalist at the *Financial Times*, who had used the term in an article about the Dresden phenomenon.

Today, Silicon Saxony is a private entity with more than three hundred members and an annual budget of €800,000. Most of the funding comes from the 80 percent of its members that are small and medium-sized business entities, but hotels and banks also contribute, and annual conferences generate revenue as well. Although the organization is tiny in size in comparison with many industry associations, it represents a first step to brand the sharing of brainpower in the revitalized Saxony region.

Gitta Haupold believes Silicon Saxony has made it possible for people to share brainpower more easily and effectively. "Now politicians, scientists, and entrepreneurs know how to find each other," she said. At the same time, she acknowledges it has taken a long time to gain the kind of attention and clout she believes the region deserves. "We are still not being heard in the German capital, Berlin, and the capital of the European Union [EU], Brussels," she said.[21] In 2014, Silicon Saxony made a small but significant step forward in this regard. Infineon was selected as the leader of the three-year, €55-million European research project eRamp,[22] a collaboration of twenty-six research partners from six EU countries. Its purpose is to develop ways to increase energy efficiency through chips and sensors. Silicon Valley has shown how local organizations that facilitate sharing of brainpower and create a brand identity can be instrumental in attracting hotly competitive funding at a regional, national, or even supranational level. This form of public-private institutionalization is much less developed in the United States than Europe.

There is still much work to be done to convince politicians in Brussels to make investments to support the chip-making industry in Dresden and elsewhere. To this end, four leading European brainbelts—Eindhoven (Holland), Leuven (Belgium), Grenoble (France), and Villach (Austria)—joined forces with Saxony to found an organization called Silicon Europe.[23]

The connector who made it happen, Frank Bösenberg, of Silicon Saxony, did much of the lobbying to create Silicon

Europe. A civil engineer by profession, he joined the Dresden University of Technology in 2005 to set up a department to work on applications for cofunding grants in Brussels. Because Saxony is classified as an underdeveloped region, based on statistical data gathered by the European Union, it was eligible for "structural funds" that could be used for infrastructural projects and research.

Bösenberg and his colleagues first focused their resources on securing these grants, then gradually shifted to other EU funding sources, such as innovation subsidies that are granted through a program called Horizon 2020, an EU initiative to stimulate innovation throughout the countries of the European Union. The department, the European Project Center (EPC),[24] employs more than forty people and has the distinction of being the German university with the most projects, 270 at last count, financed through third parties. Bösenberg eventually left the university and started his own firm, which advises small and medium-sized companies on the funding process. He also works part time with Silicon Saxony and is a strong advocate in Brussels for breaking down the barriers between sectors and countries that are an obstacle in the creation of a well-connected European economy.

Although Dresden has made tremendous strides as a center of collaborative tech innovation since its gloomy postwar period, struggles remain. When Bettina Vossberg moved to Dresden in 2008, she saw the area as a sleeping beauty, full of potential waiting to be awakened. She had earned an MBA from the University of Applied Sciences in her hometown of Cologne, then traveled the world for a series of German multinationals before considering her next move. When she looked at the state of Saxony, she was impressed by the quality of life, the well-functioning infrastructure, the cultural attractions—including top singers and actors appearing in the local performance venues—and by the world-class education and research.

Once Vossberg took the job of developing incubation programs with the Dresden University of Technology, she began to see some of the downsides of the region. For one thing, there weren't enough entrepreneurial role models. Even highly successful entrepreneurs, such as the founder of Novaled—which was sold to Samsung in 2013 for €260 million—had been slow to take an active role as mentor and model. Another disadvantage was that the global companies doing business in Dresden took their orders from headquarters based in other cities. For Siemens and Infineon, the senior leadership is based in Munich, and policy for GlobalFoundries is formulated in California. Vossberg was frustrated by her engagement with people at Siemens, for example. "They react positively, they nod yes, and they are interested in learning about the inventions involved in the development of new products," she said, but when it comes to investing in Dresden-based start-ups, the money doesn't flow easily.[25]

Such obstacles are not unique to Dresden and may be characteristic of German culture in general, Vossberg suggests. Family-owned companies with annual turnover of between €500 million and €5 billion—the so-called German Mittelstand—have very traditional, closed cultures. "They keep their R&D for themselves," Vossberg told us. They are not interested in sharing brainpower. "They do not set up joint research programs, where start-ups can participate." Another obstacle is that Germans tend to be risk-averse. Failure is a stigma. But tolerance of failure is necessary to the brainsharing approach to technology innovation. Indeed, failure is an essential part of the process. Gradually, Vossberg has been chipping away at these obstacles, and her message is being heard by the people and institutes that matter. To make students aware of the possibilities of entrepreneurship, Vossberg started a highly respected training program for developing new business pitches. The state of Saxony picked up on the idea and created a business plan competition called futureSAX,[26] to increase the visibility of regionally developed start-ups. Would-be entrepreneurs submit their business plans, and those who are selected present them at a spectacular competition. Those who propose the most promising plans receive support from the state of Saxony to help them start their business.

Vossberg's message is leading to change in other ways. Her investor-and-venture program, Hightech Venture Days, matches high-tech start-ups and growth companies from eastern Germany and other European countries with international investors active in investing in key technologies developed in Dresden. More and more innovations originated in the area are finding use in the development of new products, production technologies, and services, with applications in the fields of life sciences, environmental and energy engineering, the automotive industry, and the Internet of Things.

A number of university-based initiatives—such as Dresden Exists,[27] whose mission is to stimulate the transfer of knowledge into commercial products—are designed to increase interest, on the part of both students and researchers, in creating their own companies and then provide support in concept development and business planning. In addition, successful Dresden entrepreneurs have been recognizing the importance of acting as role models. Roland Scholz, an entrepreneur and co-owner of several start-ups, created an initiative called Sherpa Dresden[28] to coach entrepreneurs and support their start-ups. Scholz fits the bill brilliantly: he was born and raised in Dresden, graduated from the local technical university, worked in software, and is on the board of several local companies, including GK Software, which had a successful IPO in 2007.

Vossberg wants Dresden to be recognized as a world-class brainbelt, and for that, she is tackling the issue of venture capital. She would like to increase the frequency of the investor meetings she organizes from once a year to every month and, eventually, hold them on a weekly basis. (Vossberg was inspired to attempt this by a successful MIT practice: there, entrepreneurs and financiers get together once a week.) However, the resources needed to create such an aggressive program require funds that are currently not available in the region. Vossberg hopes that the programs that her organization, the High Tech Startbahn, has developed in the last five years will eventually attract venture capitalists to Dresden and that they will make a long-term commitment to the region.

Although Vossberg believes that Dresden can become a hub for technology investment, she knows achieving that goal will be a major challenge, because Berlin is currently the center of venture capital and the focus there is on app creation, which is trendy, needs little capital, and requires less patience. Making advanced chips is a far more complex endeavor and requires larger quantities of investment and has longer payouts. Companies generally need financing at several stages of their development, from seed money to pre-public investment, which can take years.

Dresden has come a long way in the last twenty-five years, and though it has not yet regained its early glory as Germany's preeminent industrial center, it is well on its way to achieving a different status—as one of the world's most advanced chip-making brainbelts.

Eindhoven: The Most Intelligent Region in the World

We took the train to Eindhoven in the Netherlands and when we exited the central rail station, it was impossible not to notice the statue of Anton Philips, the founder of the electronics company that bears his name. The Philips family and their company, Philips Electronics, dominated the business, social, and cultural scene of this region, in southern Holland, for nearly a century. Then, faced with global competition in the 1990s, Philips drastically reduced its manufacturing activity and cut its workforce by 35,000 jobs. (Eindhoven had a population of 200,000 at the time, so the impact was enormous.) The other major employer in Eindhoven, DAF Truck, fell on hard times around the same time. Within a few years, Eindhoven had fallen into that state of dormancy typical of once-thriving but hollowed-out industrial centers.

Eindhoven, however, did not remain dormant for very long, which distinguishes it from other rustbelt areas that struggled for decades before reawakening. Today, Eindhoven is known as a center for open, collaborative research in technology and, perhaps its greatest distinction, home to one of the most extensive value chains we have seen. It is also a preferred location for start-ups and ambitious entrepreneurs and the place where 19,000 researchers, hailing from all over the world, do their work. That is why Eindhoven won the designation as "most intelligent region in the world" from the American world policy research organization Intelligent Community Forum.[29]

At first, when Philips and DAF Truck cut back local production, it looked like Eindhoven was headed for permanent rustbelt status. When Philips moved its production to Asia, there was widespread fear that local knowledge would also be lost. But, as is often the case when a once-proud region faces decline, Eindhoven was down but not out. In Eindhoven and the surrounding area, there was an abundance of talent, people with extensive mechanical knowledge gained from years of industrial activity.

Then the awakening began. Many people who had spent their careers in the sheltered, even cloistered environments of Philips and DAF, had little choice but to find new opportunities, and many decided to go out on their own. Suddenly, there was a pool of entrepreneurs that had not existed before. The knowledge was not lost.

For years, Philips had operated a research facility called NatLab, and although the company shut down most of its manufacturing capability, it kept the lab open. NatLab had been a traditional corporate lab: proprietary, siloed, and closed. In 2002, however, Philips renamed it the High Tech Campus Eindhoven and opened its doors to the world, offering its services to outsiders and actively seeking collaborations with companies and knowledge institutions that were in need of innovative research.

The High Tech Campus Eindhoven[30] has enjoyed astonishing success so far. More than one hundred organizations—including global players Intel, IBM, ABB, ASML, and Philips—have now located at least part of their research activities to the campus, and more than 8,000 R&D engineers from sixty countries are employed there. In addition to the big players, 6,000 square meters of workspace have been reserved for start-ups and small and medium-sized companies. And the output is remarkable. In 2014, researchers at the campus submitted over 50 percent of all patent applications in the Netherlands.

In 2005, open innovation at the campus reached a whole new level with the establishment of the Holst Centre,[31] a joint initiative with financial support from the Belgian and Dutch governments between Imec, a company based in nearby Leuven, Belgium,[32] and TNO, a Dutch public institute for applied research, with financial support from the

Belgian and Dutch governments. The purpose of the Holst Centre is to provide a brainsharing link between the university's knowledge base and the companies' need for expertise, with a focus on two fields: wireless sensor technologies and flexible electronics. The Holst Centre employs 180 people, including thirty-five PhD students and forty researchers in residence. The corporate partners contribute more than half of the program's annual budget of €40 million, and they will take on greater financial responsibility as governmental involvement phases out.

Like Albany's NanoTech Complex, the Holst Centre provides a neutral meeting ground for companies, researchers, and leading international scientists. The knowledge gained is shared among the participants, although sometimes a single entity will sign an agreement to take exclusive rights to a specific idea or innovation. More and more companies want to participate in these programs because it is hard to match the Holst Centre's research capabilities in corporate production facilities. The Holst Centre brings a wide range of diverse entities together to collaborate, innovate, and develop knowledge that can lead to fresh new technologies and products.[33]

The changes at Philips that led to the creation of the High Tech Campus and the Holst Centre did not just happen, of course. The transformation of the NatLab[34] was led by Gerard Kleisterlee, who became CEO of Philips in 2001 and introduced a new way of thinking and a new focus for the company to address the big global social challenges, such as aging, hunger, health, and safety. He knew, however, that Philips could not solve these issues on its own. The problems demanded integrated solutions that would involve multiple disciplines.

Open innovation became the mantra at Philips, and redirecting the work of the NatLab was an essential first step in promoting brainsharing. For the first time, Philips invited competitors into the research facility to participate in joint research programs. Start-ups, which might well be competitors one day, were also given access to Philips' research facilities and its international network of brainpower. Philips proved that its belief in open innovation was not just for show by investing half a billion euros in the project.

Gradually, others in the region began to embrace the Philips mantra. In 2002, Amandus Lundqvist, the former head of IBM Netherlands, was appointed chair of the Technical University of Eindhoven. He was an advocate of Kleisterlee's approach to open, collaborative innovation and wholeheartedly supported joint initiatives between the university and the High Tech Campus. He also strengthened ties with the Technical University in Aachen, Germany, and with high-tech institutions in Leuven, Belgium. In 2003, a new mayor was elected in Eindhoven, Alexander Sakkers, and he, too, proved to be an effective advocate for open innovation. He reached out to local authorities, leaders in the business community, and centers of knowledge to promote the "rough diamond" that was the High Tech Campus.

With Philips, the Technical University, and the city itself all preaching the same gospel of open innovation, the power of brainsharing began to attract important new players into the fold, and a key one was ASML.[35]

ASML has been a presence in the region since the early 1980s, when it was spun off from Philips to produce photolithography equipment, which, as we've discussed, is essential to the manufacture of chips. ASML has surpassed its Japanese rivals Canon and Nikon and is now the leader in this market.

As the quest for smaller chips and lower-cost manufacturing intensified, ASML realized that it could not supply the vast financial resources required to develop the next generation of chip-making machines. That's when it began to look to its suppliers to help fund the research. Martin van den Brink, a member of ASML's board, made public statements about the importance of finding new ways for established companies and suppliers to work together. "This new form of collaboration is a process in which suppliers are accountable for part of the research," he said in an interview.[36]

The brainsharing between manufacturers and suppliers got an unexpected boost in the economic crisis that followed the bursting of the dot-com bubble in 2000. The big Asian manufacturers of chip-production equipment cut back on their research budgets. ASML, however, boldly defied this trend and increased its research expenditure. Although it looked like a risky bet at the time, the research led to the creation of new equipment that could produce larger silicon wafers (jumping from 200 millimeters to 300 millimeters in diameter), which we have seen is a key factor in chip making and was an important technical breakthrough.

Today, ASML continues to innovate and is working on further improvements to its machines in order to produce even more powerful and efficient chips at acceptable cost. To do so means creating the 450-millimeter silicon wafers and developing the extreme ultraviolet lithography technology.

These technical innovations are so complex and expensive that ASML needed to collaborate with partners that could contribute resources and expertise beyond those available in the supplier network. ASML turned to the world's largest chip makers (and the company's three largest clients)—Intel, Samsung, and TSMC—for financial support. The three companies committed to an investment of €1.4 billion over a five-year period and, in return, took a 23 percent ownership stake in ASML, with limited voting rights.

Even with this massive influx of capital, ASML still faced a daunting challenge: finding enough talent to support the endeavor. The company estimated it would need 1,200 expert technicians, and there simply were not that many available in the Netherlands or, indeed, in Europe. ASML went on a global talent hunt, recruiting employees from as far away as KAIST, South Korea's technical university.

Traditional Supply Chains Transform into Value Chains

As ASML expanded its activities in chip-making equipment and as Philips shifted its focus from manufacturing to research and marketing, it became clear that this approach to open innovation and collaborative research would require a different kind of network of support and suppliers. Gradually, the Eindhoven supply chain transformed into a value chain. What's the difference? In a traditional industrial supply chain, the manufacturer designs a product, writes specifications for that product's components, and works with suppliers to produce the components to spec, on time and on budget. In a value chain, however, suppliers also act as research-and-development partners. They get involved much earlier in the process, contribute their knowledge to product design, and collaborate in developing the best methods of manufacture. In other words, suppliers become collaborators who add value throughout the process.

Hans Duisters has witnessed and helped foment this evolution. Duisters is a serial entrepreneur, technician, innovator, communicator, and man with a mission: to help build a closely knit network of highly competitive enterprises that reinvent the word *innovation*. "It is my dream to build, together with other entrepreneurs and scientists, a high-tech sector in Eindhoven that is able to deliver the best high-end equipment for precision engineering in the world," he told us.[37]

Duisters has made remarkable progress toward that goal. In 1996, he founded his first company, Sioux,[38] a multidisciplinary firm that now brings together technical software, mechatronics, electronics design, and industrial mathematics to manage supply chains. But when he founded Sioux, the company focused on manufacturing components for two major clients: Philips, which had continued to manufacture scanners and medical devices in Eindhoven, and ASML, a producer of high-precision industrial machinery used in the fabrication of silicon wafers. At first, Sioux received the specs, submitted a bid, and conducted the work under clients' direction.

"Gradually a new relationship emerged," Duisters said, "in which we would do some of the R&D ourselves." One of the first such collaborations began when Rob Fastenau, a director at FEI, a maker of electronic microscopes, approached Duisters with an idea. FEI had developed a small microscope in collaboration with Philips but had not gone to market with it, largely because it was aimed at a low-end market and FEI did not want to confuse its position in its primary high-end market of professional researchers. NTS, an Eindhoven-based mechatronics company, and Sioux formed a collaboration with FEI and a group of companies in the region to further develop the microscope and eventually produce and market it. They refined the small microscope, manufactured it, and created another entity, Phenom-World—owned jointly by FEI, Sioux, and NTS—to market and sell the product,[39] which they have done successfully since 2006.

Sioux began to be seen as an innovator and was approached to develop other products. One involved applying technology from one field, photocopiers, to another, 3D printers. Inkjet photocopiers operate using a technology that puts down as many as fifteen layers of ink to create an image. Canon Océ, a maker of copiers, wondered if the technology could be adapted to print the inner and outer layers for a printed circuit board (PCB) for a computer or a chip for a smartphone, replacing the thirty-step analog process that was then the standard. Canon Océ proposed the possibility of developing this new type of 3D printer but suggested that before plunging into development, the company wanted to test the waters. Sioux talked with a number of potential users of such a machine and they all expressed interest and commitment. One of them even proposed that it could handle the marketing of new product when the time came.

With a reasonable certainty that there was a market for a 3D chip printer, Sioux developed prototypes[40] and spent five years of intensive evaluation and testing and refinement, with financial support from the Brabantse Ontwikkelings Maatschappij (BOM),[41] the public-private partnership that promotes new economic initiatives in this southern province of the Netherlands. In the printing process, every miniscule drop of material counts, and the researchers of Canon Océ were able to develop an incredibly reliable print head, with a failure rate of one-in-a-billion droplets. As good as that may sound, the machine delivers up to 50 million drops per second, which means an error could occur every twenty seconds, an unacceptable failure rate in chip manufacture. This problem was solved with the use of a software program called Predict that identifies errors and fixes them before they can cause an imperfection on the PCB. When the business case was ready, Sioux and Océ Technologies created a partnership with the BOM under the name MuTracx, and, in early 2014, the first machines were shipped under the brand name Lunaris.

Sioux and other suppliers proved they could not only manufacture components, they could also successfully bring complete new products to market. This changed the game still further, and the concept of a "supplier" continued to evolve. Companies and research entities, large and small, were all members of an ecosystem where sharing brainpower was the only way to bear the costs of technology development and to meet the complex challenges of high-tech manufacture.

In Duisters' view, companies like ASML, Philips Healthcare, FEI, DAF, and Canon Océ that are successful in world markets will increasingly focus on the beginning (R&D, prototype, and proof of concept) and end (product sale and marketing) stages of the production chain. Established, highly focused manufacturers will make "first-tier" components, as the German lens manufacturer Zeiss does for ASML. But the intermediary stages of product development and industrialization—involving design, fabrication of prototypes, structuring production, and integrating all the different production phases—will be handled by other companies, like Sioux. "In that way," says Duisters, "the supply chain evolves into a value chain."

Creating Community:
Associations and Foundations

As suppliers played an increasingly important role in the Eindhoven brainbelt, they came to a similar conclusion reached by small and medium-sized companies in other regions such as Dresden: they needed a new type of association to constantly improve their brainsharing and also represent the companies' interests. Hans Duisters, along with several others, founded Brainport Industries,[42] whose purpose is to support members, the great majority of whom are based in the Eindhoven region, in the fields of people, technology, and market strategy. One of Brainport Industries' top priorities was improving the relationships between

Rob van Gijzel, mayor of Eindhoven and chairman of Brainport Eindhoven Foundation.
Credit: Hollandse Hoogte

its members and the Technical University of Eindhoven, which it accomplished by holding joint meetings and regular conferences on key technological topics.

Eindhoven is an example of a brainbelt that has its act together and is flourishing enough to take on a role beyond its own region in related industries. That is why the Brainport Eindhoven Foundation was established in 2004, chaired by Eindhoven's mayor, Rob van Gijzel. Its dual purpose is to help outsiders navigate the Eindhoven brainbelt and to create working relationships with other like-minded centers of innovation and European funders.

Van Gijzel told us about the two roles he now plays, as city mayor and as chair of the foundation. When in Eindhoven, van Gijzel behaves like an entrepreneur, working to coordinate brainsharing among twenty-one neighboring cities, high-tech companies, and universities, which are all foundation members. When he travels outside the region, he acts as an ambassador for the area. As a former member of parliament, van Gijzel knows his way around the country's political center, the Hague. He also frequently travels to Brussels to advocate for Eindhoven and the surrounding region and, when necessary, open doors to facilitate EU funding for innovation.

Although we now think of sharing brainpower as a regional activity, and indeed a phenomenon mostly seen in developed economies, its future must be global and extend to innovation activities of all kinds.

Hans Duisters, founder of Sioux, foresees that technology companies based in Silicon Valley, Israel, Singapore, and elsewhere will come to Eindhoven to explore whether a high-end precision product they are developing can actually be manufactured and how they might refine their designs for optimal manufacture.

Duisters, while well aware of the trials the region has been through and the threats it still faces, is proud of what has been accomplished here and is optimistic about Eindhoven's future. When we asked Duisters what drove him in his work, he pointed to the bronze figure of Anton Philips, founder of Philips Electronics, standing outside the train station. "I would be very honored if they build me a statue one day."

Chapter Three

MAKING A NEW MOVIE
OF AN OLD STORY

*Dramatic Scenarios of New
Materials Development*

It didn't take long for us to come to expect the ubiqui-tous coffee shops and wine bars, repurposed warehouse spaces, futuristic labs, and robotized fabs that we encountered in the brainbelts we visited. But one of our most striking experiences took place in Akron, Ohio, on that first foray into the American rustbelt.

There, in a trendy restaurant in the renovated downtown area, we sat down with Luis Proenza, president of the University of Akron (he retired soon after our interview in 2014 and became president emeritus). He was not alone. He had invited several of his senior advisers and colleagues to join the dinner conversation, and the cultural makeup of the group blew another antiquated rustbelt image out of our heads. We had, without even thinking about it, expected to meet with a group of Ohio's born-and-bred, but our dinner hosts came from Mexico, Greece, and India, as well as the United States. We had assumed we would have a

Luis Proenza, president emeritus of the University of Akron.
Credit: Beijing Forum, 2009

casual conversation and, truth be told, believed we were beginning to be experts on this emerging brainbelt trend. Ha. Proenza's team was meticulously prepared, armed with documents and data, and knew all about the brainbelt areas we had visited or were planning to study. Needless to say, we learned a good deal during the course of that dinner.

It was in Akron that we really got a sense for the emotional underpinnings and social drivers of the awakening of a sleeping beauty. Proenza talked about how Akron had gone from glory to ghost town and back to glory again. The Akron area had once been an American industrial powerhouse, with a strategic location between New York City and Chicago that made it a key link in the supply chain for Detroit's car industry and a critically important transportation hub for many American-made goods. Akron was home

An employee working in one of Akron's tire-manufacturing plants, 1945.
Credit: Getty Images/Keystone-France

to global tire giants Firestone, Goodyear, and Bridgestone and was also a major railroad hub for transporting the region's grains, a significant percentage of which was stored in the silos (physical, not organizational) of the Quaker Oats company.

Like the other brainbelts we have described, everything changed for this part of Ohio in the latter half of the twentieth century. At that time, the major tire companies had been so dominant for so long they had become insular, siloed, and inward focused. They barely heeded the growing competition from abroad and did little to reduce costs through automation. By the time they woke up to the threat, it was too late. Much of the supply chain had moved overseas, particularly to Mexico and China. As the turn of the millennium approached, Akron was hurting badly. The tire plants had been abandoned. The Quaker Oats silos had lost their original function. The freight trains didn't stop there any more.

For some years, Akron struggled along. There was capital available for development, Proenza told us, but there wasn't much drive to do anything with it. "Hardly anybody was willing to take risks," he said, "beaten down as they were by memories of failure."[1] However, just as we saw in Dresden, there were still plenty of smart, skilled people in the Akron and Youngstown area, and many of them *were* willing to take risks, if largely out of necessity. They began to start their own companies, usually based on the technical skills they had developed in their years in the rubber and steel industries.

Little by little, and then by leaps and bounds, northeast Ohio came back. Today, this brainbelt is one of the top five industrial markets in the United States, home to 10,000 manufacturing companies (one-fourth of them exporters) and a workforce of 3.9 million people. Proenza was instrumental in getting the ball rolling, but what saved the region from its death sentence was sharing brainpower—among businesses, educational institutions, and government agencies—and building on a singular and valuable expertise that remained. That expertise was polymer science.

And, just as deep research in one discipline tends to push forward the scope of inquiry (as we saw in Albany, where the work on nanotechnology is pushing toward new achievements in semiconductors), Akron's work in polymers has broadened out into the wide-open field of new materials that consist of many types of molecules and take many

University of Akron Polymer Center.
Credit: Kevin Quinn

forms, including fibers, composites, coatings, powders, liquids, films, crystals, and plastics. These new synthetic materials will transform products and open up a wide variety of applications from paints to medical devices to aerospace components. The creation of these new materials goes hand in hand with discoveries in advanced research and new manufacturing methods, particularly 3D printing.

In this chapter, we'll visit four brainbelts that are involved in materials research in different ways. Akron, the polymer capital of the United States, has a particular concentration on materials for power generation systems, medical applications, and anticorrosion coatings for steel. In the North Carolina Research Triangle brainbelt, the materials activity intertwines with another of the three major areas of activity we studied: life sciences. There, new materials are being developed for application in sophisticated textiles, more efficient energy sources, and nanomedicine—the fabrication of materials to be used in vaccines and therapeutics for the treatment and prevention of disease. The Lund-Malmö area of southern Sweden was propelled into materials research after its premier corporate resident, Ericsson, the mobile telephony pioneer, went out of business. Its path was quite different from that of the others, however, because it chose to focus on a facility (as Kaloyeros did in Albany), the Max IV particle accelerator, Sweden's biggest and most ambitious research initiative, which will enable researchers to study the properties and interactions of materials, gases, surfaces, and biological substances as never before. And we'll also visit the European equivalent of Akron, eastern Holland. What Ohio is to the American polymer market, the Netherlands is to Europe. But just as Akron built its reputation on the basis of its long history and knowledge of making rubber tires, the Dutch expertise on new materials was built on its long-term research experience in aviation and the chemical expertise that was built up in the postwar period by companies such as Shell, Akzo, DSM, and Dow Chemical.

As we'll see, smart new materials will be increasingly ubiquitous in our daily lives. The clothing we wear, our cars and aircraft, the medical procedures we undergo to replace joints and receive implants—and even the art we create—all will be transformed by brainsharing partnerships based in these former capitals of rubber and steel.

The Northeast Ohio Brainbelt: Creating Akron's Polymer Valley

Northeast Ohio is a quintessential rustbelt turned brainbelt, and one of the most telling symbols of its story is the Quaker Oats building in downtown Akron. For years, the thriving company stored oats, ready for shipment by rail throughout the country, in the huge silo complex there. After the industry left the region and the facility fell into disrepair in the 1970s, real estate developers turned it into a hotel. This is where we stayed during our visit, just before the silo was reinvented once more as a residence hall for students at the University of Akron. But there it stands, not only as a visible reminder of the past but also as a marker of the future: the Quaker Square complex today houses shops, restaurants, offices, and apartments, and bustles with street life.

Like Albany, a university played a major role in awakening the sleeping beauty of Akron, but Luis Proenza thought about the role of his institution more broadly than did Kaloyeros, who was focused on the SUNY Poly NanoTech Complex. When Proenza came to the University of Akron in 1999, he vowed the institution would be a major force in reshaping the region and wasted little time in developing a written plan he called the "Akron Model: The University as an Engine for Economic Growth."[2] In it, he argued that a university should not be an ivory tower but rather an open source of knowledge and a connector among the public and private entities and that it should, and could, drive growth for the region it served. The university was well positioned to play this role, and materials research was a natural fit: the university had been a leader in polymer research for years and trained thousands of scientists and engineers. Many of them had gone on to staff the research labs of the big tire companies. Because the labs were so deep in talent and so rich in expertise, the companies had not shut them down when they relocated their manufacturing operations. So the Akron area, Proenza knew, had a tremendous knowledge base, and much of that knowledge pertained to the materials involved in tire making: rubber, synthetics, steel. All that was needed was to reawaken and repurpose the knowledge asset, by applying it to marketable products that were urgently needed in the twenty-first century.

Today, the College of Engineering and the separate College of Polymer Science and Engineering at the University of Akron, with a combined 120 faculty members and over seven hundred graduate and postdoctoral students, has grown into the nation's largest academic program devoted to the study of polymers and is acknowledged as one of the world's most important concentrations of polymer expertise. Researchers at the two colleges are working on advanced materials that include high-temperature ceramics, composites, and novel metal alloys. These are transforming the auto industry, and the aerospace and defense industries as well.

However, when Proenza described the Akron Model as being university-centric, he did not mean that the university must control or lead all initiatives, only that activity and initiatives would radiate out from and around the university and that a quest for knowledge would always be involved. One of those initiatives was the Austen BioInnovation Institute, founded in 2008—a collaboration of the University of Akron, Akron Children's Hospital, First Energy, the Knight Foundation, and Summa Health System. The institute's mission is to "bring together the best minds and the most creative thinkers" to tackle health-care issues, by combining "entrepreneurial spirit with scientific innovation to achieve powerful results."[3]

An important part of the research conducted at Austen BioInnovation centers is on the advanced polymers that will be essential in medical devices and biomedical applications. And the research there can get pretty wild, with explorations into paints that emit light, coatings that are self-healing, and contact lens materials that change color based on the wearer's insulin levels.

Further, Proenza did not suggest that university-centric activities always center on the University of Akron itself. Kent State University, also based near Akron, has its own programs for polymer research. Its Glenn H. Brown Liquid Crystal Institute is named after the inventor of the liquid crystal display (LCD) and is the birthplace of this now-ubiquitous material, which is increasingly used in advanced materials and sensors. At Ohio State University (OSU), based 150 miles to the west of Akron in Columbus, scientists are also deeply involved in polymer research, focusing on the link between polymers and nanotechnology.[4] The Wright Center at OSU has brought together six educational institutions and over sixty corporate partners (including Goodyear,

GE, Boeing, DuPont, Battelle, and Honda) and played a key role in creating several new companies.[5]

As the research in these initiatives began to bear fruit in the form of new knowledge, Proenza saw that another element was needed in the university-centric model: a bridge between academia and business. Researchers could not be expected to create breakthroughs in materials, openly share the knowledge with their corporate partners, and then stand by as the advances were turned into lucrative products in which they shared no gain. That smacked of the old days, when academics were forbidden from sullying their hands with commerce. Accordingly, Proenza created an independent research foundation, which provided a mechanism for professors at the state university to financially benefit from their inventions.

The state government, too, played a role in the realization of initiatives like the Akron Model. In 2002, Governor Bob Taft launched a project called Ohio's Third Frontier, a $2.1 billion initiative to "create new technology-based products, companies, industries and jobs,"[6] then the largest state effort of its kind in the United States. Third Frontier, which was renewed in 2010, provides funding to Ohio technology-based companies and helps connect them to universities and nonprofit research institutions.

With grants from Third Frontier, two professors at the University of Akron, Frank Harris and Stephen Cheng, founded Akron Polymer Systems. They hired twelve PhDs and many other scientists from Akron's enormous pool of polymer talent. Their mission was to develop special films for flexible LCD screens for use in solar cells and medical and aerospace applications. Their research was licensed and generated $1 billion in sales over the years.[7]

Akron Polymer Systems is just one of a whole new generation of materials—focused start-ups that have risen from the ashes of the tire-manufacturing industry, thanks to the combination of Proenza's visionary work, revitalized research initiatives, opportunities for commercial gain, and government support. Akron Surface Technologies (ASTI), for example, is a start-up formed through a collaboration between the $5 billion manufacturer Timken[8] and the University of Akron. Timken moved some of its research labs onto the university campus to facilitate collaborative research that focuses on corrosion, sensors, and coatings. The arrangement combines open knowledge sharing with proprietary research. Timken retains certain commercial rights for the use of its knowledge in specific applications, such as bearings, while allowing others to apply the knowledge in other applications, such as biomedicine and aerospace.

But not all the commercial action is in start-ups and in the retained labs of the big tire companies. Other large and long-established companies with a presence in the area, such as Akron-based A. Schulman, which manufactures high-quality specialty plastics, saw that they, too, could benefit from the Akron Model. Although A. Schulman operates plants around the world—including in Mexico, Asia, and Europe—the company chose to build a new plastic-fabrication facility in Akron, precisely because of its university-centric environment. Joseph M. Gingo, A. Schulman's chairman and CEO, said the company sees great value in "having one of the leading polymer research institutions in our own backyard." The company engages interns from the University of Akron and hires many graduates to staff its facilities in Akron and around the world.[9]

According to George Haritos and Ajay Mahajan of the University of Akron's College of Engineering, companies in Ohio have learned so much and are so committed to the sharing of brainpower, they now share their knowledge widely. They teach other companies how to measure and minimize pollution, use sensors to develop clean energy sources, and produce fuel-cell components from polymers.

As we mentioned earlier, one of the beneficiaries of this brainsharing is the steel industry. Akron has applied its expertise in polymers to create corrosion-resistant coatings for the region's steel producers, so they can produce next-generation steel that has superior performance characteristics and that better resists rust as well as minimizes wear and tear in bearings, a little-known problem that some analysts estimate costs the US economy 1 percent of GDP each year.[10]

Tom Stimson, who was vice president of technology and operations at Timken when we spoke with him and who remains a passionate believer in collaborative innovation and brainsharing, told us about his company's joint research with researchers at the University of Akron. The goal is to develop special polymer-based coatings for bearings that are 40 percent more resistant to wear and corrosion. The company invested $5 million to build the Timken Engineered Surfaces Laboratories (TESL), a joint venture with the University of Akron. The arrangement required eighteen months of often difficult negotiations to address intellectual property issues, but the resulting solution is becoming a national model for knowledge sharing.

Akron's breakthroughs in this little-heralded field of anticorrosion coatings is important for a wide variety of industries, not just the automotive sector. Polymer-based coatings are used in everything from personal-care products such as hair spray and lipstick to antimicrobial surfaces for surgical devices. The University of Akron's independent research foundation, which we mentioned earlier, is starting to unlock the huge commercial value of this research. Artificial stent producer Boston Scientific paid $5 million for access to the university's work on coatings, and the US Department of Defense is also keenly interested in this area and has sponsored a program at the university to further develop anticorrosion coatings.

The Road Ahead: Realizing Northeast Ohio's Unique Innovation Potential

"Ohio is still making things," said Barbara Ewing, COO of the Youngstown Business Incubator. The companies that couldn't make the transition from the old model to the new have been left behind, but the ones that could manage the change have grown smarter and found new paths to success. "People are more optimistic again," Ewing remarked. "The sense that we can't compete with the Chinese is gone."[11] This was confirmation of what the Chinese themselves had told us and reaffirmation of what we had heard in other brainbelts on our journey. In Albany, the NanoTech

Complex and Global Foundries demonstrated that the edge in semiconductor research and production was not irretrievably lost to Asia; in the Research Triangle Park in North Carolina, a company like Cree Inc. was confident that constant innovation in the light-emitting diode (LED) meant that the future of lighting would not be in China; large firms like GE, Apple, and Caterpillar were bringing back some of their operations.

The result of this extraordinary fifteen-year period of activity in Akron, which began with Proenza's articulation of the vision of the Akron Model, is that Ohio is today the acknowledged polymer capital of the United States. Ohio is the largest producer of polymer and rubber products of any state in the country, the second-largest producer of plastics, and polymer manufacturing is the state's leading industry.[12] Ohio is recognized as the global leader in the polymer and specialty chemical industry, with about 1,300 companies that employ over 88,000 people.

One of Akron's greatest strengths is that it is keenly aware of how quickly a once-proud industrial area can find itself facing an existential crisis and, equally important, university and city administrators have learned that, through brain-sharing, such threats can be overcome and whole regions can be successfully transformed. Akron will likely never feel the sense of invulnerability and superiority it had when it was the world's tire capital, and that is certainly a good thing in today's ultracompetitive world. But people in Akron have also rid themselves of the self-doubt and risk aversion that became so prevalent after the automotive bubble burst. According to Proenza, Akron now employs more people in the many small polymer companies than the big tire companies did at the height of their dominance.

This is not only a reawakening, then, but a revitalization.

NRT: A Brainbelt Forms Around a Struggling Pioneer

As our aircraft approaches the Raleigh-Durham International Airport in North Carolina, we're rewarded with a pastoral view of pine forests. But what really gets our attention is the built environment, especially the modern, sunlit terminal, with its soaring ceiling, that serves as a stunning gateway to the once-struggling towns that are evolving into hubs of knowledge creation in this area.

The North Carolina piedmont has evolved dramatically over half a century, in a story similar—but with distinct differences—to that of the other brainbelts we visited. During the 1950s, North Carolina was a mostly agricultural state and the third-poorest in the nation. It was the rural equivalent of an urban rustbelt state: textiles, tobacco, and furniture manufacturing were as critical to the Raleigh–Durham–Chapel Hill economy as steel, autos, and other heavy industries were to the Midwest. And like the economic mainstays farther north, these industries faced a challenging future and many had already begun to falter. State officials and businesspeople understood that without new sources of revenue, the region's economic survival was at risk. "We were pretty much in a rut," said William Little, a University of North Carolina chemistry professor.[13]

Little and others hit on a striking and novel concept: to create the first full-fledged science park in America. The proposed park would build on the strengths of the three major local universities—health care at Duke University in Durham, education at the University of North Carolina in Chapel Hill, and materials and agriculture research at North Carolina State University in Raleigh—to establish a unified research community within a science-based economic zone. The intention was not to "throw away our traditional industries," says Little, but instead to encourage more diversity.

Creating the Research Triangle Park was a monumental effort that required the involvement of the three universities, a succession of governors and other state officials, bankers, old-money investors, and corporations based in North Carolina and outside the state, as well as real estate developers. The park did not immediately spring up on the 7,000-acre site in Durham. "We were running a bluff game in the beginning," recalled George Simpson, the first director of the Research Triangle Committee and widely acknowledged as the brain of the Triangle. With little more than a brochure in hand, featuring images of the three university towers to give it an appealing Ivy League aura, Simpson and his fellow advocates visited over two hundred companies to solicit their support and encourage their participation.[14]

The process of populating the park continued over the period of a decade. As it gained more tenants, its reputation grew, attracting the attention of some of America's leading companies. An important breakthrough came in 1965, when IBM decided to build a plant in the RTP for production of its recently introduced System/360 mainframe computer. Big Blue, as IBM is known, had looked carefully for a new production location, and its requirements were stringent: strong universities; high quality of life; good working relations among government, academia, and business; an industrious workforce; and nonunionized labor. The Research Triangle offered it all, and IBM took the plunge. System/360 became a runaway success, at least in part due to IBM's operations in North Carolina, and the success justified the investment that *Fortune* magazine[15] had described as a "$5 billion gamble." To some, risk taking may look like simple gambling, but IBM saw the potential in the RTP and made a smart bet—a move quite similar to the judicious bet GE made on Batesville a few decades later.

IBM's commitment to the RTP had an impact far beyond the success of its computer system. It opened the way to the brainsharing future, a new way for corporate, government, and academic research entities—which had been isolated and siloed—to collaborate, and it legitimized the research-park concept in the United States.

A Research Cluster Is Not the Same as a Brainsharing Ecosystem

Today, the Research Triangle Park no longer has a monopoly on innovation in the Raleigh-Durham area. And what attracted the brightest minds to the RTP in the 1950s and 1960s—the suburban setting, trees and landscaped greens, isolation—is not what appeals to today's young researchers. As we've seen, they prefer a lively, urban setting, with open

The American Tobacco Campus, the year before its $200 million renovation in 2004. Credit: Ben Casey, 2003

work spaces, coffee shops and cafés, where the environment stimulates informal communication and facilitates open and collaborative innovation.

What's intriguing about the Raleigh-Durham area is that brainsharing environments have sprung up near the Research Triangle Park, including the Centennial Campus in Raleigh, as well as locations and facilities in Durham. In 2010, the old Lucky Strike factory, just a few miles from the RTP, was reopened as part of the 1-million-square-foot American Tobacco Campus, which that company calls "one of the most ambitious, largest and farthest-reaching historic preservation and renovation projects in the history" of North Carolina.[16] "That's where the action is now," said Richard Brodhead, president of Duke University.[17]

A revitalized American Tobacco campus. Credit: American Tobacco

However, the RTP's management is well aware of the cultural shift toward a different approach to innovation and is working to enhance the park's environment so that it will connect with and benefit from the new beehives of activity that surround it. Many of the RTP enterprises are investing in materials research. For example, we met with Chuck Swoboda, the wiry and enthusiastic CEO of Cree, a maker of LED materials for semiconductors. Swoboda, who has been with the company since it went public in 1993, works out of the headquarters offices sited next door to the company's manufacturing and R&D facility. Gaining new knowledge is king at Cree, Swoboda says, which is why the company is located near North Carolina State, where researchers focus on advances in the materials essential to the fabrication of LEDs.[18]

Cree has come a long way since its early days, when it introduced the first blue laser to the world. At the time, most researchers thought the idea of using LEDs for lighting was crazy. Then came one of those serendipitous, sideways breakthroughs in product development. Ursula Piëch, wife of then Volkswagen CEO Ferdinand Piëch, caught a glimpse of a blue LED and found the light appealing. Soon enough, they were gracing the dashboards of the new Volkswagen Beetle.

The North Carolina area, then, has plenty of corporate muscle, but it would not be a brainbelt without the participation of its three original university members, as well as other nearby educational institutions that have joined the action.

NC State University, for example, is home to the fourth-largest engineering school in the country[19] and runs the top program in one of the world's most ancient and also most futuristic materials: textiles, a discipline that most other universities abandoned when textile manufacturers moved out of the area. NC State's colleges of engineering and management also offer a joint program in entrepreneurship through its Centennial Campus, which is a cross between a college campus, an industrial park, a research facility, and a company incubator—an updated, more intense version of the Research Triangle Park environment.

Although Stanford and MIT led the way in bringing universities, start-ups, and research-oriented companies together in collaborative and often physically co-located relationships, the Centennial Campus is the only such initiative led by a state university. "This is a true live, learn, and play environment," Randy Woodson, NC State's chancellor, said of the Centennial Campus, which has as many as sixty-four companies on its grounds. "You can go to class in the morning, study in a world-class library, do an internship in the afternoon, and go to work after graduation with a company without ever having to leave the campus."[20]

Not only have many companies moved to the Centennial Campus, but sometimes they are born there. Materials is an important focus. Spoonflower.com, for example, was founded in a campus residence hall nicknamed the "Garage" in honor of the favored start-up venue for American entrepreneurs. What we found particularly relevant about Spoonflower.com is that it, like so many brainbelt companies, builds on one of the legacies of the area, in this case, textiles. The company produces wallpaper, fabric, and gift wrap that its customers design.

But there is much more action in materials that are not so familiar. The Centennial Campus is home to the Nonwovens Institute, for example, which focuses on the development of startling and advanced new materials. These typically have unique properties: they are antimicrobial; filter out ultraviolet light; are resistant to chemicals, including those used in weapons; and resist heat. Everything from diapers to protective clothing will be affected by this research, and large textile companies such as Hanes, as well as the military, are keenly interested. The work of the institute is so renowned that Stuttgart-based Mann+Hummel moved its R&D center for filtration technologies to the Centennial Campus in 2013.

The Centennial Campus provides companies with all the benefits of a brainbelt environment, from research facilities to restaurants, but it has some unique twists. One-fourth of the research funding at the Centennial Campus comes from corporations, a much higher contribution than the average 5 percent that is typical for major research universities in the United States. In return, the investors gain access to groundbreaking research as well as the rights to commercialize the innovations their programs generate. To facilitate this process, NC State developed a standard contract so that companies do not have to negotiate new agreements for each deal.[21] The contract specifies that the corporate entity will retain full rights for the commercialization of an innovation but will pay the university a fee when the value of the intellectual property passes a critical threshold of $20 million. This arrangement avoids red tape, saves time, ensures consistency across relationships, and enables the process of transforming research findings into marketable technologies and products.

Today, the area is developing into a full-fledged brain-belt—with the Centennial Campus, cutting-edge manufacturing facilities, associations with educational institutions throughout the state, and the transformation of disused facilities like the Lucky Strike factory—and is, as a result, provoking changes in the original Research Triangle Park itself. Bob Geolas, president of the RTP, sees its future in the eighty start-ups and early stage companies that have been nurtured in the park's five incubators, more than 40 percent of which employ fewer than ten people. Some of these companies have a new and distinctive character: small-scale, low-capital manufacturing. Dick Daugherty, former head of manufacturing at IBM, describes it as "local craft

Bob Geolas, president and CEO of the Research Triangle Park.
Credit: Research Triangle Park

manufacturing" conducted by young companies with only a few employees that make a limited number of high-quality components on demand.

In sum, the Research Triangle Park is looking to move beyond the repurposing of fragments of the old approach to manufacturing to create a new model that brings together academia, global business, nanobusiness, government, and social engineering in an environment that still features rolling hills but is better known for its brainsharing. "We need to be highly collaborative, authentic, unique, and inspiring," said Geolas, "if we want to keep it fresh and attractive to the smartest young creative minds."[22] And, as it does, the area can continue to build on the knowledge it has amassed over the decades—much of it related to materials—and push it into the applications of the future.

Lund and Malmö: Supporting Materials Research with a World-Class Tool

Every rustbelt needs a connector to coax or cajole it into transformation. In Akron, the connector was Luis Proenza; in Lund and Malmö, it was Nils Hörjel. In the early 1980s, Sweden was undergoing an economic downturn. As governor of the southern region of the country at that time, Hörjel was convinced that the area could be headed for rustbelt status, as shipbuilding and other heavy industries went into decline.

Whereas government ministers in Stockholm tried to manage the national economic crisis with traditional, Keynesian, policy-driven measures, Hörjel developed a vision of the future for his cities that involved a different approach. He imagined a new economic structure with two pillars: first, the computer and electronics industry, and second, the disciplines of chemistry and biotechnology, both of which are still key research fields of Lund University.

A first step, Hörjel thought, would be to establish a science park where for-profit companies could collaborate with the researchers of the not-for-profit university. As Hörjel imagined it, the park would encourage and support research and business creation and eventually produce the area's next big, knowledge-based industry. Hörjel was well positioned to bring businesspeople and academics together. Former colleagues describe him as an atypical politician,[23] a cross between a civil servant and an entrepreneur, a man who sat on the board of several Swedish firms, including Ericsson, the electronics company. As a result, he had built an extensive

A tanker under construction at Kockums Shipyard in Malmö, Sweden, 1961.
Credit: Getty Images/Winfield Parks

network of people in both the public and private sectors. He was a successful connector.

Hörjel identified a good location for the science park—near the university and convenient to private companies—but it was zoned for residential housing. He worked with Lund's local authorities to change the zoning designation and then gained the financial support of Ingvar Kamprad, the founder of IKEA, to buy the parcel. Next, Hörjel brought together the leaders of several local construction and development companies, many of them competitors with one another, and worked with them to form a consortium to develop the park.

Hörjel conferred with the local business leaders about what the commercial focus of the park's activity should be. Chips? Medical devices? A member of the prominent Wallenberg family sat on Ericsson's board of directors, and Hörjel knew him well. When the board gathered for a dinner at the family's castle, Wallenberg made a persuasive argument to his fellow board members that Lund's industrial focus should be mobile telephony and that Ericsson, in desperate need of young, skillful engineers, should locate its research center at the new science park that Hörjel was developing. That way, Ericsson might be able to enter the market early and gain a leadership position.

Within two years, the science park, now named Ideon, achieved lift off. Like the Research Triangle Park in North Carolina, it was born through a collaborative effort of developers, entrepreneurs, local politicians, established companies, and a nearby university. Lund University may be local, but it is the largest in Scandinavia and its 48,000 students make up nearly half of the city's population. It is one of the top one hundred research universities in the world, with a history of innovations that include ultrasound, the artificial kidney, Bluetooth, and the nicotine medication Nicorette.

Mats Lindoff, then Ericsson's chief technology officer, was one of the first to join the company's team at Ideon. Lindoff's boss, Niels Rubeck, showed him a prototype phone and told him their assignment was to take the clunky prototype that was "as big as a brick" and make it "as small as a matchbox." As the project gathered momentum, Ericsson hired as many as twenty engineers a week, initially from

Sweden and then from all over the world. At the peak of its activity, Ericsson employed 4,000 engineers. Ericsson worked closely with the scientists at Lund University and benefited in particular from the contributions of Sven Olof Orvik, a leading academician in radio technology. He, with his top students, solved several of the thorniest technical challenges as part of their research. After graduating, they made a swift transition to the Ericsson labs.

Ericsson's activity on the mobile phone created an extensive ecosystem of partners and suppliers in Lund and the surrounding area. For every research engineer employed at Ericsson, there were ten more working at nearby suppliers and other mobile technology companies. The demand for phones exploded, and Ericsson sought to ramp up production to 100 million phones a year. Even with a highly automated production line, however, the company could not meet this production target. They investigated sourcing capacity from China and found they could produce phones there at a lower price, with higher quality and more reliability. So, in 1999, Ericsson began production in China. Although the move enabled the company to rapidly increase production, it had a serious downside: it separated engineering from manufacturing. With the disciplines operating in isolated silos, Ericsson could not benefit from multidisciplinary collaboration. So, as smartphones began to appear on the horizon, the Ericsson engineers rejected the idea of getting involved in that market, because they saw too many technical barriers. "We lost our dominance in mobile because we took too much of an engineering approach," Lindoff said.[24]

The rest is history. In 2007, Apple introduced the iPhone and, by 2009, Ericsson's mobile division became a part of Sony. Still, just as we have seen in other brainbelts, the research expertise in Lund was so great that Sony retained the Ericsson research center at Ideon and 2,500 engineers continued to work there.

The members of the Lund brainbelt began to consider new initiatives. Hörjel had originally proposed two pillars to the new economic structure: electronics and computer science, and chemistry and biotechnology. The global outlook for biotechnology was bright, so they refocused their efforts on life sciences.

In 2014, AstraZeneca consolidated its research and moved its R&D scientists from Lund to Göteborg, vacating its facility, Medicon Village, which was located right next door to Ideon. Lund joined with other players from Sweden and Denmark in a new life-sciences initiative known as Medicon Valley. It is home to several leading pharmaceutical companies, including Novo Nordisk, the Danish company that is the global leader in diabetes research and is the largest pharmaceutical firm in Scandinavia; Bioinvent; Active Biotech, a developer of new drugs in immunology; Camurus; and major medical device makers such as Gambro. There are also hundreds of other small biotech startups that have high hopes of making it into the big league. More than 40,000 people work in the valley—nine out of ten life-science workers in Denmark and one out of five in Sweden. They seek to succeed in the face of the onerous risk-reward ratio in life sciences. Only one of fifteen drugs that enter clinical trials succeeds, and very few of those become blockbusters in the market.

Ideon is home to, and an incubator for, companies in a range of technology industries, in clean technology, software, and new materials, as well as life sciences and telecommunications. Richard Mosell, a patent lawyer and the son of an inventor, is head of the Incubator at Ideon. "Innovation mostly takes place at the boundaries," he said. "At Ideon, we create an environment where engineers talk to creative people and entrepreneurs." Sharing brainpower, says Mosell, is nothing like the rigid hierarchical process of the rustbelt industries of shipbuilding or tire making. "It's really much more like making a movie."[25]

This approach has led to the creation of a remarkable project of the kind you might *see* in a movie, the $300 million Max IV particle accelerator. It is a circular, Coliseum-sized structure that looks every bit the biggest research project ever undertaken in Sweden, which it is. The Max IV promises to shift the center of gravity in the world of particle research. Its users will include not only university professors but also companies that do research on new materials and want to study nano-size molecules. According to Katarina Noren, a chemist who manages relations between the accelerator and its corporate users, the Max IV "beats all but a handful" of the latest accelerators in the United States, Europe, and Japan.[26]

What happens within this beyond-space-age device? "What we offer here is light," Noren explained. "We rev up electrons to nearly the speed of light, use magnets to channel them into circular paths through narrow pipes, and produce light that is more than 1,000 times more intense than normal daylight." Max IV can produce light all along the spectrum from ultraviolet to infrared, light that enables scientists to study all kinds of gases, surfaces, and biological materials. Researchers can explore how atoms and molecules interact when they are mixed, and they can even tinker with their structure to produce new materials with specific properties. "MaxIV will be the standard way of studying new materials at the nano level," Noren claimed.

You might imagine that knowledge gained in such a facility would be jealously guarded by the companies that sponsor it, just like in the old days of secretive, behind-closed-doors R&D. With Max IV, however, companies have two choices. They can use the facility for free if they agree to share the knowledge that results from their experiments. But certain kinds of research would be flat-out impossible without an accelerator of this caliber, and companies will likely be willing to pay substantial fees for that kind of initiative, which will help defray the costs of managing and constantly improving the facility—which will, in turn, benefit all users.

The Netherlands: The Akron of Europe?

The coal-mining district in the southern part of the Netherlands is a classic example of a sleeping beauty searching for a prince to unleash its potential. The Dutch government closed the mines in the early 1960s after the biggest natural gas reserve in Europe was discovered in the northern part of the country. Initially, the closure was seen as a disaster, especially for employment, because the owner of the mines, DSM, was the largest employer in the area. DSM, however, turned to the production of basic chemicals, using a site near the abandoned mines. This provided employment for many years, but in the 1990s DSM decided to transform again, this time to the production of vitamins and bio-based materials. The unions and local authorities feared that the most important employer in the region would now leave and jobs would be lost forever. But Feike Sijbesma, who became CEO of DSM in 2007, convinced all concerned that his company would not only stay in the region but would enhance its role in the region. How? Sijbesma proposed the establishment of a research campus where companies and researchers could advance the field of bio-based materials, and which would be sited on the former DSM chemical-production site, near the city of Maastricht.

The Netherlands has a long history of leadership in new materials development. Almost a century ago, the government created the National Aerospace Laboratory[27] (NAL) to conduct research with two partners: KLM, the Royal Dutch Airlines, which was one of the first commercial airline companies in the world; and Fokker, the pioneering aircraft builder. The goal of the research was to make aircraft more reliable and efficient, and one of the most important contributors to these characteristics is the performance of the materials that make up the aircraft. In the 1980s, materials research focused on synthetic fibers. Two Dutch chemical companies, Akzo and DSM, introduced the synthetic fibers Twaron and Dymeera, which are similar to Kevlar, created by DuPont, but even stronger. Those fibers became key ingredients in the thermoset composite materials that became standard in the automotive and aerospace sector.

Since the late 1990s, Sijbesma has been the connector in the southern region. His greatest contribution was to eliminate the skepticism prevalent in the trade unions and with the local authorities. He always thought in terms of solutions rather than about problems. This enabled him to shape the circumstances that ultimately led to a deal bringing the University of Maastricht, the local authorities, and his own company together as equal partners in the research campus, which is strongly focused on bio-based material research. Open innovation became the mantra, and the campus on the former chemical production site was named Chemelot, a combination of the words *chemical* and *Camelot*, the legendary city of King Arthur and his knights.

Eventually, more than fifty companies moved to Chemelot, creating over 1,100 high-quality jobs. Among them is Avantium,[28] a spin-off of Shell Oil company. It specializes in research on catalysts for companies such as BP, Shell, DSM, and Coca-Cola. Leveraging this knowledge, researchers at Avantium discovered how to substitute PEF—a plant-based, renewable material—for the ubiquitous PET now used for plastic bottles. In 2012, Avantium built a pilot plant on the Chemelot campus with the support of such partners as Coca-Cola, Danone, and the Austrian packaging firm ALPLA. The construction of a commercial facility got underway in 2015.

Another Chemelot company is QTIS/e, a start-up whose goal is to develop new materials for health-care applications.[29] Two bioengineers, Mirjam Rubbens and Martijn

Cox, are conducting breakthrough research into living heart valves. In close cooperation with materials experts, they developed and patented a biodegradable polymer that merges with healthy body cells to create new vessel-and-valve tissue. Gradually, the new tissue takes over the original body function and the polymer melts away. The huge advantage is that young children who are born with a heart defect (4,000 each year in Europe alone) can have the problem corrected with a single operation, instead of the two or three operations that are commonly required with other plastic heart valves. The new technology has been tested in animals, and ten human patients have been successfully treated. Cox, now chief scientific officer of the company, said that in 2016, clinical tests with a larger group of heart patients will be done: "If these tests are successful, the commercial introduction of the valves will start in 2018."[30]

Collaboration among local authorities, the university, and private companies was a critical ingredient in the creation and success of Chemelot. In recent years, the university has established some of its master's programs in Chemelot, and both research and teaching are done in close collaboration with the companies located on campus. With a generous ten-year, €600-million investment from the deep-pocketed province of Limburg, the initiative has been able to attract top-notch talent. Professor Peter Peters, for example, made the move from Amsterdam where he was working at the Free University and the famous cancer hospital Antoni van Leeuwenhoek AVL, to Maastricht to assume leadership of the newly created Institute for Nanoscopy.[31] Peters and his team will be exploring how cancer and some infectious diseases originate, and their work will be enabled by the use of specialized microscopes, thanks to financial support from DSM. Another big academic fish, Clemens van Blitterswijk—named the most entrepreneurial professor in Holland—left Twente Technical University to go to Maastricht University with a group of twenty researchers to specialize in tissue engineering.[32] The group is using stem cells to create smart materials that can rebuild tissue and repair bones. Beyond his own research, van Blitterswijk's goal is to work closely with DSM and other companies at the Chemelot campus to create a "pool of spin-offs."

From Textiles to Thermoplastics

As we have seen, the polymer research in Ohio is not confined to the Akron area but is spread through the region, and there are strong ties between the different areas and institutions—the same is true for the Netherlands. In addition to the former coal-mining rustbelt of the south, there is much materials activity in Twente, located in the eastern part of the country near the German border, where the textile industry had blossomed for more than a century. In the 1960s and 1970s, cheap labor competition from countries in Southern Europe had a devastating effect on employment, just as it had in Maastricht. TenCate, one of the companies located in Twente, had been focused on the creation of thermoset composite materials. But these were difficult to manufacture and could not be recycled. After ten years of work, an engineer of TenCate patented a new production procedure for a material called Cetex, a more flexible thermoplastic composite that could be more easily produced in a variety of configurations.

The production process for making Cetex, like the thermoplastics that came before it, is based on traditional weaving methods long practiced in the area. The first step is the weaving together of very thin synthetic fibers. Loek de Vries, CEO of TenCate, explained that weaving thin silk without breakage is an art.[33] Expertise in weaving creates thermoplastic materials that are strong and highly shock resistant. And through application of a patented coating, the material can also be made resistant to dampness and fire.

TenCate has focused its application of Cetex on three global niche markets: defense and security, aerospace-automotive, and artificial turf of the kind used in fields for American football and European soccer, as well as for public lawns in hot regions such as the Middle East. TenCate, which has become a world leader in artificial turf, continues to work with partners to make the material more flexible, durable, and safe for users.

TenCate has built a strong position with its thermoplastics in the aerospace components market, where the materials must perform in extreme conditions and where failure can lead to catastrophe. The materials must withstand wide temperature fluctuations, from −55 degrees to +45 degrees C, or −67 degrees to +113 degrees F. In extreme cold, the fiber must not become so brittle that it might crack or shatter. In high heat, it cannot become overly flexible or reach the melting point. The material must also be able to endure the intense forces that an aircraft experiences during takeoff, landing, and turbulence.

TenCate has always worked in brainsharing relationships with its clients, one of which is the Dutch company Fokker. Fokker went through a bankruptcy in 1996, then emerged as a components company, focused on fuselage, wing parts, and landing gear.[34] Fokker's chief technology officer, Wim Pasteuning, explained the importance of the collaboration with TenCate in the research into thermoplastics for its products. TenCate was required to test the materials frequently to achieve the certifications required for use in aerospace applications. "They were prepared to do this," Pasteuning told us, "even when they knew we would order only in small quantities."[35] But for TenCate, it was a way to improve its product and reach the highest standards, and to expand its commercial activities gradually to enter the profitable automotives market.

Over the years, TenCate and Fokker also worked closely with the National Aerospace Laboratory and the technical universities of Delft and Twente. In 2009, these partners shared their brainpower with Boeing in the Thermoplastic Composite Research Center (TPRC), which is located on the campus of Twente University, not far from TenCate's head office.

Now TenCate is building on its materials expertise in the aerospace sector to expand the use of thermoplastics in automobiles. In 2013, TenCate and the Swiss automotive parts producer Kringlan signed a cooperation agreement to produce molded composite structures, such as car wheels, and in 2011 BMW, the German carmaker, took a 17.5 percent minority stake in the start-up. BMW seeks to replace steel wheels with the lighter composites, and Kringlan is the first company that can produce them in the necessary volumes. The wheels will be 30 to 40 percent lighter than steel ones, which will reduce fuel consumption and CO_2 emissions.

The sharing of TenCate's expertise with materials and Kringlan's skill in manufacturing, combined with their deep knowledge of the automotive and aerospace industries, is sure to contribute to a safer, more fuel-efficient generation of vehicles on our roads and our aircraft in the skies.

Chapter Four

WHITE COATS AND
BLUE COLLARS

Cross-Boundary Collaborations in
Bioscience and Medical Devices

Not every brainbelt emerges from a rustbelt and not every seminal figure in the story conforms to the profile of a prominent, larger-than-life connector such as Alain Kaloyeros or the governors in North Carolina or Malmö. In Minneapolis, for example, the presence of a large company, Medtronic, loomed large. No single person played the role of connector; rather, there were several doctors, researchers, entrepreneurs, and venture capitalists who were leading figures in the talent pool and helped put Minneapolis–St. Paul on the map as a life-sciences brainbelt, in particular for medical devices.

The Minneapolis area had long been a center for health care, and this focus owes a lot to a key figure (if not exactly a connector)—a doctor and self-promotional maverick named C. Walton Lillehei (1918–1999). Lillehei was known as a brilliant surgeon, a talented teacher at the University of Minnesota (UMN), and a pioneer of open-heart surgery

techniques and tools, especially for children with birth de-
fects.¹ He was, in other words, a triple threat: practitioner,
academic, and entrepreneur, but he was not so much the
nuts-and-bolts builder of ecosystems—those people would
come later. (Lillehei was also known to "live large" and had
some disputes with the IRS, details that add to the complexity of his character but are not particularly relevant to
our story.)

In the 1950s, heart surgeons relied on a cumbersome,
electrically powered piece of equipment to control the patient's pulse during surgery. One day in 1958, Lillehei was
operating on a child when the hospital's power shut down.
The equipment failed, the patient's heart stopped, and the
child died on the table.

Lillehei did not intend to let that happen again. One of
his nurses was married to an electrical engineer named Earl
Bakken, who ran a company that repaired medical instruments for the University of Minnesota hospital. Lillehei
asked Bakken to devise a small, portable, battery-powered
device to replace the stationary, electrically driven clunker
that had essentially caused the death of his young patient.
Working from Lillehei's napkin sketch, Bakken repurposed
the mechanics of a metronome—the little machine that
helps music students keep a regular beat—into a prototype.
This was before the days of US Food and Drug Administration (FDA) regulations, so Lillehei was free to test the gadget
the next day, and it worked. Eventually—after much refining
of the device and convincing skeptical surgeons of its reliability and effectiveness—the product became the central
product of Medtronic, now the world's leader in pacemakers.

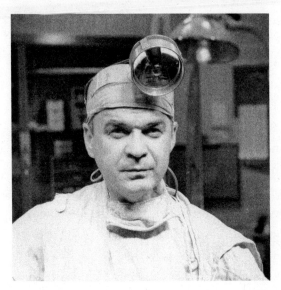

*Dr. Lillehei,
known as the
Father of Open-
Heart Surgery.*
Credit: University of
Minnesota, Lillehei
Institute

In the process, Lillehei's innovation sparked the creation of a network of doctors, scientists, hospitals, and universities that made Minneapolis a center of the life-sciences industry, with a particular focus on medical devices.

Life sciences, the newest and most explosive area of brainsharing activity, encompasses bioscience, biotechnology, biomedicine, and medical devices. Biotechnology is an area of inquiry as ancient as the fermentation of beer, which dates from around 7000 BC, but the term *biotechnology* was coined only in 1919 by Károly Ereky, a Hungarian engineer who believed that the fermentation process could be used to develop a wide variety of products, including medicines.[2] He was right. In the 1940s, the process gave us not only steroids and hormones but also penicillin, which has saved millions of lives over the years and has delivered billions of dollars in revenues and profit to pharmaceutical companies.

We have seen tremendous advances and breakthroughs in biotechnology over the years since then. In the 1960s, the study of molecular biology[3] eventually gave rise to the creation of biotechnology firms such as Genentech, Biogen Idec, and Amgen. Starting in the 1990s, the mapping of the human genome and advances in immunotherapy led to the development of new drugs, particularly for the treatment of cancer.[4] Research continues into cloning, stem cells, and genetic modification. In the past decade, computing and data analytics have become important elements in life-sciences research and product development.

Because we made great progress in the twentieth century in developing treatments and cures for infectious and communicable diseases, such as cholera, tuberculosis, malaria, venereal disease, HIV, and many others, today the world's biggest health challenge is chronic diseases—cancer, diabetes, heart disease, stroke, and obesity—and those account for more than 60 percent of deaths worldwide and 75 percent of medical expenses.[5] The development of new products and technologies in this sector depends on brainsharing. Clinical research is often too expensive, too complicated, and too multidisciplinary for any single player to pursue alone—just as we have seen in chips and sensors and new materials. The big pharma and life-sciences companies have cut back on their own research activities, especially in new fields and riskier ventures, preferring to focus on a smaller number of surer bets. But they still need the research that creates new knowledge, and so they increasingly buy the "R" in R&D and work in close collaboration with start-ups that are often founded by professors and students to pursue unorthodox ideas. These smaller companies typically do not have enough talent (particularly in management), the necessary technology, or deep enough pockets to pursue their research as they would like. So they, in turn, seek collaborations with bigger players to help fund development and also work with them to manage the process that takes a concept from an early trial to a marketable product. The big companies sometimes take a financial stake in their smaller partners or purchase them outright.

Some of today's most exciting action in the life-sciences field is in medical devices, now a $300 billion industry. These devices will bring major changes to medical practices and procedures. Sensors will collect far more useful medical data than ever, thus taking much of the guesswork out of diagnosis and monitoring the effects of treatments and medications. Surgeons will rely on implantable, disposable sensors to precisely position and monitor implants.

Wearable devices—such as watches, clothing, and patches—with sensors embedded in them, will monitor and track various bodily organs and functions, analyze performance, and provide health alerts. Just as the portable pacemaker replaced the operating room machine, these small and unobtrusive wearables will replace the stand-alone testing equipment that has been confined to the doctor's office and the patient's hospital room. They will wirelessly transmit large amounts of data to your health-care provider, the device manufacturer, regulators, and others. (Security and privacy issues are already being hotly discussed.) "Soon all medical devices will be collecting real-time information," Johnson & Johnson CEO Alex Gorsky told us. "The era of dumb products is over and the era of remote medicine is upon us."[6]

In this chapter, our journey takes us to Minneapolis, pacemaker capital of the world, as well as to Portland, Oregon, where big data reigns; Zurich, Switzerland, home of an extraordinary science park; and the BioSaxony region in Germany and Oulu, Finland, where a life-sciences brainbelt emerged from the remains of the mobile telephony industry.

Minneapolis: Self-Reliance Can Be Key to Collaboration

Minneapolis–St. Paul has experienced economic upturns and downturns over the years, but the area never fell into the kind of rustbelt status experienced by cities and regions such as Akron and Malmö before it began to emerge as a brainbelt. The metropolis was long a center for milling grains, brewing beer, and sawing lumber. Although activities in those sectors slowed down, the city avoided a devastating decline, because important Fortune 100 companies—including 3M, General Mills, and Cargill—which had long been headquartered in the Twin Cities (as the neighboring communities of Minneapolis and St. Paul are known)—did not abandon the area. Minneapolis also had an early role in the computer industry, as the home to Control Data, the creator of the first supercomputer. The company's presence—along with the many spin-offs it created—attracted venture capital firms and IT talent to Minneapolis that later benefited the region's medical-device companies.

Railroad yard in front of Minneapolis's Gold Medal Flour mill, ca.
1940. Credit: Corbis Images

Minneapolis became a brainbelt for the life sciences, medical devices in particular, through a combination of factors. In the late 1940s, in response to data that showed a rising incidence of heart disease in the United States, the National Institutes of Health (NIH) boosted funding for research into heart health and related medical procedures. The grants created a cottage industry of medical-device developers in Minneapolis, as well as other areas in the country, and also encouraged the actions of pioneering, even swashbuckling, surgeons such as Lillehei.

Norman Dann was a venture capitalist in Minneapolis in the 1950s and watched as surgeons became "king of the hill," as he put it. These entrepreneurial doctors secured research grants, had little bureaucracy to contend with, were infatuated with medical technology, and spent lavishly on new devices that offered the latest features and capabilities. Their spending, in turn, fueled the rise of the small, emerging medical-device makers that invested much of their profits in further research.

The creation of the Minneapolis brainbelt also involved the participation of several innovative, world-class hospitals in the area—including the Mayo Clinic—as well as a key educational institution, the University of Minnesota, and its surgeons and students.

The local culture—which can be described as one of "careful risk taking"—also proved to be well suited to the development of complex, innovative, life-and-death products such as medical devices. This attitude stems partly from the work ethic of immigrants from Northern Europe who were talented tinkerers and self-reliant inventors, parsimonious with their resources. They preferred to fix things themselves before calling in a repairman or buying a replacement.

A Company as Connector and Catalyst of the Ecosystem

Although Lillehei was an important player in the early Minneapolis story, it is the talent pool associated with a single company, Medtronic, that can be seen as the essential connector.

Medtronic was founded in a garage in 1949 by Earl Bakken, who created the first pacemaker prototype for Lillehei, in partnership with his brother-in-law, to manufacture the pacemaker. Medtronic grew to become the global leader in medical devices and implants, but its most important and profitable product is still the pacemaker. The devices have gotten far smaller and more reliable than the gadget cobbled together by Bakken from Lillehei's specifications, but they are still expensive, selling in the range of $10,000–$25,000, not including hospital costs and surgeon's fees. About 1.5 million pacemakers are sold annually and Medtronic produces 40 percent of them. In fact, the United States has a virtual monopoly on making pacemakers.[7] Medtronic also leverages its expertise in pacemakers to produce other medical devices, including stents, defibrillators, brain and spine stimulators, and insulin pumps.[8]

As Medtronic grew into a global manufacturing leader, it spurred the creation of a great deal of new knowledge. When we asked Ellie Pidot, vice president of strategy at Medtronic, about the term "University of Medtronic"— which some say rivals or even surpasses the contribution of the University of Minnesota—she declined to rank the two, saying simply, "There is more innovation in cardiac R&D within a 50-mile radius of Minneapolis than anywhere else in the world."[9]

The two institutions work in constant collaboration with one another, and the flow of innovation goes both ways. For example, an insulin pump developed at the University of Minnesota was commercialized by Medtronic. It is just one of the many technologies that have emerged from UMN's Medical Devices Center, which is an invention "mill," whose scientists have generated more than 125 patents. The university also teaches entrepreneurship and is a sponsor of the Minnesota Cup, the largest statewide new-venture competition in the nation, which has attracted more than 8,000 aspiring entrepreneurs since 2005.[10]

The collaboration of Medtronic with UMN and other players is an extremely successful business generator. In 2000, there were 450 life-sciences companies (predominantly focused on medical devices) around Minneapolis; by 2014, that number had risen to 2,500. St. Jude, the world's largest heart-valve company, and Cardiac Pacemakers[11] were founded by former Medtronic researchers. The founders of several other companies making stents and implants— including CVRX, EV3[12] and SurModics—began their careers at the local pacemaker producers. Because there is so much activity in medical devices in Minneapolis, start-ups can draw on its huge talent pool, gain access to venture capital, and get feedback from academics, entrepreneurs, and other mentors with deep knowledge and long track records in the industry.

Acquisitions of small R&D firms with innovative teams are a key part of Medtronic's brainsharing strategy, as is the case for many other life-science companies. In 2014, for example, Medtronic purchased the Dutch start-up Sapiens SBS (Steering Brain Stimulation), which specializes in neuro-modulation, the targeted delivery of electrical pulses and drugs to specific sites in the nervous system. It is also developing next-generation deep brain stimulation with as many as forty individual contact points. Jan Keltjens, Sapiens CEO, explained that getting financing had become a problem, so it made sense to get help from Medtronic to take its products over the "finish line."[13]

Large legacy organizations make such acquisitions mainly because they can't match the innovative spirit of small research firms and they rely on their acquisitions to do much of the innovative research, usually with better results and lower costs. With his early experience still fresh in his mind, Norman Dann, now in his eighties, expressed a view that is held by many others, that "the best R&D is done by a small band of researchers without hierarchy who can correct mistakes rapidly and work in a culture that understands that mistakes are unavoidable in research."[14] Large organizations tend to be siloed, slow, and hierarchical, places where researchers get punished for being wrong rather than for being late. Medtronic's CEO, Omar Ishrak, an alumnus of GE Healthcare, believes that the yield on the company's R&D was too low and, even as he acquired smaller firms, he fired several thousand in-house researchers.[15] However, when it comes to organizing huge clinical trials and building support systems, big companies like Medtronic have overwhelming advantages—of expertise, reach, and resources.

In addition to the contributions made by Medtronic and the University of Minnesota, specialized research and training institutes, patent lawyers, regulatory specialists, venture capitalists, and the local government have also played important roles in forming "a whole culture," said Dale Wahlstrom, who was a vice president at Medtronic and then became CEO of a Minneapolis trade association called LifeScience

Alley.[16] Public-private partnerships are of particular importance. "When I was working as a scientist in the private sector," Wahlstrom told us, "I had no idea what a public-private
partnership could do." But he has come to see that it's crucial
for companies and universities to "band together" to develop
new ideas and reach out to the regulators. "I am a believer,
now," he said, echoing what we discovered about other brainbelts around the world.[17]

Portland: A Philanthropist
as Enabling Connector

Portland, unlike Minneapolis, did go through a rustbelt period. The state's economy was once driven by forestry, aluminum smelting, shipbuilding, and automotive assembly,
which were gradually replaced by apparel and technology
companies. An extensive network of suppliers and distributors grew up around Tektronix, a manufacturer of test and
measuring equipment. In 1974, Intel set up a chip fabrication plant in Portland to supplement its operations in California, when the US government required the company to
establish a backup facility in an area not vulnerable to earth-
quake. Under the leadership of Governor Barbara Roberts,
who served from 1991 to 1995, Oregon attracted other high-
tech companies by offering tax breaks in exchange for setting up plants according to mutually agreed-upon goals.

Sometimes it takes an outsider to bring parties together,
even when they have been operating in proximity to each
other for many years. That was the case in Portland, where
researchers at a leading university and businesspeople at

Phil Knight, founder of Nike and the Knight Cancer Institute.
Credit: Paul Morigi

semiconductor giant Intel had long been working in the same area, without collaborating. It was Phil Knight, co-founder and chairman of Nike, icon of the sportswear industry and another leading company in the region, who served as a catalyst in bringing people out of their silos. An important moment in that effort came on a September evening in 2013, when Knight took the stage at a fund-raising event honoring Brian Druker, director and star researcher of the Knight Cancer Institute, who famously said: "There is no question that we can defeat cancer. What it requires is knowledge. When we understand what is broken, we can fix it." Druker might have added that the required knowledge had two prerequisites: deep funding pockets and tight collaboration between the worlds of bioscience and high-tech manufacturing.

The Knight Institute had been named in Knight's honor five years earlier when he made a $100 million gift to the institute, which is a part of OHSU, and focuses on early stage cancer research. That earlier gift proved to be a watershed moment for the Portland area: the increased funding put the Knight Institute on the map as one of the top cancer research centers in the United States, and it brought the Portland life-sciences research community into closer collaboration with crucial partners outside the field of medical research. To be successful, OHSU needed the kind of smart manufacturing that Intel, the chip maker, and FEI, a company that makes electron-beam microscopes, were engaged in. In turn, Intel was eager to collaborate because it was seeking to develop the next generation of chips that are critical for genomics research and needed to work with large sets of patient data to aid in chip development. FEI saw an opportunity to refine its microscopes so that cancer researchers could better observe cells and their interaction with drugs.

In part thanks to Knight's 2008 gift, the biotech sector in Oregon did not suffer a decline during the recession; in fact, employment in the industry grew by 31 percent during the past decade.[18] However, even with Portland's success in life sciences during that difficult period, the region faced new financial challenges when, in 2010, the National Cancer Institute (part of NIH) began to reduce the size and quantity of its grants.

So, on that evening in 2013, Knight upped his commitment to the Portland area and challenged others to do the same. He pledged $500 million to the Knight Institute, if a matching amount could be raised over the next two years, a goal it was able to reach in June 2015.

Although Knight's gift is substantial, Portland's life-sciences brainbelt is still relatively small in comparison to areas like Boston and San Diego, but it is teeming with ambition and growing fast. Today, bioscience in the state is a $4 billion industry with a workforce of 15,000 people, 40 percent of whom work in medical instruments and 26 percent in the creation of drugs, making Oregon one of the leading states in biomedical manufacturing in the country.[19]

The Oregon Health & Science University grew and transformed as Portland's industrial landscape changed. OHSU was established in 1974 as the University of Oregon Health Sciences Center, then assimilated several state programs—including dentistry, medicine, and nursing—into its offerings. In 2001, the institution merged with the Oregon Graduate Institute of Science and Technology. Today, OHSU employs 2,500 faculty, enrolls 3,000 students, and has a $350 million annual research budget, and its three on-campus hospitals manage nearly 1 million patient visits annually.[20] OHSU is the sole National Cancer Institute–designated cancer center between San Francisco and Seattle and is recognized as one of the leading medical university research centers in the United States.

The growth of the high-tech industry, especially the presence of Intel, combined with the steady development of OHSU, put in place two essential elements needed to create the Portland life-sciences brainbelt: smart manufacturing and powerful academics. However, until the turn of the millennium, the technology community and the life-sciences players had not cohered into a "whole culture" of the kind Dale Wahlstrom talked about in Minneapolis. In

2001, the state of Oregon sought to close the gap between the two by strengthening the life-sciences ecosystem. A $200 million bond issue called Oregon Opportunity was proposed that would provide funds to develop a new biomedical research facility and recruit talent, and it was overwhelmingly approved by the voters. Local philanthropists contributed an additional $375 million to the pot.

The Oregon Opportunity initiative resulted in an explosion of activity and achievement. Not one but three new research centers and an incubator space were established, researchers brought in over $400 million in grants, and more than fifty biomedical companies started up and others moved in. Genentech produces two cancer drugs, Avastin and Herceptin, in a $400 million plant in the Portland suburb of Hillsboro. Biotronik, a Germany-based maker of the first wireless pacemakers,[21] operates a state-of-the-art plant near Lake Oswego, south of Portland. Sam Medical Products was founded by Sam Scheinberg, a battlefield trauma surgeon who developed a new generation of lightweight splints to replace the bulky, ill-fitting models he had used during the Vietnam War. Medolac Laboratories is a human milk bank, which collects breast milk from an extensive network of women and distributes it to nourish prematurely born babies.

Portland is also rapidly moving into remote medical monitoring, which requires multidisciplinary brainsharing among software engineers and medical researchers, and the coming together of wireless technologies with distributed computing power. We visited the offices of a company operating in this sector, ReelDx, located in a former rope factory that is now home to more than sixty start-ups. Bill Kelly, CEO of ReelDx, is a Harvard Business School graduate and serial entrepreneur[22] who founded the company with David Spiro, chief of pediatric emergency medicine at OHSU. Their purpose was to document patient treatment through smartphones or GoPro cameras worn by paramedics. Although they conceived their product as a teaching tool for medical students, they soon recognized its potential for use in ambulances and clinical trials, and in monitoring incapacitated and elderly patients. The plan is to enable the sharing of video through a secure, cloud-based platform that is compliant with HIPAA (the Health Insurance Portability and Accountability Act) regulations and to help make health care less costly and more efficient.

A Big Data Trade:
The OHSU-Intel Collaboration

Perhaps the most emblematic initiative of Portland's academic-manufacturing brainsharing is the one between OHSU and Intel. Mary Stenzel-Poore,[23] senior associate dean for research at the OHSU School of Medicine, helped get the program off the ground. She is a person who describes complex problems as "delicious" and regards the reduction in grants from the NIH as a positive development. Why? Because it forced the sharing of brainpower. As we saw in so many other brainbelts, it is often necessity that forces the emergence of team science, cross-disciplinary collaboration, and knowledge sharing. "People will only partner when they can't get there alone," Stenzel-Poore told us. But these relationships-of-necessity can be a lot of "hard work," she said, and they knew they needed a connector, a "matchmaker who could make the magic happen."

That's what they found in Joe Gray, chair of OHSU's Department of Biomedical Engineering, a scientist with over eighty patents to his name and a background in engineering and nuclear physics. As Gray described it, OHSU's goal was to create a "Google map for cancer" that would combine a microscopic view of the billions of mutations in cancer cells with a big-picture analysis of the entire cancer system.[24] Data visualization on this scale requires a tremendous amount of computing power, which is why Gray reached out to Intel and connected with Stephen Pawlowski, then Intel's CTO.[25] Pawlowski saw that the collaboration would combine Intel's strength in "developing energy-efficient, extreme scale computing solutions" with OHSU's ability to visualize and understand complex biological information.[26] Today, the Intel-OHSU program brings together computer scientists, biologists, and experts on biophysics, bio-informatics, and genomics, and they work side by side daily. Twenty Intel engineers are embedded on the OHSU campus.

Both partners see this kind of brainpower sharing as the way forward. For Intel, health care is a key future market, one it wants to lead by creating the next generation of high-powered chips. The goal is to be able to analyze an individual's DNA in a period of hours, rather than weeks, and to do so for tens of dollars, rather than thousands. OHSU provides the patient data that Intel needs and, in return, gains the ability to treat its patients more effectively. To realize the potential of personalized medicine, Gray says, it is

Joe Gray, on the right, chair of OHSU's Department of Biomedical Engineering. Credit: Oregon Health & Science University

necessary to collect data on millions of patients to identify cells that are similar to those of the patient you're treating and to understand the outcome of different kinds of treatments. Only by working together can the researchers gain the insight they need to better help patients and the chip makers gain the expertise they require to produce more capable chips for health-care applications.

Collaborations of this kind have helped scientists in the Portland area see that the ability to transform research into marketable products is essential for securing corporate funding. (There are still traces of the old academia-business divide in Portland and other brainbelts.) But the complexity of the projects and the regulatory hurdles that must be overcome in the health-care industry can make for a slow transition from research to product. Still, according to Andrew Watson, director of OHSU's Office of Technology Transfer, OHSU has granted eighty-four licenses to for-profit companies to commercialize research conducted by OHSU scientists and technologists and has spun off start-ups at a rate of three or four per year. (Not bad as a start when compared to longtime champions Stanford or MIT, where as many as twenty start-ups are spun off annually.) Most of OHSU's start-ups are located in Oregon, so they contribute to the region's economic development and also bring OHSU as much as $3 million in license fees annually.[27]

There are many success stories. Orexigen Therapeutics, for example, offers a weight-loss drug called Contrave for diabetic and obese patients. MolecularMD commercialized the university's patents on methods for detecting cancer mutations that are resistant to Gleevec, a drug for treating chronic leukemia. Another start-up is testing Richard Wampler's design for the first non-pumping heart, which could help overcome the shortage of donated hearts.[28]

The key to all this activity is brainsharing among entities and disciplines. Joe Gray told us that when he was in school, there was no life-sciences curriculum that embraced all the related disciplines. "We know now that you need interdisciplinary collaboration," he said, "because a single human mind simply can't grasp the complexities anymore."

Brainsharing Requires Infrastructure, Too

Start-ups need more than just brilliant scientific minds. Indeed, young companies need market knowledge, infrastructure, and the capital to create it. In this regard, large-scale philanthropy (with Phil Knight as the leader) has played a significant role in providing the needed funds to develop Portland's biomedical infrastructure. In addition to Knight's contributions, gifts made by Daniel K. Ludwig, Bill Gates, Paul Allen, and others[29] have helped create facilities that encourage the sharing of brainpower. The new buildings of the Knight Cancer Institute, for example, will be located close to the downtown area, rather than on a campus hilltop outside the center. The effect will be to link OHSU's cancer research activities into the ecosystem of start-ups and bioscience incubators and enable connections with chemistry and engineering at other universities nearby.

OHSU's Collaborative Life Sciences Building, too, will be an important component of the university's downtown presence and a hub of its collaboration with Intel. There, engineering and computer science are integrated into the curriculum, and the building is designed with features that accommodate the most advanced health-care-related equipment. The floors, for example, "float" within the superstructure so as to eliminate environmental vibration, which can disturb the operation of extremely sensitive microscopes. Most important, OHSU's star researchers, including Joe Gray, have offices at the facility. Gray showed us a photo of the view from his office just a few years ago, which looked out on the Willamette River and the remains of the shipyard that operated there for decades.

That view has been transformed. According to angel investor Eric Rosenfeld, Portland was once characterized as a "smaller version of Cincinnati," meaning that it was bland

Portland waterfront, 1898.
Credit: Library of Congress, LC-USZ62-120205

and without the amenities that are necessary to creating brainbelts. No longer. City officials and university administrators are working together to revive abandoned parts of the city, improve transportation, and promote opportunities for young entrepreneurs to open farmers' markets with locally produced food and to create good restaurants. Portland already has the most bike riders per capita of any American city and is a magnet for well-educated graduates who like working in start-ups. "This is a fun place for creative geeks," Rosenfeld says. "and we also attract affluent, retired CEOs who love to take on a new management challenges."[30]

Portland has been known for years as a hotspot for athletic pursuits, sportswear, specialty beer brewing, and wine making. Now it is gaining worldwide attention as a hotspot of brainsharing activity in life sciences.

Portland streetcar in front of OHSU Life Sciences Building.
Credit: *Teresa Boyle, City of Portland/NACTO*

Zurich: A New Kind of Currency

Fred's first trip outside Holland as a financial journalist, in the spring of 1981, was to Switzerland. There, as he interviewed bankers and financial analysts, he saw that confidential banking was a sacred asset. Thirty years later, under heavy pressure from American authorities, Swiss banks were forced to change their private banking practices and lost some of that traditional advantage. The 2008 financial crisis dealt another painful blow to the local banking community.

Therefore, when we visited Zurich in 2014, our purpose was not to interview members of the financial industry but rather to learn more about the Technical University that had become a start-up engine of biotech firms. Traditionally, fundamental research had been done by the global pharmaceutical

View from Peter Church, Zurich, Switzerland.
Credit: Library of Congress, Prints & Photographs Division, Photochrom Collection
LC-DIG-ppmsc-07927

companies, such as Roche and Novartis in nearby Basel, but in the previous two decades Zurich developed as a life-science brainbelt. Just as we saw in other cities, Zurich's abandoned manufacturing sites now were home to a science park, theaters, and restaurants. These long-forgotten areas had become vibrant and attractive places to live and work.

Zurich, and the other life-sciences brainbelts we investigated in Europe—Dresden and Oulu—developed in ways quite distinct from the life-sciences brainbelts in the United States and the brainsharing centers that had focused on different industries. Although Zurich did not go through a rustbelt phase or face an existential crisis, it did lose some

Mario Jenni, center, with Gian-Luca Bona (CEO of Empa), left, and Peter Frischknecht (managing director of Feld3), right.
Credit: © Empa, 2013

of its traditional manufacturing industries and the banking industry lost some of its dominance, but it was still a banking center and was also headquarters to luxury businesses with world-class brand names like Rolex and Lindt.

The emergence of Zurich as a life-sciences brainbelt was largely due to the initiatives of the Swiss Federal Institute of Technology (ETH), based in Zurich. ETH Zurich is one of the world's leading universities for technology and the natural sciences, a magnet for talented individuals, a hotbed of start-up activity, and a desirable location for established organizations as well. As we learned in other brainbelts, the genesis of the change could be traced to an individual connector and, in this case, it was Charles Weissmann, founder of Biogen, as we saw in Chapter 1. Weissmann's name came up immediately when we spoke with Mario Jenni, part-time CEO of the Bio-Technopark Schlieren-Zurich, where much of the regional action in life-sciences research takes place. As director of the Molecular Biology Institute at ETH, Weissmann had been an academic who had turned entrepreneur to found Biogen in 1978. His colleagues thought Weissmann had "sold his soul to the devil," Jenni told us.[31]

However, as typically happens in the development of a brainbelt, Weissmann's bold move eventually brought people of differing opinions together. Although universities do not change quickly, over the period of a decade Biogen's success caused other academic researchers and administrators to reexamine their attitudes about the relationship between research and business. Their conversion was hastened with the passage in 1991 of legislation that required ETH, a state-funded institution, to apply its research to the creation of products that would benefit the taxpayers who funded the research and the society as a whole. Gradually, ETH took on the institutional connector role that Weissmann had pioneered and became like a benign spider in the web, the essential player in an ecosystem that includes the usual suspects: academics, authorities, entrepreneurs, scientists, and financiers.

Just as important as the role of the university was the establishment of several science parks. The first was Technopark Zurich, which opened its doors in 1993. It was developed by Thomas von Waldkirch, long a professor at ETH and one of the few academics who applauded the founding of Biogen by his colleague, Professor Weissmann. Von Waldkirch had visited the United States in 1985, and what he experienced there convinced him that Zurich needed a science park where young entrepreneurs could be mentored and flourish. He began by establishing the Technopark Foundation in 1988, with support from Zurich mayor Thomas Wagner and ETH president Heinrich Ursprung, as well as entrepreneurs, politicians, researchers, and bankers.[32] The venture found a home in a manufacturing facility vacated by the Swiss industrial group Sulzer, and as soon as the renovations were completed, companies began moving in. In 2001, von Waldkirch was ready to take on a different challenge. As his successor, he selected Lesley Spiegel, then thirty-one, because she was a contemporary of the entrepreneurs in the facility. During Spiegel's tenure as leader of the Technopark Zurich, the number of company tenants has doubled to over three hundred, primarily in science and technology but also in financial services.

The Bio-Technopark Schlieren-Zurich, which is devoted solely to life-sciences companies, was the brainchild of Leo Krummenacher, a retired entrepreneur. He purchased several buildings from the Swiss Rail Carriage and Elevator Factory when it went out of business in 1984. He knew the university, ETH, was desperately in need of space at the time and it was one of the first tenants to move in, but it soon moved to a brand-new complex north of the city. Krummenacher kept in touch with some of the professors he had gotten to know during ETH's brief tenancy, and they told him that what was really needed was an incubator that could provide specialized laboratory equipment that many start-ups did not have access to or could not afford. Krummenacher did some calculations. "I felt the risks were limited," he said, "so I stepped in."[33] The incubator proved immediately attractive, and since then, tens of millions of Swiss francs have been invested in equipment.[34]

Mario Jenni has been part-time CEO of the Bio-Technopark Schlieren-Zurich since 2003. Perhaps his most important duty is identifying and accepting tenants for the park. "The selection of companies remains very focused on life sciences and we cannot dilute that," Jenni has said. More than thirty companies are now based in the park, including producers of drugs, medical devices, biodegradable bones, and diagnostics. Ninety percent of the companies that started up there have survived.

Because land is limited, the park is building upward into high-rises. Jenni wants to add more offices and laboratory space as well as features that will enhance the campus-like atmosphere, with informal meeting areas where people can interact informally and an auditorium for large meetings, lectures, and conferences.

One of the success stories at Bio-Technopark is the start-up company Molecular Partners, which develops proteins whose purpose is to guide medications to locations in the body where they can do their work most effectively.[35] The company has research agreements with several pharmaceutical companies, valued at about $50 million each.

In 2012, Molecular Partners formed an alliance with Allergan, based in the United States, to develop more effective treatments for diseases of the eye, a research collaboration that could be worth as much as $1.4 billion in revenues to the company.

But Bio-Technopark is not solely a haven for start-ups and university-led initiatives. In 2005, the Swiss pharmaceutical company Roche bought Glycart, whose mission is "to become a world leader in the development of antibody products that address unmet clinical needs with increased efficacy."[36] That research will be concentrated at the Bio-Technopark. Novartis made its debut at the park in 2009 with the purchase of ESBATech, which plays an important role in preclinical research on a wide range of eye diseases.[37]

The explosion in research, start-ups, and big-company facilities has created a need to do just as they're doing in Portland: develop ways to bring academia and industry closer together to better exchange information and collaborate on initiatives that build the ecosystem. To that end, ETH created the Technology Transfer Department to support students and professors in developing commercial projects. The university also launched a trial incubator in 2012, called the Innovation and Entrepreneurship Lab (ieLab), whose purpose is to help students learn entrepreneurship by translating their ideas for products into business models. One of the focus areas of the ieLab is life sciences: molecular biology, biotechnology, biochemistry, pharmaceuticals, and diagnostics. Undergraduates with an idea can apply for an eighteen-month stint at the ieLab. Those who are accepted receive seed capital of 150,000 CHF (about $160,000), free room and board, and access to advice and mentorship from a variety of experts on such matters as law, patents, finance, and entrepreneurship.

In Zurich, though the promoters, most of whom were professors of biology, saw the need for multidisciplinary collaboration, it was still difficult to lure the academics and researchers out of their silos. In Portland, Joe Gray faced the same problem, and his solution was to create the new buildings on the river's edge to make it virtually impossible for its inhabitants *not* to collaborate. The installation of a state-of-the-art multidisciplinary laboratory—featuring the latest FEI microscopes—sealed the deal and removed any lingering reservations that some still might have had. The ETH employed the same tactic. In 2006, the Swiss government donated 100 million CHF ($107 million) to open a new university site in Basel. That same year, the president of the university, Ernst Hafen, a molecular biologist, created a multidisciplinary institute, the Department of Biosystems Science and Engineering, where biologists, physicists, chemists, and computer scientists now work closely together on big-data research.[38]

Unlike some of the former rustbelt cities, the Zurich brainbelt does not need much in the way of improvements to the city environment. Professionals in their thirties and forties, both Swiss and foreign, love to work in the area. "Let's be honest," said Mario Jenni, "Switzerland is a great place to live."

BioSaxony: State Support Stimulates
Private Action

Saxony, the former East German state with its capital city, Dresden, suffered deeply from the Communist period that lasted until the fall of the Berlin Wall in 1989. Free enterprise and private ownership had not been allowed under the Communist regime, and this meant that the market economy had to be built up from scratch. It was an experienced politician, Kurt Biedenkopf, prime minister from 1990 to 2002, who focused this process on fundamental research.

Saxony had a rich history in this regard, and Biedenkopf wanted to build a new economic order on this tradition. It was a smart and successful bet. Dresden is now home to the largest chip-production sites in Europe, as we saw in Chapter 2. But what is less well known—we only learned about it on our first visit—is that Dresden and nearby Leipzig also developed a brainbelt in the life-science field.

Dresden is working hard to bring this "sleeping beauty" to life. The man who is leading the charge is André Hofmann, an energetic engineer in his mid-thirties who is CEO of BioSaxony, an association founded in 2009 to boost the life-sciences sector.[39] When we met, it was a surprise, if not a shock, to see such a young man in the role of connector. Other connectors we had met were typically businesspeople, administrators, politicians, or scientists with many years of practical experience and large networks of colleagues and associates.

But Hofmann has a personal quality that is a great asset for any connector—empathy, a quality that is needed to bring people, companies and institutions together and to unite often opposing or conflicting views and interests into a new, inspiring identity. He showed this aspect of his personality when we asked him about his experiences with the two political systems—Communist and capitalist—he had lived in. Hofmann was in elementary school when the Berlin Wall fell in 1989, and he praised the way that kids helped each other during the Communist era. That group cohesion has been eroded by competitiveness and a greater focus on individualism. Yet life was far from rosy in the Communist era. Hofmann remembers how his older brother was not allowed to attend college, because their father was not a member of the Communist Party. By the time Hofmann was ready for college, seven years later, he had freedom of choice.

The buildup of the life-sciences brainbelt in Dresden has similarities to that of Portland. In Oregon, it was Phil Knight's philanthropy that catalyzed the creation of new infrastructural elements such as research facilities and helped attract more scientists. In Dresden, a €100 million investment made by the state had a similar effect.

In the late 1990s, scientists and entrepreneurs in Saxony saw there were tremendous business opportunities in life sciences, and in 2000, the state government provided €200 million to set up the necessary facilities and attract top-notch life-sciences researchers. The funds were to be equally divided between the cities of Leipzig, in western Saxony, and Dresden, in the center of the state.

The stimulus had dramatic results in both cities. In Leipzig, an incubator was opened in 2003, called Bio City Leipzig,[40] which soon became home to forty start-ups, bio-tech service companies, and six professors who conducted research in the incubator's labs, and the start-ups are further supported by a technology transfer organization called Bio-Net Leipzig.[41] Seeing the success of the incubator, the city of Leipzig, in conjunction with the state, provided an additional €200 million in support of life-sciences activities.

The most exciting initiative came in 2005, when the medical school at the University of Leipzig launched an initiative called Innovation Center Computer Assisted Surgery (ICCAS).[42] Its mission is to bring together scientists from several disciplines—including engineering, material sciences, and medical sciences—to conduct research toward a common goal: developing the operating room of the future. ICCAS has become the leading authority in model-based automation and integration (MAI), an initiative to "integrate standardized patient and process models and to make them available to surgeons before and during operations," for standardization of surgical methods and the development of patient and process models in oncology.[43]

In Dresden, the focus has been on molecular biology. The driving force behind the work in that city has been Kai Simons, a Finnish-born doctor and biologist who spent much of his career as group leader at the European Molecular Biology Laboratory in Heidelberg.[44] In the late 1990s, he collaborated with several colleagues to develop a plan for a new molecular-cell biology and genetics center that would be associated with the Max Planck Institutes, an independent, nonprofit organization based in Munich. A key characteristic of the new facility was that it should be open to other universities, research institutes, and for-profit companies—in short, a brainsharing organization.

Possible locations were debated. Simons and his colleagues decided against Heidelberg, because they doubted the brainsharing concept would work in that traditional city. They knew about Saxony's interest in life sciences, however, and considered Dresden as a possible site. The problem, however, was the area had no tradition of research in molecular biology.[45] They overcame their reservations because the commitment to sharing knowledge was so high on the agenda in Dresden and because the state of Saxony was willing to invest €100 million in the project—a strong incentive. The Max Planck Institute of Molecular Cell Biology and Genetics, Dresden[46] opened its doors in 1998, near the University of Dresden's hospital, on the banks of the river Elbe. In 2004, another life-sciences innovation center, the Bioinnovationszentrum,[47] moved close by, and, in 2009, BioSaxony located its offices in the same building. The concentration of life-sciences activities in the neighborhood has now become so great, people refer to it as Biopolis.

The Max Planck Institute in Dresden acts as an accelerator of new brainsharing life-sciences initiatives. Physicists, biologists, and physicians work closely together there and their research is coordinated by colleagues from four institutions: the Technical University, the Faculty of Medicine, the University Hospital Carl Gustav Carus, and the Helmholtz Institute. In 2005, the interdisciplinary research initiative OncoRay was started at the institute, to promote personalized cancer treatment using radiation therapy.[48] OncoRay was financially supported by the state of Saxony, the federal government in Berlin, and the EU in Brussels.

In 2006, brainsharing got another boost when the interdisciplinary network CRTD (Center for Regenerative Therapies) was founded in Dresden.[49] Although it is administered by the Technical University, it operates independently, collaborating closely with a number of other research institutes, including other Max Planck Institutes (there are many of them, each focusing on different disciplines and studies) and the Max Bergmann Center for Biomaterials.[50] In addition, a dozen companies—including Novartis, Amgen, Qiagen, and Boehringer—are involved in the project.

The development of the life sciences in Saxony continues to this day. In 2014, a new facility was opened on the grounds of the University Hospital to house a laser-driven particle accelerator. With this advanced equipment, treatments can be accurately targeted on cancer cells, causing little or no damage to healthy tissue.

But in the past couple of years, André Hofmann, of BioSaxony, has seen there are still many more beauties to be awakened, so he started the Bioconnection to showcase start-ups to investors and other companies.[51] At the first meeting of the Bioconnection, sixty researchers made their pitches—limited to ten minutes—to the audience in a casual environment. There were also workshops in which experienced entrepreneurs shared their business experience with scientists, as well as a fair at which companies presented their work.

Not all of the action in the region is taking place through BioSaxony or in the Biopolis area. Wilhelm Zörgiebel, a highly successful entrepreneur, founded Biotype, in close collaboration with doctors from the University Hospital Dresden.[52] They developed a test that can determine DNA in a single day, a sharp reduction from the four weeks it took before their discovery. In addition to his own entrepreneurial efforts, Zörgiebel transformed an old furniture factory located near the international airport in an area north of Dresden into a life-sciences incubator. Now, fifty companies have been established there, employing more than four hundred people. Two of the start-ups are Zörgiebel's own. Qualitype creates software to improve forensic research and Rotop creates products for nuclear medicine diagnostics.[53]

Hofmann says he is satisfied with what has been achieved in the region, although there is still much to be done so that the world recognizes the Saxony region as an important life-sciences brainbelt. Before 2000, there was no life-sciences activity in the region. Within fifteen years, one hundred life-sciences companies—in biotech and pharma—have established themselves there. And that is a great distinction of this area: it was not a rustbelt area that had to come back from a great decline. It was, instead, a beauty that was created from scratch.

Oulu: From Wireless Talk to Connected Health

In the late 1990s, when Ericsson, Sweden's mobile phone leader (a company we also discussed in Chapter 3), and Nokia, Finland's wunderkind, were about to announce their quarterly earnings reports, the scene on the editorial floor of the Swedish financial publication *Dagens Industri* looked more like the inside of a sports pub toward the end of a soccer game than a newspaper office: the place buzzed with excitement as everybody waited to hear the final score. But in this case, it was not about which team had scored the most goals, but which of the two companies had sold the most mobile phones. Ten years later, Samsung and Apple had replaced the Scandinavian companies as the global leaders in mobile phones, and the Oulu region, where Nokia was based, had to look for a new focus, which it eventually found in wireless health-care facilities and devices.

Harri Posti, director of the Centre for Wireless Communications at the University of Oulu, began his career at Nokia immediately after his graduation from the University of Oulu in 1989. Nokia centered its research efforts in Oulu because the Finnish government provided incentives for it to launch a cable company there. Nokia's success kickstarted Finland's rapid transition from traditional industries like paper and pulp to high tech. When Posti joined, Nokia was a young company—most of its engineers were in their twenties and its managers in their thirties—that had boldly moved into the nascent mobile phone market.[54] At its peak, the company employed 15,000 IT people in Oulu. It was an early brainbelt, but then, when it missed the boat in smartphones, it fell into a rustbelt-like decline, affecting the entire ecosystem and causing great anxiety about Oulu's future. Like Lund-Malmö and the Research Triangle, it went through a double transition: the center of agriculture and traditional manufacturing went into decline and reemerged as a technology brainbelt, which ran into trouble and made another transition to a different brainbelt activity.

Good engineers are not the same as bold entrepreneurs. So, when Nokia reluctantly laid off employees, it not only gave them a two-year severance package but also provided seed capital to some of its engineers to help them set up new businesses. "The downfall of Nokia is definitely a mixed blessing," Posti explained. "Several thousand jobs disappeared from Oulu, but a lot of the expertise in base stations and radio frequency remained."[55]

Traditional Finnish perseverance transformed the fallout of Nokia's implosion into many start-ups in IT, medical technology, and clean technology. Nokia, bolstered with solid cash flow from its patents (which it did not sell to Microsoft), rebranded itself as Nokia Networks, focusing on the intelligent networks that form the backbone of the Internet of Things.

Today, Oulu is once again of interest to the editors at *Dagens Industri*. Located in northern Finland just below Lapland and the Arctic Circle, Oulu's cobblestone streets, bicycle paths, and traditional wooden houses—juxtaposed with modern Finnish architecture—belie the city's transformation from a sleepy rural town historically known for producing sailing ships and tar for the British Royal Navy into a high-tech hub that hosts world-class research centers.

The University of Oulu houses 17,000 students and 5,000 faculty in a group of low-rise buildings in the forested outskirts of town located next to a business/technology park for start-ups and close to Nokia's R&D Center. Large numbers of foreign students from all over the world now find their way to Oulu, filling the streets and crowding local hangouts.

Nokia and the University of Oulu, in collaboration with a forward-looking city administration, created a modern version of the ancient Greek Acropolis—the nucleus and citadel of the capital city of Athens—but this one a haven for start-ups.

Technopolis comprises two business parks, which provide space for the sharing of brainpower between the University of Oulu's science and technology researchers and the practical skills of the faculty of the University of Applied Sciences.

There are other types of support for start-ups, including a vocational training center, the VTT State Technical Research Centre (a public nonprofit institution that helps companies to apply the newest technologies), the Institute for Management and Technological Training, and a business incubator, Oulu Innovation Ltd.

There is considerable activity in Oulu, and much of it is in the life sciences. WellTech Oulu, an institute within the University of Oulu, coordinates the research conducted in the departments of science, medicine, and technology. It also works closely with companies to stimulate and improve education.[56] The region boasts a major academic hospital and four medical centers.

The Oulu region now produces thirty to fifty start-ups in the life-sciences sector every year, and Finland's medical-device industry achieved growth as high as 20 percent in 2012, outpacing the global average of 5 percent. This exceptional growth rate was achieved partly because the process of European and FDA approval for medical devices proved to be less of a hindrance than expected. In the past, it could take as long as seven years to gain approval for a new device, but one recent product, a heart monitor, was approved in less than a year.

Oulu, like other brainbelts, has built on its legacy: expertise in wireless technology that was gained during its Nokia days. It then moved beyond the original applications of that knowledge to apply it to a new activity, life sciences. Tuula Palmen, director of BusinessOulu's bio-health cluster, agreed that Nokia's implosion unleashed innovation in the medical technology field. "Our aim is now to marry advances in medicine with cutting-edge mobile technology," she told us.[57]

The members of Oulu's life-sciences brainbelt recognize the importance of personalized health-care delivery, and their approach is to give patients as much responsibility for their own health as possible. The start-up iSTOC has created software that reads diagnostic strips that continuously monitor vital information that the user's smartphone instantly analyzes. Assisted by real-time medical coaching transmitted through the smartphone, patients (or nurses, if present) can perform most routine tests on the spot, which iSTOC claims can reduce overall costs by up to 70 percent.[58] Odosoft has developed a fetal monitor that, together with a smartphone app, allows a pregnant mother to monitor her unborn baby's heart rate, displaying the information in a graph of each week of the pregnancy. Spektitor monitors the heart rate of adult patients for emergency rooms or other triage situations, and Polar Electro produces heart monitors contained in bracelets, watches, and smartphones. Otometri CEO Manna Hannula, motivated by the experience his children had with recurring ear infections, worked closely with the Oulu University Hospital and the University of Applied Sciences to develop an ear-infection detector for home use. Finnish doctors now use his device extensively to minimize the use of antibiotics in treating ear infections, as they are unnecessary in 80 percent of cases.

To learn more about how such companies go about the arduous process of developing ideas for life-sciences products into production-ready goods, we visited Optomed, a start-up that designs and manufactures a hand-held retinal imaging device called the Smartscope™. Seppo Kopsala, the company's thirty-five-year-old founder, is as soft-spoken and understated as he is serious and determined. Together with Markku Broas, a physician at the University of Lapland, he wanted to create a device that could replace the expensive, heavy desktop imagers that were then standard. (His approach is reminiscent of Lillehei and his pacemaker.) With its remarkable power, portability, and versatility, the Smartscope™ is to existing imagers what the smartphone is to the desktop computer. China and India have expressed interest in Optomed's scanner, given the importance of remote diagnostics for their massive (and underdeveloped) rural areas. An initial lack of interest from Western doctors worried investors, but many of them have since come around and the Smartscope™ has been increasingly accepted.

Kopsala's story is similar to that of many start-up founders in Oulu. He began his career at MyOrigo, a Finnish company that developed an early touchscreen and user interface for smartphones. Samsung and Apple passed on the technology (Steve Jobs said, "We don't want to get involved in mobile

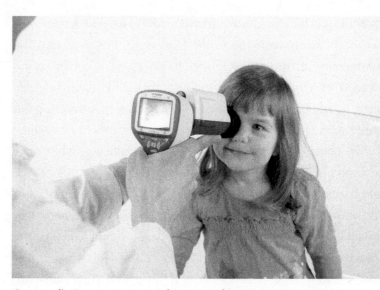

Optomed's Smartscope retinal imaging device. Credit: Optomed

phones"), and MyOrigo eventually went bankrupt. Kopsala learned that even with a working prototype of a good idea, the real work has only started. This realization served him well when he founded Optomed, as he worked out several technical kinks and nearly went bankrupt more than once.

In addition to personal qualities—an ability to think differently, optimism, and persistence—the entrepreneur needs government assistance, marketing partners, and, very important, money. Kopsala thought he could develop a prototype in two years with a €1 million investment and half that amount from Tekes, a Finnish agency that finances innovation, but it ended up taking five years and €12 million to create a prototype that was credible to potential customers and partners, and a total of eight years to become a financially viable business.

During those years, Kopsala spent as much as 70 percent of his time talking to potential investors. In October 2010, his colleagues completed a prototype with an outstanding optical design and, with the last of his money, Kopsala traveled to the United States to meet with Volk, a well-regarded lens manufacturing company based in Cleveland, which had been considering Optomed as a supplier. Kopsala joined Volk's CEO and CTO on a journey across the United States, visiting clinics, doing demonstrations for ophthalmologists and optometrists, and calling on university professors to talk up his product. "I went through the wringer," Kopsala remembered, but Volk was convinced.[59] Volk acquired exclusive distribution rights for the device in North and South America, and its English parent company, Halma Plc, invested €2 million to bring the product to market.

Optomed launched its first viable, if imperfect, commercial product in the spring of 2011, and it gained acceptance in the market, particularly from pediatric ophthalmologists, who liked using the handheld product with children because they have difficulty sitting still before the traditional retinal scanner. It also proved popular with doctors who perform outreach screening for eye diseases in villages in developing countries and with customers in emerging markets. The Aravind Eye Care System, based in India, performs more cataract surgeries than any company in the world. Seeking to become the "McDonald's of eye surgery," Aravind uses Optomed's handheld scanners to streamline its surgeries into an assembly line–like process that reduces the duration of the average procedure to two minutes (it usually takes forty minutes) and cuts costs by 99 percent.

Today, Optomed's growth in sales and presence—along with its success in attracting partners in Europe, the United States (Volk), Europe (Zeiss), and Japan (Canon)—gives Kopsala confidence that the company has a bright future and could disrupt the life-sciences market. It also introduced him to the concept of smart manufacturing. Although he originally assumed that production would take place in China or Thailand, he started manufacturing in Austria and will soon bring it to Oulu. Why? "The plant needs to be close to the engineers who designed the Smartscope™," he said. "You need a lot of engineering support and also must be able to get to market fast."

Peril and Potential

Although there is great excitement about the developments in the field of medical devices, wearables in particular, there is also plenty of concern and uncertainty. How will all that data be handled? What about payment through government and insurance plans?

Despite concerns, the need for innovation in life sciences and medical devices is urgent and the opportunities enormous. Today, the United States and Northern Europe are world leaders in the medical device industry. Although uncomplicated medical products such as rubber gloves, thermometers, and syringes can be made in countries throughout the world, Western companies are dominant in the creation of complex, high-value medical devices such as pacemakers, prostheses, implants, and surgical robots.

In life sciences, perhaps more than any other industry, smart trumps cheap.

The life-sciences industry has a reputation for employing creative thinkers, paying good salaries, and driving GDP growth, exports, employment, and innovation. Over 400,000 people work in the medical-device industry in the United States alone, mostly in well-paid, high-tech jobs (despite considerable outsourcing of assembly to Mexico, Ireland, Costa Rica, China, and Puerto Rico). Two-thirds of the world's forty-six largest medical device makers are based in the United States, with over 6,500 companies in the industry.[60] The United States has 137 medical schools, and nearly four hundred major teaching hospitals are important partners for industry innovation.[61] Europe has a similarly impressive record in the field. More than 575,000 people in Europe are employed in the life-sciences sector, as compared to 520,000 in the United States. There are more than 25,000 companies involved in life-sciences work, 95 percent of which are small or medium-sized, and most of which are based in Germany. Yearly turnover of these European companies is €100 billion. Considering the total global market, the United States has about a 39 percent share; Europe, 28 percent; and Japan, 10 percent.[62]

The medical-device industry would not exist without the sharing of brainpower between top-notch universities and world-renowned hospitals, which is why it is so concentrated in knowledge centers such as the ones we have explored in Minneapolis and Portland in the United States and leading centers in Europe, particularly Zurich, Eindhoven,

Dresden, and Oulu, as well as the well-known centers in Cambridge/Boston and Silicon Valley.

If the industry is to continue on its successful trajectory, however, there are a number of important issues that must be addressed—indeed, they impact all of the focus areas we have discussed—including matters of policy, education and training, funding, infrastructure, and culture.

Chapter Five

A SMARTER WORLD

*How Brainsharing Can Meet the
Challenges of the Twenty-First Century*

The future is being created in brainbelts and innovation zones around the world—in the ones we visited and have talked about in this book, in others we were only able to mention, and in still more that are forming but have yet to emerge—presenting us with mind-boggling opportunities, uncertainties, challenges, and questions. How will these high-capacity chips, new materials, and bioscience discoveries affect our daily lives, the way we work, and the world we live in? Will they enable human beings to function more effectively and happily throughout their lives? Will they ease some of the social strains and inequities of our societies? Will they reverse the twentieth-century exodus to the suburbs and help create better-functioning cities? Will they help mitigate the negative effects of climate change and address the challenges of the planet's aging populations?

Many people worry that the advances in technology create as many problems as they do solutions, but it is our belief that smart products developed through brainsharing are—by the very process of how they are created—more likely to offer solutions than those created by entities working in traditional, siloed, and isolated models. That's because many voices and disciplines are involved throughout the process, each one contributing to and counterbalancing others.

So, in this chapter, we'll show how smart new products, services, and technologies conceived and created through sharing brainpower initiatives will help us meet many of the challenges we now face. Some of the impact we have already witnessed, and some we can reasonably speculate on. We'll look at five key areas: housing and communities, offices and workplaces, cities and agricultural areas, the environment, and transportation. Will smart products and services solve all our twenty-first-century ills in these areas and create a utopia? Not exactly. Will they introduce *new* problems directly associated with the processes themselves, just as mass production methods, even while meeting important human needs, also had harmful effects on the environment and human health? Likely. But will they make great contributions to dealing with the known challenges of the twenty-first century? We believe the answer is yes.

Smart Energy and Climate Change: Consumers Become Producers

One of the greatest challenges of the twenty-first century— if not the greatest—will be to minimize our dependency on energy sources that contribute to the effects of climate change. That will only happen if homes, buildings, planes, cars, and machines become more energy efficient and we continue to use more solar, wind, biofuel, and other renewable sources while reducing their cost. These new sources will yield far greater benefits than any of these advancements could have on their own if they are combined with new energy storage technologies. From the Hudson Tech Valley to Raleigh and Portland and from Dresden to Oulu, we saw researchers and start-ups working toward the goal of more efficient use of energy and, ultimately, turning energy consumers into energy producers. On the Centennial Campus in North Carolina, for example, the Swedish-Swiss company ABB is working in a joint program with university researchers to develop elements of the smart grid; in Dresden, a group of firms is working in an EU-sponsored research program on energy-efficient chips and sensors.

In 2014, there was an unexpected but welcome sign of progress on climate change. Largely because of improved energy efficiency in the developed economies, combined with the results of greater commitment in China and other emerging economies and the increasing role of renewable energy technologies, the world saw no rise in carbon emissions (unrelated to an economic recession) for the first time.[1]

Improved energy efficiency, a shift from dirty coal to shale gas (at least in the United States),[2] and the steadily declining cost of renewable energy sources, particularly solar panels and wind turbines, will fundamentally transform how we power our societies and the impact that our energy consumption has on the planet. Vastly more efficient LED lights, recapture of heat from server parks and heating systems, air-conditioning finely calibrated through the use of sensors and data analytics, better battery storage and distributed generation of electricity in homes and buildings—all of these advances will reduce demand. Renewable energy systems such as photovoltaic farms and wind turbine fields will add to supply as they are becoming price-competitive in many areas and are on their way to becoming a viable economic option for large-scale energy generation.

The electric grid will also need to become smarter. Increasingly, the system will be a hybrid, in which traditional users of electricity will become energy producers as well. Individual households, businesses, and even cars will generate and store energy, sometimes contributing excess energy back to the grid, sometimes purchasing energy from the grid when their own sources cannot supply enough. The use of solar roof tiles and glass windows in buildings and homes, in combination with low-cost battery storage,[3] will go a long way toward this end.

It remains to be seen how quickly industrial-sized battery storage technologies will be embraced in the marketplace. General Electric built its GE Energy Storage plant in the heart of the Schenectady rustbelt where GE turbines were once made, and the company was hoping its battery business would achieve $1 billion in revenue by 2020. We visited the plant in August 2013 and met with the general manager, Prescott Logan, who was enthusiastic about the prospects for the sodium-nickel-chloride Durathon battery produced there.[4] He believed it had the potential to create an important niche market, as a backup energy source for cell towers and windmills and for use in microgrids and solar-energy storage. But GE's technology partners struggled, sales were disappointing, and production was stopped. Although some states—including California and New York—have pushed for mandates to require that solar power generation facilities be equipped with batteries with gigawatts of storage by 2022, the procurement process has been slow.

Thousands of researchers have been pursuing advances in battery technology, but breakthroughs have proved elusive. Yet-Ming Chiang, professor of material science and engineering at MIT and the chief scientist and cofounder of 24M Technologies, has taken a different approach: he has developed a simpler and cheaper process for manufacturing lithium-ion batteries, a method that will also make them sturdier and more efficient. Chiang has secured eight patents, has raised $50 million in venture capital, and has been awarded a $4.5 million grant from the Department of Energy. More than 10,000 users are testing Chiang's invention, and he has high hopes that production will begin by 2017.[5] Chiang's company, 24M, will initially produce batteries for the smart grid but, in the longer run, has its eye on the electric vehicle market. Venkat Viswanathan, of Carnegie Mellon, believes that 24M's innovation could disrupt battery manufacturing just as "mini-mills did to integrated steel mills." Production time could be reduced by 80 percent and costs cut by over 50 percent, savings that would help make battery-equipped electric vehicles competitive with carbon fuel-based vehicles.[6] Another development that could boost local energy production is the availability of massive batteries—the size of refrigerators—and Tesla is scaling up to produce these. According to Shell, such batteries have a promising future in regions with abundant wind or sun.[7]

The electric vehicle's battery has the potential to make a significant impact on the energy grid. Between 2009 and 2012, Danish researchers conducted a research program called Edison, whose goal was to evaluate a variety of methods for enabling vehicles to contribute energy back to the grid (these are referred to as vehicle-to-grid, or V2G, technologies).[70] A team composed of members from IBM, the Danish energy group Dong, Siemens, and the Authorities of the Island of Bornholm—an island off the coast of Denmark where the study was conducted, due to its exclusive use of renewable energy sources—sought to evaluate the potential of storing excess electricity produced by wind in the batteries of electric vehicles. Their owners would be reimbursed for supplying power back to the grid, when it was needed.

This system has not yet become operational, but it is a good example of how the electricity industry could eventually develop into a decentralized grid. The lion's share of energy would not be produced by traditional utilities, but by a network of individual home and business consumers. They would generate electricity for their own use and also for supply to the grid. This would have revolutionary consequences for utilities, which would become system stabilizers and energy redistributors, rather than power generators. They would generate energy only when supply and demand are in need of alignment.

This emerging evolution of the market prompted the German energy producer RWE to reorganize in 2014, consolidating its traditional generation facilities into a separate holding unit and focusing the core of the company on sustainable energy production. Other utility companies will similarly have to reevaluate their missions, structures, and processes in order to survive in a world in which their consumers are also their business partners. In this new world, sensors and data analytics for optimal distribution will become even more important than the traditional centralized energy generation. In several cities in the United States and in Europe, people have organized cooperatives with the goal of making these energy initiatives as productive and successful as possible. As more and more producers join, they will have less need of the subsidies and incentives they rely on now. As these cooperatives expand and become ubiquitous—and as we become less and less dependent on carbon sources of energy—there is no doubt that energy policy, business models, and fee structures will have to change fundamentally. The communications market experienced a similar transformation when the traditional telephone network was disrupted by the advent of mobile telephony.

The Automobile: Most in Need of a Radical Redesign

A survey of the coming challenges must include the most obvious and ubiquitous of all: transportation and, specifically, the automobile. At the Aspen Ideas Festival in July 2013, Silicon Valley venture capitalist and billionaire John Doerr posed the following question to the four young industrial designers on the panel he moderated: "Which everyday technology could benefit most from a radical redesign?"

The immediate answer: the automobile.

As we learned while doing our research, the reinvention of the automobile and, indeed, the entire transport system, is a focus of activity in advanced chips and new materials research and development in brainbelts around the world— in the California labs of Google, Tesla, and Apple; at Uber, where they hired robotics scientists away from Carnegie Mellon in Pittsburgh; and in the research centers of automakers Mercedes, BMW, and Toyota.

For decades, car ownership has been a symbol of middle-class prosperity. But the mass production—carried out by hierarchical, siloed, megalithic, noncollaborative companies—coupled with private ownership of gas-combusting cars that expanded throughout the twentieth century has created many challenges for the twenty-first: highly congested urban areas and mind-numbing traffic jams (also deleterious to the health, according to some studies), road accidents that cause more than 1 million deaths worldwide every year, and greenhouse-gas emissions that contribute to the effects of climate change and global warming.

There is no denying the utility of the automobile as a personal transport vehicle, but neither can its problems be ignored. Only 1 percent—1 percent!—of the gasoline that goes into the fuel tank is required to transport the weight of the driver (roughly 75 percent of car owners drive alone) from point A to point B, with the remaining 99 percent providing the energy to propel the 4,000-pound steel-plastic-glass container along the road. Additionally, a car sits idle for most of its life. Even during peak use periods, such as morning and afternoon rush hours, 80 percent of the cars on the road are stationary. The impetus to radically redesign the car—and the transportation system around it—is huge and urgent.

The creation of the next-generation automobile is, without doubt, one of the industrial activities that requires brainsharing. It must involve established companies with vast resources, small companies with focused expertise, effective and engaged government entities, educational institutions with breakthrough research insights, advanced manufacturing facilities, and canny leaders who can bring all these disparate elements together into productive initiatives. And we saw just such activity at Google in Mountain View in California, and Pittsburgh; at Tesla in Palo Alto and Fremont, California; at Mercedes in Stuttgart; and in the polymer initiatives at the University of Akron.

There is no question that the next-generation vehicle will be created; it is already well on its way to becoming a reality. This should not be a great surprise. Smart technology has been making its way into cars at least since the advent of anti-lock braking systems in the early 1970s and now includes interactive dashboard displays, rear-view cameras, and GPS. Tesla,[9] Mercedes, Volvo, and BMW are using a combination of GPS, radar, and sensors to perform a wide range of functions such as maintaining a fixed distance between cars, parallel parking, automatic cornering correction, and anticipatory braking for "objects"—such as cyclists and pedestrians—that the car can detect even before the driver is aware of them. Just like Google and other newcomers to the car industry, they are working closely with local universities and research centers, chip makers, and big-data crunchers.

Now comes the autonomous, or "self-driving," vehicle. In 2004, the Defense Advanced Research Projects Agency (DARPA),[10] the US military's main research organization, jump-started the development of the self-driving car by establishing the Grand Challenge. This groundbreaking competition teamed researchers from universities such as Stanford, Carnegie Mellon, and MIT with major industry players (including, among others, General Motors (GM) and Volkswagen) to realize ambitious concepts as working prototypes that could compete in a road race. The challenge, however, proved too great, and none of the driverless vehicles completed the 150-mile course through the Mojave Desert. The farthest any one of the prototypes was able to travel was 7.3 miles. The leading vehicle failed to negotiate a turn, got marooned on a rock, and threw in the towel. The $1 million cash prize was not awarded that year.

In 2005, Congress upped the ante by doubling the prize to $2 million to further encourage Grand Challenge competitors. The results were encouraging. Five cars, led by teams from Stanford and Carnegie Mellon, successfully navigated the entire 132-mile course—which featured narrow tunnels, winding mountain passes, and more than one hundred turns. After these two challenges, Google took the lead in the driverless-car crusade, building on the Challenge prototypes to develop the first fully functional, street-legal vehicles. In 2007, Google hired Sebastian Thrun—who had led the development of Stanford's Grand Challenge Champion robotic vehicle in 2005—and other engineers from his team. DARPA's Grand Challenge continued and, in 2007, moved out of the desert onto a 60-mile urban course.

It was not until 2011, however—after intense lobbying from Google—that the state of Nevada enacted legislation legalizing the operation of autonomous cars on public roads. In 2012, the states of Florida and California followed suit. Since then, Google's fleet of twelve test vehicles has driven more than 800,000 miles, negotiating heavy traffic, hairpin turns, and the vertiginous hills of San Francisco, without causing an accident. There are still problems to overcome, however, including responding to traffic signals and driving on snow-slick streets.

Google is poised to radically change how we think about cars on our roads. In a May 2014 interview with the *New York Times*,[11] Christopher Urmson, the leader of Google's autonomous car project, said the company had, as its initial priority, designed, from the ground up, an electric car without a steering wheel for urban and suburban use only—not for highways—with a maximum speed of 25 miles per hour. The cars navigate using advanced radar and sensors with a 360-degree, 600-foot range. The passenger selects a destination through a mobile app, and the car—which complies with all US federal and state regulations—sets off.

As we've seen, brainsharing has been essential in the development of the smart car. Government agencies, academic institutions, automotive and technology companies have all collaborated to provide capital, the latest technologies (sensors and radars, chips, wireless instruments, high-performance electric engines), and the cooperation and willpower to bring the smart, driverless car closer to reality.

As these models develop, and new ones emerge, it is likely the vehicles involved will share one important characteristic:

they will be electrically powered. Tesla is best known for that assertion. Tesla's all-electric car has made waves throughout the industry and around the world. It has set up free supercharging stations around the United States, and the company has announced it will build four hundred such stations in China over the next few years to boost its lackluster sales in Asia.[12] In European countries—including Denmark, Sweden, and Holland—electric vehicle infrastructures in and around metropolitan areas are also expanding. After many years of trying to build enthusiasm for their electric vehicles, the major carmakers are now gaining traction with the electric models. Google's self-driving car is powered by electricity and, not to be left behind, Apple has committed huge resources (involving a team that is being staffed up with 1,000 engineers) to building its own electric, self-driving car.[13] The car of the future is almost certainly electric.

Sharing brainpower plays an essential role in the development of these alternative models of the automobile, particularly the autonomous car, in a very important respect we should talk more about: road safety. A major goal is to reduce the number of traffic accidents and, above all, cut the number of fatalities to zero. To achieve such an ambitious result will require contributions from a diverse set of integrated players, including owners and distributors of a number of data streams, such as those providing traffic and weather information; GPS software developers; sensing and monitoring chip manufacturers (such as NXP and Intel); technical universities; tech giants, including Apple and Google; and automotive industry leaders such as GM, Mercedes, and Volvo. All must be involved in the development, smart manufacturing, and management of these elements if the autonomous vehicle is to operate effectively and safely. In other words, when it comes to their design and development, these vehicles are the opposite of autonomous—they rely on sophisticated, integrated, collaborative, brainsharing ecosystems of the kind we visited and have described in this book.

This transformation of the auto industry provides a vivid illustration of how disparate new technologies can combine to create a powerful new paradigm whose value is far greater than the sum of its parts. Many things will be different about the cars of tomorrow: how they are manufactured and propelled, what they are made of, how they are owned, and how they are operated. These changes, in turn, will have an effect on key twenty-first-century challenges, including climate change (through the reduction of carbon emissions), urbanization (by easing congestion in ever-expanding urban areas); public health (by reducing accidents and road fatalities, cutting down on the stress of commuting, and providing better mobility for an aging population); and social cohesion (by providing more convenient access to safer cars at lower cost).

The smart car, then, is a key element to a more intelligent, productive, equitable, and safe society.

Smart Farming Closer to Home

Another thorny challenge of the twenty-first century is how to feed the 9 billion people expected to live on the planet Earth by 2050. What role can the development of technology through brainsharing play in that effort? As the global population expands and demand for locally sourced produce rises, innovations such as next-generation greenhouses and automated milking will redefine how and where we produce our food to meet an ever-growing demand. This issue, too, is being explored in the world's smartest places, not only near Silicon Valley, where tech start-ups deploy drones and analyze big data to help farmers increase their yields, but in lesser-known spots like Wageningen, in the Netherlands, where extensive studies are conducted on the greenhouse of the future, and Lund, Sweden, where the focus is on robots for milking cows.

Not surprisingly, the United States is the world's largest producer of agricultural and food exports, with about 11.5 percent of the world's total, but the nation that comes second on the list is a surprise: the Netherlands. A country with a tiny, densely populated land area (less than 0.5 percent that of the United States) contributes about 7.5 percent of the world's food exports. This outstanding performance results from many factors, including the high productivity and efficiency of the Dutch agricultural sector, the brainsharing collaboration between the agricultural university of Wageningen, and cooperative farmers' organizations and private companies, as well as effective marketing.

The University of Wageningen started as a professional school for farmers, and its students came mostly from the Netherlands. Today, however, it is ranked second in the world in its field, and its programs are so highly regarded that nearly half its graduate students come from outside the country. It is one of only a handful of universities whose students can transfer their credits to any other educational institution in Europe. It collaborates with state-of-the-art local agricultural institutes and with similar institutes in Sweden and elsewhere in the world. Wageningen researchers explore ways to make Dutch agriculture more sustainable, in addition to addressing issues of food security in Central Asia in light of climate change and methods of improving yields in Africa. They also work closely with startups like Plant-e, which is studying the ways in which living plants generate electricity, and Micreos Food Safety, which is looking into how "good" bacteria can be used to replace antibiotics. This work is being done in the light of the tons of new data generated by the Microbiome Project, a global initiative that is defining the genetic footprint of the all-important microbiomes that jam-pack the human gut.[14]

Holland is well known, of course, for the stereotypical image of a country characterized by lovely fields of tulips and daffodils. However, as with so many stereotypes, this one, though not wrong, is incomplete and out of date. Today, the majority of the flowers, plants, and vegetables produced in Holland are grown in greenhouses.

They are not, however, just any greenhouses—they are advanced greenhouses, developed through an initiative called the Greenhouse of the Future, which was established after a 1997 resolution of the Dutch government and Dutch grower organizations to reduce pollution and increase energy efficiency. The initial goal was to develop methods to control the temperature inside the greenhouses to suit the specific needs of diverse crops while storing heat created during warm periods to use during colder weather. These goals could be achieved, it was believed, through the combination of co-generating heat and power with thermal energy storage of excess heat in an aquifer for feeding it back to the grid.

This concept eventually became known as the "closed-circuit greenhouse," and the Dutch tomato grower Themato was the first to construct one in 2001.[15] During the following decade, more and more growers modernized their greenhouses, with the result that flower and vegetable growers now generate 9 percent of Holland's electricity.

A new wrinkle was introduced when Casey Houweling, a former Dutch citizen who had moved to the United States, made plans to start growing operations in a town just north of Los Angeles, California. Houweling asked the Dutch company KUBO to design a greenhouse specifically for use in very hot climates, like that of Southern California.[16] KUBO responded by focusing on climate-control options that used fans to regulate the greenhouse's interior temperature. In 2009, these warehouses opened under the name of Ultra Clima, and similar projects are now operating in Utah, France, Slovenia, Mexico, and Russia. Houweling's tomatoes have earned the "Best" rating for sustainability at Whole Foods. With a year-round growing season, Houweling produces as many tomatoes at a 125-acre California facility as a conventional 3,000-acre farm could produce in a regular season. What's more, water in the greenhouses is recycled in a closed loop, an extremely important feature in a state where water is scarce. After little more than an hour's drive from Los Angeles, we were impressed to see how the ripening tomatoes in his massive greenhouses contrasted with the surrounding drought-parched land during our visit in September 2015.[17]

The greenhouse advances continue. The character and intensity of the light inside a greenhouse are also important to the efficiency of its operation and the quality of its products. In 2014, Chicago-based Green Sense Farms (GSF) and Philips announced a partnership to develop indoor commercial farming installations that utilize LED lighting to maximize plant productivity.[18] For its part, Philips is developing its knowledge of the effect of light on plants and their ability to produce. According to Udo van Slooten, director of horticultural lighting at Philips, each type of plant is most productive when exposed to the specific wavelength of light that it favors. "We have developed light 'recipes' for different plant varieties," he explained.[19] Meanwhile, partner GSF has set up an experiment in an old warehouse to study hydroponic production technologies using vertical stacks that replace traditional soil with a mineral nutrient solution and do not require any direct sunlight. By using multiple levels, this approach maximizes the interior volume of a greenhouse and thus increases productivity. It also eliminates the need for harmful pesticides, fertilizers, and preservatives. As a result, the plants can be organically grown and are virtually chemical free. And that is another benefit for consumers and for public health.

Such reinvented facilities have the potential to yield twenty to twenty-five harvests per year (in comparison to two or three annually) while consuming 85 percent less energy. Food shortages in developing countries and water shortages in states like California provide powerful testimony that "smart" matters not just in manufacturing but also in farming, to make it more productive, sustainable, and energy efficient, with the additional benefit that consumers can enjoy locally grown foods at supermarket prices.

Smart production embraces many ways of making things, not all of which rely solely on machines and electronics. The push for mechanical innovation in the dairy sector during the 1990s gave rise to advances such as individualized electronic necklaces that control cows' eating habits and the first milking robots. The leading companies in this field are the Swedish DeLaval and the Dutch Lely group.[20] They have developed automated barns—in which sensors monitor and control the quality of the milk, self-navigating robots clean the floors, and other robots spread the cows' forage according to their individual needs. Such facilities have become the rule rather than the exception in many developed countries. Farmers are able to track their animals digitally and manage the information they gather to create more effective milk-producing facilities.

The productivity gains and enhanced value in the dairy sector do not stop at the farm; the entire process has undergone a revolution. Emmo Meijer, CTO of FrieslandCampina,[21] explained Holland's global leadership in agricultural research to us during our meeting with him in Amersfoort: "In this country, you find the best knowledge and research on food issues in the world. The food sector in Holland spent 6 percent of its sales on R&D in 2013—only Denmark spent more (7 percent)."[22]

FrieslandCampina applied this expertise to resolving the long-standing trade-off between production volume and production quality. Until recently, for example, dairy producers' focus on maximizing their output of milk, butter, and cheese substantially diminished the quality of the product. Whey, for instance—a "byproduct" of milk production in the current model—is a substantial and nutritious dairy product, and it is not utilized in the existing production process. In 2005, FrieslandCampina initiated research into alternative processes that would deliver optimum quality for all outputs.

After a new approach had been developed and its positive results verified at a test site, the company opened a full-production installation in 2010 that has the characteristics of a milk "refinery." After separating out the milk fat, the remaining fluid passes through membranes with successively wider holes. The bacteria, relatively large microorganisms, are the first component to be filtered out, followed in successive steps by the casein, whey-proteins, and lactose. "The new process delivers product streams of high quality," Meijer explained, "[including] casein for the production of cheese, whey-proteins for infant food, and lactose for the preparation of medicines." Boosting efficiency through innovations like FrieslandCampina's milk refinery is critical to ensuring that our limited natural resources will meet our ever-growing demand.

Smart farming is a good example of how advanced technologies such as robots, sensors, clean energy, water management, biotechnology, and information technology can be brought together in ecosystems that include businesses, local communities, and universities to yield enormous productivity gains. Innovations like smart greenhouses, stacked hydroponic production, and next-generation lighting will greatly increase the efficiency of modern farming and will play a significant role in localizing and maximizing food production—and these technologies are applicable around the world. Vegetables and other produce can be harvested in warehouses or on rooftops in the middle of our largest cities, addressing the growing desire to eat locally grown food, while simultaneously diminishing the need for fertilizers and pesticides. There will be less need for transportation over long distances, reducing the industry's overall carbon emissions. By offering developing countries with hot climates the opportunity to produce their own fresh vegetables anywhere they want, smart farming will contribute greatly to addressing the twenty-first-century challenges of global hunger, food shortages, and inequitable distribution.

Smarter Cities: Technology Serves Community

One of the major trends of the twenty-first century is urbanization. Cities are growing in population, area, and influence—especially in emerging economies—and they are transforming in ways that defy traditional definitions of cities: sprawling over huge areas, comprising multiple centers, separating into distinct subentities of wealthy enclaves and underserved districts, and growing to populations of unprecedented scale. In the "old" economies, millennials are reversing the twentieth-century exodus to the suburbs. Urbanization poses tremendous challenges, including housing, the provision of services, food production and distribution, public health, and even individual resilience. All the smart technologies we have discussed in this chapter—energy, transportation, food production, data analytics—and many others we have not covered, will come into play in the creation of the city of the future.

In cities, the challenge of transportation, for example, is better described as one of mobility: the creation of systems that enable citizens to make their way from place to place conveniently, safely, and in a way that is integrated with a compact city design and customized to the needs of those who are very young and very old. The issues associated with cars and traffic look very different in suburban and rural areas than they do in urban settings, where getting from place to place within a relatively contained area is a constant struggle involving cars, trucks, taxis, buses, vans, trains, subways, bicycles, pedicabs, motorcycles, skateboarders, motorized wheelchairs, rickshaws, three-wheel vehicles, and in some cities, cable cars, bus rapid transit, moving walkways, and escalators, as well as, of course, pedestrians of every size, description, and capability—all plying the streets and contending with congestion and pollution. Products or technologies that improve mobility, through cleaner, smaller, more convenient, safer, and cheaper methods of conveyance should be pursued, and the autonomous car as well as car-sharing are promising solutions.

Food production for city populations is replete with tensions: there is a need for huge quantities of food, in a wide variety of types and price points, available 24/7, that contributes to a city's health and appeal. The rise of urban agriculture and local farmers' markets in public spaces where residents can find locally grown produce have the capacity to improve our diets and enhance our sense of community. The reinvigoration of these public spaces—including parks, transport hubs, and entire neighborhoods—as well as the priority placed on crime reduction in Europe and the United States, will reinvent how we think about our city systems and organizations, and the people within them, and by extension, this will completely transform our concept of a city.

The reimagining and repurposing of public spaces has become a collaborative initiative involving artists, architects, developers, residents, businesses, and local politicians. In Eindhoven, for example, an organization called STRP—which is located in the Strijp, one of Philips's old factories—aspires to bring together art, science, and community.[23] To that end, STRP organizes the Biennale, a biannual art and technology festival, as well as regular meetings where practitioners of both "high tech" and "high art" meet to create solutions and products that are as efficient and productive as they are aesthetically appealing.

Lighting is another important element in improving public spaces. Companies such as GE, Philips, and Osram (formerly Siemens) are currently investigating new, smart lighting configurations that will be more adaptable and capable of providing diverse light environments, unlike traditional fixtures and bulbs that are not particularly flexible in adapting to different circumstances and environments. These companies are consulting closely with local authorities and residents to develop proposals for lighting solutions that can respond to people's desires for variations in the color, quality, and intensity of light in an area, using sensors integrated into the system to adjust the lighting instrument, depending on the season, time of day, the amount of activity on a street or square, and other inputs—typically using LED elements that are more economical to operate than halogen bulbs. Borrowing a page from the sharing economy, they lease lighting equipment to municipalities. The city pays for the energy, and the lighting suppliers maintain and update the equipment.

These emerging elements of the smart city—including new approaches to transportation, energy management, food production, and infrastructural design—can only be developed through the sharing of brainpower among all city constituents. The result, we believe, will be the return of a "village" mentality in large cities, particularly among young people. We already see this as part of the "sharing economy" that is composed of sharing services such as Airbnb and ZipCar and that has extended to many products and services, including tools and real estate. It is a form of sharing brainpower and collaboration that goes beyond technological innovation to city reinvention.

Data: Big and Smart?

The extensive Internet research required in writing this book made us acutely aware of how online search tools have changed over a period of just a few years. Basic Google searches are now enriched with information beyond the scope of the original query, and the same is true for other popular sites including Facebook, Amazon, and LinkedIn. But Google is not alone in providing its users with a richer world of related possibilities—other companies such as Apple, Samsung, and Microsoft are doing the same. By allowing these companies increased access to your personal behavior and information through GPS data, e-mail, contacts, and calendars, the information they deliver to you will become richer and more precise.

The collection, analysis, management, and leverage of all this information is generally known as "big data," and along with many benefits, it raises many prickly questions regarding privacy and security. And the collection of data is becoming more pervasive, such that it is no longer the exclusive domain of information technology companies. In both Europe and the United States, producers of various kinds of hard goods are adding service-oriented products to their portfolios. By leveraging new technologies such as embedded sensors, these companies are collecting vast quantities of data to create new customer services.

In 2003, a project driven by the Federation of Finnish Technologies, the Finnish government, and Tekes,[24] the Finish agency that finances innovation, helped a number of companies make the transition from being providers of specific solutions to becoming "value partners." Thirty companies took part in the initiative, including Kone, Wärtsilä, Nokia, Finn-Power, Fastems, and ABB.

The example of Kone, an elevator manufacturer, illustrates the results of the project. The company, which had long offered elevator maintenance services, developed a set of solutions that helped its customers better understand the flow of people in highly populated buildings, such as offices and hospitals. The company began working with contractors and architects on a design for a medical facility—including, of course, the distribution of elevators—incorporating input from doctors and nurses to optimize movement within the buildings. Ultimately, Kone reimagined itself as much more than an elevator mainte- nance company but rather as a "people-flow" company. This new focus is readily apparent in the skills required of its employees, who must possess client-facing skills in addition to their technical capabilities.

As the Internet of Things grows in ubiquity, it will further increase our capacity to gather data from a global network of billions of connected objects and devices. To be effective, however, we will need to settle on a set of standards and protocols for data sharing so that the massive amount of information being created can be communicated flawlessly among systems and machines. In 2014, the Internet Indus- try Consortium—an open-membership group including companies such as Intel, Cisco, IBM, AT&T, and GE—was founded to develop this framework. In Germany, a similar initiative was announced by the federal government in early 2013 under the name Industry 4.0, referencing the Fourth Industrial Revolution of the Internet of Things.[25]

The avalanche of data that modern technology provides is one of the reasons that traditional sector distinctions have become increasingly blurred. As we discussed in the introduction, the idea of information technology, service, manufacturing, and agriculture as separate branches of the economy or industries is outdated. The future economy will be dominated by smart manufacturing, that is, the fusing of information technology and new technologies, materials, and discoveries with these traditional branches, built on a foundation of sharing brainpower.

Much More to Come

In this chapter we have touched on only a few key areas of activity that are related to some of the most important twenty-first-century challenges we face—and, in particular, those that are being developed and will continue to be refined through the sharing of brainpower, and the use of sensors and chips and advanced materials, as well as the phenomenon of smart manufacturing. There is no doubt that these activities will change—and, we believe, improve—the societal structures that define our lives.

Beyond the technologies and processes involved, there is the profound change that is taking place in the way people address our greatest challenges—through sharing brainpower and collaborative decision making. In the brainbelts we have studied, we see that a collaborative and entrepreneurial spirit has awakened in politicians, scientists, professors, and students, and it will have far-reaching consequences for the way organizations, societies, and economies function. Local political leaders will gain influence and prestige, and federal authorities will increasingly become facilitators (if they choose not to get in the way). We even believe that the dominant assumption of our working life—that globalization is accelerating whether we like it or not—is coming into question. Automation will make cheap labor increasingly irrelevant. As new materials replace long-used commodities (as carbon takes over from aluminum in aircraft, and bio-materials substitute for carbon-based plastics), there will be less need to ship production components, semifinished products, and finished goods around the world. Food, clothing, and shoes will once again be made closer to home. Local production will grow and global trade will slow. In other words, globalization will not accelerate forever; it will reach a peak and then level off and even decline. Worldwide, brainsharing and collaboration will increase in variety and degree, creating stronger ties between old and new economies, transforming traditional workplaces into innovation zones, and remaking rustbelt areas into brainbelts.

If, that is, we can successfully address a number of key practical issues—including education and training, policy, funding, and culture—that are essential to supporting and spreading the practice of sharing brainpower.

Chapter Six

AWAKENING THE BEAUTIES

Could Your Region Be One of the
Smartest Places on Earth?

Somewhere, something incredible is waiting to be
known.

—CARL SAGAN, ASTRONOMER

We have entered a new era in which many forces are
at play: the sharing of brainpower, smart manufacturing, the simultaneous interaction between thinking and
making, the rise of the brainbelt, and the decline of the
low-cost labor advantage. But this new era is still patchy in
places and struggling to emerge against a backdrop of structures, practices, organizations, skills, and attitudes left over
from earlier times. This new era, like other transformational
moments before it, did not come about as the result of a
grand plan or globally unified effort. How could it have?
The new era evolved, happened, was pushed.

What really struck us on our journey through the brainbelts, however, was that on the local and regional levels there
were always ideas and a willingness to take action, even if

federal initiatives in the United States or (to a lesser extent) European-wide efforts sometimes languished. People found ways to break loose from the stagnation and negative thinking that had been prevalent in the rustbelts. Individuals with vision and commitment brought institutions, authorities, and companies together.

Necessity played a major role in the rise of the brainbelt phenomenon. The need for jobs, revenue, and clout—combined with the complexity of technologies and a lack of resources—forced people and groups to put aside their differences, step over their organizational barriers, and reach out to unaccustomed colleagues, in order to collaborate on research, share knowledge, and work together to make things and push forward initiatives. This sharing of brainpower across an ecosystem of participants to achieve innovation is very different from the kind of innovation that is so talked about these days—the kind that Apple, Google, Amazon, and other iconic technology leaders practice. These players already possess the talent and resources to build *internal* innovation engines. They are not weighed down by the memory of stagnation or hampered by the presence of abandoned facilities or faltering infrastructure. What they lack they can acquire. They do not need to open up, share knowledge, reveal their secrets, reach compromises, and forge win-win deals. Indeed, they continue to operate as "lonely heroes." They have power and influence. Such companies may form partnerships and allegiances, but they remain at the center of them. They call the shots.

Although we tend to revere the lonely hero, there are limitations and drawbacks to the model. The lonely hero organization can amass too much power, squash outside innovation when it becomes threatening, limit the range of action of partners, become complacent, and put a chokehold on consumers. Brainbelts may not be as tidy in their process or as burnished in their image, but they have every bit as much (or more) potential to create breakthroughs and game-changing technologies and products as any lonely hero.

However, in order to fully realize the potential of the world's brainbelts, to awaken beauties that are currently slumbering, and to extend and leverage the practices of sharing brainpower that have been pioneered in those innovation hubs, there are many of those leftover structures and practices we need to think about, alter, clear away, or improve. We need to start with the recognition that *today's innovation is more bottom up than top down*. It takes place mostly at the local level, in proliferating brainbelts where academia and business share brainpower and are hard at work to invent and design the smart products that address the challenges of the twenty-first century. But national (or, in the case of Europe, European Union) brainbelt initiatives that support the continuous process of innovation through funding of fundamental research, challenge grants, an emphasis on crosscutting technologies, teamwork and collaboration, and modernization of physical and digital infrastructure— these remain immensely helpful. The payoffs in innovation from top-down support from DARPA and EU programs to Chinese and South Korean innovation policies stand out. National government support for innovation should no longer be mired in ideological debates. Moreover, the thrust of education and training programs must be rethought. More funding needs to find its way to potential brainbelt areas. Organization design, leadership, and cultural attitudes and assumptions need to be adapted. And, very important, we must find better ways to measure and evaluate the performance of collaborative activities such as brainsharing, even in the early stages. Here are a few thoughts about where we are now on these issues and how we might make change.

Policy and Guidelines

The idea that a country should have a common framework and policies to stimulate and support innovation in brainbelts is hardly a radical one. On the contrary, almost every country in the world has a set of innovation guidelines and objectives, with one notable exception: the United States. Why is it that, in the world's largest economy, politicians and business leaders seem to have an allergic reaction to the notion of a national innovation policy? Perhaps it's because things seemed to be working pretty well without a national policy in places like Silicon Valley, where entrepreneurs and researchers were quick to claim credit for projects that would not have happened without government funding. Or perhaps it's because such policies are sometimes confused with industrial policy, which focuses on specific industries or economic sectors and is often seen as a form of governmental interference in private enterprise. But the goal of innovation policy is not to regulate or to interfere but rather to encourage, motivate, and support innovation.

Critics love to cite government's failures, such as the support for solar-cell maker Solyndra, but there are far more examples of successful government participation in helping innovation than there are of misfires. However, *even without* a fully articulated national policy, the US government has pursued many initiatives over the years to promote growth and innovation in areas as diverse and as world-changing as transistors, lasers, the Internet and search engines, jet propulsion, space exploration, drones, horizontal drilling for oil/gas, new materials, robots, and the autonomous car.

Over the last decade or so, the federal government has been sharpening its focus on innovation. As early as 2006, the National Science Foundation (NSF) began to issue warnings about the risk of cutting back on basic R&D. The 2012 Presidential Task Force on Advanced Manufacturing highlighted the need for the creation of manufacturing institutes (they were eventually implemented by the Obama administration, with the first one for 3D printing opening in Youngstown, Ohio, in 2012 and the second one for digital manufacturing and design in Chicago in 2014). But while Congress dithered and debated over policy, governors and mayors found ways to take action on their own, supporting innovation initiatives in their states and cities, and collaborating across political party lines. Sharing brainpower, after all, is an inclusive and nonpartisan activity.

Still, we believe that a set of initiatives along the lines of various proposals made by presidential commissions and think tanks for the federal government in the United States and various national agencies (and also for the European Commission) would further spur and support innovation. We suggest, in particular, to:

- Develop *guidelines* and articulate *best practices* for regions and localities that want to create a positive environment for brainsharing ecosystems. The practices developed in Akron, Eindhoven, Portland, and Dresden are useful models.

- Provide *incentives and rewards* for groups that take an interdisciplinary, collaborative approach to the creation of technology products and services. The Swiss example of bioscience in Zurich is illustrative. One idea is to encourage that some goods and services be purchased from brainsharing entities.

- Encourage and facilitate *public-private partnerships* based on the model of the German Fraunhofer Institutes.

- Favor *open* innovation platforms when providing funding. The Open Innovation Pavilion of the US Air Force Research Laboratory is a good example, as is the Horst Institute in Eindhoven.

- Enable educational institutions to serve as *antitrust umbrellas*, through tax-code revisions and new guidelines, in a way similar to SUNY Poly's Nano-Tech Complex or the Akron Model.

- Provide financial support, expertise, and incentives for the *transformation of rustbelt areas*, facilities, and infrastructure into twenty-first-century innovation districts, as North Carolina did when it revitalized the old tobacco factories and established the Research Triangle Park.

- *Remove regulatory barriers* that prevent the testing and adoption of innovations such as the self-driving car, as California, Nevada, and Florida have in the United States and Sweden and Germany have done in Europe.

- *Encourage the use of new technologies* and products through regulations and incentives. Examples include accepting payment by smartphone for government transactions and incentivizing charging stations for electric vehicles.

- *Recognize brainbelts*, the sharing of brainpower, and smart manufacturing with awards and praise. For example, Startbootcamp has initiated a program for young entrepreneurs in five European cities and Israel.

The Need for New Metrics for Efficiency, Productivity, Creativity, or . . . ?

We are convinced of the far greater pervasiveness of technology, but the productivity statistics have been dismal the last dozen years. I have not heard these two observations satisfactorily reconciled, but we have to figure it out.

—LAWRENCE SUMMERS, HAMILTON PROJECT CONFERENCE ON THE FUTURE OF WORK, FEBRUARY 2015

Former treasury secretary and Harvard economist Lawrence Summers is not alone in recognizing a big hole in the statistics that policy makers rely on to evaluate the economy and its performance. Martin Bailey, a Brookings scholar and former chairman of the Council of Economic Advisers, along with its current chairman, Jason Furman, expressed similar concerns when we asked them about the issue, as did Federal Reserve Board member Lael Brainard. They agree that we do not currently have the tools to effectively gauge how we're doing in terms of efficiency and productivity, let alone understand the status of our efforts in innovation, creativity, and other important aspects of economic activity. In Europe, researchers have long complained that the models used by organizations—such as the Central Planning Bureau in the Netherlands—are missing something important but have been told, essentially, to mind their own business. The European Commission has made a start on the issue by engaging a group of leading economists to review the current evaluation methods and come up with recommendations for better ones. The work will involve a major study and may take two years or more to complete.[1]

Nobody likes to admit to flying blind or even to operating without the right navigational instruments, but, given that so many people acknowledge the problem, it's hard to understand why there is such a lack of urgency to tackle the issue. It was in 1987 that MIT professor and Nobel laureate Robert Solow famously quipped that "you can see the computer age everywhere except in the productivity statistics."[2] That was well before the advent of the smartphone and apps like Google Search, Wikipedia, and Google Maps, which are supposed to be huge time-savers and productivity boosters. We have devices that enable us to connect with anyone (or anything) from anywhere; we can access vast stores of knowledge remotely and almost instantly; we can navigate our way from point A to point Z without getting lost or wasting time folding and refolding maps. At the National Institutes of Health and major pharma companies, robots can accomplish complicated trials of new compounds in a few round-the-clock days, tests that a human lab technician would need a decade or more to complete. Not only does the robotic approach save time and money, it opens up possibilities. As NIH director Francis Collins has said: "There are too many potential leads to take them on one at a time."[3]

It is hard to argue that all of these technologies and tools have not helped our productivity in truly revolutionary ways. Yet Solow's MIT colleague Erik Brynjolfsson and many others have wondered why the productivity statistics don't support the argument. Is there perhaps a time lag between the introduction of a technology and an improvement in results? Is it possible that the headaches that computers and information technology create are so big they offset the gains? Could it be that there as many winners as there are losers, so there isn't a net gain? Or are there real gains, but our current methods of measuring them are inadequate, out-of-date, completely useless? Which of these explanations is the worst? What if our metrics are not taking into account the most dynamic and competitive part of developed economies?

We believe that we need a new set of metrics, that we can develop them, and that there is tremendous urgency for us to do so. With greater computer power and new methods of data analytics, we should be able to directly capture the crucial contribution of innovation and smarter products rather than measure them as a residual as we do now.

The productivity paradox, as this lack of alignment between the huge increase in computer power and marginal improvement in productivity is called, is usually defined as the discrepancy between measures of investment in information technology and measures of output at the national level. We would go one step further and call it the missing hole in a doughnut. Like a magic trick, the *more* productive or efficient innovation activity is, the *less* it shows up in statistics like gross domestic product (GDP) or the Consumer Price Index (CPI), two key numbers that policy makers and business executives use every day. In fact, traditional macroeconomic statistics reward inefficiency and punish efficiency and creativity. Why? Sectors such as health care and education with rising prices are so bloated that they weigh more heavily in the total. The opposite is true for the innovation economy, from information technology to smart manufacturing, where prices are constantly falling.

We will leave it to one of the next winners of the Nobel Prize in Economics to solve this riddle, but there is something weird about the way we measure the productivity of innovation if a new drug sold at an exorbitant price shows up prominently in GDP or inflation statistics, but free services like Google Search or Google Maps that have become part of everyday life are not accounted for in consumer spending simply because they do not cost anything.

Let's look at this a little more deeply. When consumers buy a chair, a cup of coffee, a bottle of aspirin, or a theater ticket, the transaction is included in GDP because each item has a known price. But what happens when they do a Google search on the Internet? It is free, so it does not count. But could you write a report, find a nearby restaurant, or look up a recipe without a search? Doesn't this have a value to most people that may be greater than a book, a newspaper, a theater ticket, or even a new couch?

When we talk of a "residual" value, it sounds like an afterthought—the foam on the beer (or cappuccino, if you prefer)—but this hard-to-measure component encompasses qualitative improvements in the labor pool and machinery, new inventions, better materials, less waste, preemptive repairs and all types of new discoveries. Innovation is in fact the main driver of growth, typically trumping capital (from new investment) and growth of the labor pool. So it matters whether innovation happens, how much of it there is, and how we make it happen.

What about inflation? Larry Summers famously cites the example of how, using 1983 as a 100-scale basis, health-care and higher education costs have increased to 600, while the cost of a television or computer has dropped to 6—a one-hundred-fold rise in their relative prices. Do those two new prices reflect the value these two "goods" have to us? Summers worries that the very success of the sectors that have been most productive has made them statistically so small in the overall economy that they do not really matter anymore—and will matter even less in the future. Aneesh Chopra, chief technology officer of the United States, sees this as an enormous opportunity. As he put it, "health care, energy, and education have not yet been plugged into the

Internet until recently, but now we see an explosion of innovation in health care."[4]

It would not be the first time that new metrics become part of the dashboard of policy makers and business leaders. National Public Radio's *Planet Money* told the story of how it took several decades before the consumer sentiment index (developed by researchers at the University of Michigan and published since 1952) found its way into "mainstream" economic metrics simply because it measured emotions—how people felt—and many economists were of the opinion that feelings don't measure anything.[5] Now it is an indispensable tool for businesses, markets, and policy makers.

Not only is macroeconomic productivity too important to be a residual, the impact of sharing brainpower and integrating new production techniques, new materials, new data analytics, and new discoveries into everything—from agriculture to manufacturing and services—is becoming increasingly visible in revitalizing whole cities and regions. Just as data analytics and wireless data collection can be used to measure productivity better, peer group analysis would provide useful insights into the contribution of the established and emerging brainbelts.

The relative success of brainbelt ecosystems could be evaluated in a qualitative manner by a questionnaire that would include questions covering such issues as:

- Focus/specialization

- Collaboration at various levels

- Ability of local universities to attract research funding

- Corporate funding of research activities

- License activity of universities

- Success record of incubators

- Number of spin-offs and start-ups and their three- and five-year survival rates

- Ability to attract private funding for new inventions from venture capital, angel investors, and other sources of capital

- Integration of a local supply/value chain

- Role of academic hospitals in stimulating innovation

- Scope, type, and success of on-the-job training programs

- Success of local community colleges and other post-secondary-school training in placing workers in the region and elsewhere

- Ability to attract foreign and out-of-state knowledge workers to the local talent pool

In Europe, Eindhoven and Dresden scored high on this list, and in the United States, Akron did better than others, but when we rated the brainbelts we visited and studied, each had its own strengths and weaknesses, even if most of the basic ingredients were present. Particularly revealing were, for example, the differences between government funding and licensing income as well as the development of local supply chains. Obviously, the importance of hospitals was paramount in places like Cambridge, Portland, Minneapolis, and Oulu, with their life-science orientation. Brainbelts in Northern Europe scored high on work-study programs; in the United States these initiatives were often based on European models.

Economic productivity can no longer be reduced to a simple spreadsheet that measures the most effective use of labor and capital. The coming decades will be just as much about the creative use of talent, knowledge, ideas, and new technologies in the most effective way. From now on, it is not about being cheaper anymore, but about being smarter.

Infrastructure and Environment

Just as innovation requires a new set of metrics, innovation hubs require physical infrastructure that is very different from the kinds of workplaces and ecosystems of traditional industrial centers and even the innovation parks of the twentieth-century model. Today, many people with creative minds prefer cities to suburbs and respond to urban diversity more than to the sterility of the corporate campus. They favor public transportation, bicycle-friendly cities, and access to vehicle sharing. They expect ubiquitous high-speed wireless access, seek affordable housing, and also want easy access to recreational spaces and the great outdoors. They would rather shop at a farmers' market than at a supermarket and at affordable local boutique-type specialty stores than at monster shopping malls featuring national chains.

This is precisely why rustbelt cities like Akron, Lund-Malmö, Portland, and Zurich have become brainbelts. This is far from an exclusive list. We could easily add the area surrounding Carnegie Mellon in Pittsburgh, Washington University in St. Louis, Drexel University in Philadelphia, Cambridge University in the United Kingdom, and many others. Seoul in South Korea, Tel Aviv in Israel, Berlin in Germany, and Stockholm in Sweden are other examples of innovation hotspots. They offered just what was needed: low-cost facilities, convenient urban locations, and abandoned warehouse and factory districts that could be transformed into flexible, roomy work-and-live spaces where people could engage with one another in many ways. In other words, sharing brainpower and smart manufacturing are largely about connectivity, both digital and physical.

In the brainbelts we visited, we saw many examples of ways in which states, localities, companies, and individuals contribute to environments conducive to brainsharing. In North Carolina, for example, the state supported the rebuilding of the old tobacco factories, warehouses, and textile plants with a subsidy of more than $1 billion. In the Netherlands, entrepreneur Rattan Chadha, founder of the international textile company Mexx, is setting up a chain of flexible office facilities called Spaces. It is Chadha's vision that young people think of their laptop as their workplace. At Spaces, you can rent the physical setting you need—perhaps just a chair and a desk, or maybe an entire floor—and pay by the day or month. You can make use of shared administrative services, get some coaching, and meet up in the wine bar. Examples of popular shared working spaces in the United States are New Work City in New York City, Work Bar in Boston, Independents Hall in Philadelphia (no, this is not a misspelling), Office Nomads in Seattle, and Hera Hub in San Diego.[6]

As we have seen, large companies are almost always important participants in the brainbelt environment, and we are seeing more and more of them establish facilities close to universities in city centers such as Pittsburgh, reversing the decades-long trend to locate in suburbs and corporate parks. Local authorities are encouraging and responding to the inward flight by creating light-rail connections, protected bike lanes, and other infrastructural elements that meet the needs of employees and their families.

The digital environment is created through the cloud, which is available to everyone and provides smaller players with services and capabilities that only the big companies could previously afford. Led by Amazon, a constellation of international and local telecommunications companies offer storage, sharing, download, and backup services. Arsenal Digital Solutions, based in Durham, North Carolina, is a good example of a company offering pay-as-you-go services. Start-ups and small shops that can't afford expensive investments in hardware and software can now access the same digital management tools that multinationals have been able to rely on.

Here are ways to further encourage the creation of environments and infrastructures that support brainsharing:

- Support initiatives that establish *smart manufacturing facilities*. There is still an assumption that a factory must be, by definition, big, polluting, and a lousy urban citizen. This is no longer true. Factories can be small, clean, and great places to work for people with creative minds, genuine contributors to a positive urban environment, and places where people looking to develop post-secondary-school skills can receive on-the-job training. The Buffalo Billion initiative, a collaboration of New York state with SUNY Poly's NanoTech Complex in Albany is a good example, although its largest project, Elon Musk's SolarCity, is viewed with some skepticism (as well as envy) by other cities.

- Update and adjust *state or local zoning regulations* that mandate the separation of work, residential, and recreation areas. Innovators today want to work in areas where specialized laboratory facilities, retail shops, public spaces, green zones, and a variety of housing options are proximate to one another, so as to create lively, thriving, diverse, and stimulating environments. In Portland and Zurich, different approaches led to the creation of vibrant new districts.

- *Focus developments on sharing brainpower.* When city leaders seek to develop abandoned or dilapidated districts, they should focus on approaches that encourage innovation and create diverse ecosystems, rather than taking a building-by-building approach. It matters a great deal how the economic assets of a city—including universities, hospitals, research-oriented anchor corporations, and start-ups—are configured and connected. In Dresden and Portland, for example, local authorities are very conscious of keeping life-science activities in close proximity to one another.

- *Build innovation districts* that align with the preferences of innovation-minded people and entities. The districts should be physically compact, accessible by public and shared transportation, and feature a mix of housing, workplace, and retail elements interlaced with bicycle paths, public spaces, pedestrian-friendly streets and plenty of green zones.[7] In Philadelphia, Boston, Durham, Roosevelt Island in New York, Cortex in St. Louis, and many other places, such efforts are underway.

Education and Training

"By 2020, the United States will be short 5 million workers with the necessary technical skills to meet employer demand," said Anthony Carnevale, director of Georgetown University's Center on Education and the Workforce, who has studied this issue extensively. By 2020, 65 percent of all American jobs will require some postsecondary-school education.[8] In 2011, according to the consulting firm Deloitte,[9] there were 600,000 unfilled manufacturing jobs in the United States, a number that is expected to rise to 2 million by 2025. So, rather than continuing to moan about the problem of job loss in this country, we should focus on the emerging skills gap and the growing demand for workers with strengths in the STEM—science, technology, engineering, and math—areas.

One cause of the skills gap in the United States is, simply put, college. Too many young people waste their talents and don't realize their full earning potential because so much emphasis is placed on the necessity of going to a traditional, four-year college. One problem is that only 54 percent of college students earn a degree within six years, so they lose time that might be better spent working or gaining practical skills. Colleges, in designing their curricula, and students, in deciding what college to attend and which courses to take, pay far too little attention to matching their abilities and studies with the skills needed in the job market now and in the future. To make matters worse, students often take on debt to pay for tuition, with the result that total college debt has reached $1.2 trillion in the United States.

The old assumptions about the value of a college education need to be challenged. As a four-year college education became an emblem of social and intellectual status, a work life in a manufacturing plant—which for many decades was seen as a solid and fulfilling career choice—was stigmatized. But, as Harvard's Robert B. Schwartz has said, "The proposition that most middle-class Americans bought into, that a four-year education was the ticket to success in the labor market, is no longer holding up."[10] What's more, as Lisa Skaggs, human resources director at Dow Chemical, put it to us, "Young people don't understand how many interesting jobs there are in manufacturing."[11] Parents and students, therefore, place a lot of emphasis on nonmanufacturing professions and the four-year college programs they think will ensure careers in them, especially those in the vaunted "knowledge economy." They're not aware of, don't understand, or don't value other forms of education and training that can be much more useful for many young people, particularly the offerings of two-year community colleges.

Community Colleges

To help change the view of students and parents, many community colleges are developing programs that seek to help them make different and better educational choices. In our journey, we came across many brainbelts in which a community college was an essential participant in the brainsharing ecosystem. In the Hudson Tech Valley, for example, the explosion of new smart-manufacturing activity has created a demand for, and provided a boost to, education.

Just outside the gate of the GlobalFoundries plant, for example, we visited a training program called TEC-SMART, short for the Training and Education Center for Semiconductor Manufacturing and Alternative and Renewable Technologies, which is part of the Hudson Valley Community College.[12] Penny Hill, TEC-SMART's associate dean, showed us around the facility, which is housed in a Leadership in Energy and Environmental Design (LEED) Platinum green building and draws a significant portion of its energy from the solar panels and wind turbines arrayed outside, benefiting as well from a passive-solar design. We observed a group of twelve students, new GlobalFoundries hires, who were engaged in a one-week work-study course on the company's manufacturing process. One of the enthusiastic instructors told us how the course came to be. When a plant technician checked the gauges of the air circulation system, he saw the pressure had fallen to zero. Worried, he swapped out all the gauges, but that didn't solve the problem. Others realized that the pressure had been at zero because the air system had been unintentionally shut down. Time and money had been wasted.

GlobalFoundries found that many of its new hires did not have the necessary skills and training to work in such an advanced facility. Many even lacked basic abilities such as how to use simple tools like wrenches. Although many new employees hold master's degrees, others concluded their formal education with a high-school diploma. Now, all of GlobalFoundries new hires, whatever their level of education, undergo seven weeks of training, including the two-week manufacturing class.

TEC-SMART offers a range of courses and programs, in addition to the two-week GlobalFoundries orientation. It runs a two-year course in semiconductor manufacturing for midcareer students that prepares them for jobs at GlobalFoundries as well as other companies such as GE and Applied Materials. The course is constantly being fine-tuned, as Hudson Valley Community College works with the companies to determine what knowledge and skills their employees will need. The college also offers a program for juniors and seniors at nearby Ballston Spa High School. Five mornings a week, 140 young people hop on buses that transport them to the TEC-SMART facility, where they learn the basics of automated manufacturing. The program, which is modeled on an IBM initiative established in Brooklyn, New York, combines classroom knowledge of STEM concepts with critical thinking and hands-on summer internships.

The main campus of the Hudson Valley Community College is in Troy, near Rensselaer. The college boasts a state-of-the-art $35 million science center, a faculty of 650 and over 13,000 students, half of whom work part-time. The college offers seventy different two-year associate degree and vocational tracks, as well as worker retraining programs and long-distance learning for those who work full-time. Many companies pay tuition for their employees' educational activities.

David Larkin is an instructor at Hudson Valley, where he has taught a course in advanced manufacturing for more than twenty years. He holds advanced degrees in mechanical engineering and had a successful career in manufacturing before turning to teaching. He told us that for many years, students were not interested in learning the skills of toolmakers and machinists because they knew that these kinds of workers were being laid off and saw no future there. In Hudson Tech Valley, as in other brainbelts, that situation has changed, with the result that Larkin's course is now in high demand. He says there are probably a hundred programs like his in the United States. "That is totally insufficient," he told us. "The biggest problem for companies these days is to find people who can run their machines. It is no longer enough to be able to do three jobs; now you have to be able to do three hundred and be good at all of them."[13]

Larkin's program is rigorous. A typical lab course runs twelve hours per week, in contrast to the three hours in other disciplines. Students learn STEM theory, metallurgy, and practical skills such as how to shape parts, build fixtures, and inspect and test equipment. That requires regular access to $1 million worth of machinery and tools, including CAD-CAM equipment.

The problem for community colleges like Hudson Valley is coming up with the funding to equip their labs and workshops, and government support is not always available. "We needed a different approach," said Larkin. The solution was brainsharing. The college formed partnerships with companies that donate equipment, update it, and pay for their workers or new hires to take courses. One of the biggest donors of much-needed machinery to the course is California-based Haas Automation, one of the world's leading and most automated machine-tool makers. In return, the college tailors its programs to the needs of the companies. In the year we visited, every one of the thirty-three participants in Larkin's course found jobs, starting at $18–25 per hour, well before graduation. Previous graduates are earning over $100,000 on average after five years on the job.

GlobalFoundries works with several other community colleges, including Schenectady, Fulton Montgomery, and SUNY Adirondack in what is becoming one of the largest professional training initiatives in the country. Mike Russo, government relations head of GlobalFoundries, says it is a model that could be scaled up nationally to give people a better understanding of how jobs will evolve in the future.

The Work-Study Model

We need much more of the kind of on-the-job education we saw in the Hudson Valley, and this is an area where Europe has much to teach the United States. Michael Brown, senior director for talent acquisition at Siemens USA, believes that the US skills gap can better be described as a training gap. Siemens, the global manufacturer based in Germany, operates one hundred manufacturing sites in the United States, where the company builds complex, high-quality products that include electronic hospital equipment and state-of-the-art locomotives. "We were surprised by what we found in the United States," Brown told us. There were very few work-study programs, and what training programs there were had suffered from cost cutting. "I found it shocking that colleges did not reach out to us," he said.[14]

In Germany, by contrast, Siemens has a robust apprenticeship program, with 10,000 enrollees. In an effort to train more people for work in its facilities in the United States, Siemens is focusing on work-study programs. When Siemens wanted to double its plant capacity in Charlotte, North Carolina, the company worked closely with the local community college to develop a program. Now twenty-five apprentices work alongside the 1,000 regular employees of the plant. "We are just getting started," Brown said. "But there is a sea change now."

Germany, Siemens's home country, has the most developed vocational training model of any country. Its dual-track, work-study education system is known as "duale Ausbildung," and it is considered one of the "secrets of Germany's success in manufacturing," according to Jan Stefan Roell, CEO of Zwick Roell.[15] The company, based in southern Germany, is a midsized family-owned enterprise that is one of the world's leading manufacturers of sophisticated testing equipment. Roell told us that their three-year work-study apprentice program is a dream come true. Zwick Roell works with the local technical school to recruit students. In 2013, 585 people applied for the twenty available jobs, so the company could be very selective. Although the apprentices are paid less than the standard wage, Zwick Roell invests about €50,000 to train one apprentice over the three-year period, during which the students spend about 30 percent of their time in the classroom and the rest on the job.

Roell, who is the grandson of one of the company's founders, says that work-study programs have to be considered within the larger context of the entire employer-employee relationship. It's important to develop a "sense of family" in the workplace to ensure that workers want to stay with the company and that they value productivity as much as longevity. An important element of that family atmosphere is mutual respect between workers and unions and management. When we visited the company's facility in the town of Ulm, not far from Stuttgart, the sense of family and mutual trust was evident throughout the plant—in the clean and well-organized factory space, the appealing food served at lunch, and in the way Roell listened attentively to questions from factory workers and chatted with them as he went through the cafeteria line.

Engelbert Westkämper, former director of the Fraunhofer Institute for Manufacturing Methods and Automation in Stuttgart and professor at the University of Stuttgart, emphasizes the important role of technical schools (there are twelve in the Stuttgart region alone) in working closely with companies to develop and support apprentice programs. When manufacturing was hit hard by the 2008 crisis, companies survived because decisions were made jointly with the unions, which felt they had a stake in the outcome. Westkämper is aware that the relationship between a corporate board of directors and unions is very different in the United States than it is in Germany. He believes that, over the years, the cooperation "has built a trust that paid off."[16]

More evidence of the success of the work-study program is that young people like to train in manufacturing skills because they are so highly regarded. As a result, Germany may be facing a skills surplus that will intensify in the next few years. In the state of Baden-Württemberg, of which Stuttgart is the capital, there are about 225,000 apprentices in the three-year work-study system, including 50,000–60,000 in manufacturing. Only 10 percent drop out, and about 5 percent do not successfully complete the program, which means that the system is turning out a large quantity of skilled and qualified manufacturing workers.

In all of Germany, 1.6 million are enrolled in work-study programs (60 percent of those in the eligible age group), while 35 percent go to university. In the United States, 40 percent of people ages sixteen to twenty-four attend college. Of this total, 60 percent are in four-year colleges and 40 percent in community colleges. Of this last group, only 41 percent had the money to attend full time. In sharp contrast with Germany, only 500,000, or less than 2 percent, find their way into post-secondary, non-degree vocational training.[17] And, unlike students in the United States, German students and their families do not have to take on debt to pay for their dual-track education. The average annual cost per trainee in a work-study program is $27,000, of which the national government contributes 90 percent and the state picks up the remaining 10 percent. Companies put in $20,000 per year per student, plus some additional costs for workshops. The training is completely free to students, and they earn a wage that may start at $800–$1,000 per month and rise to as much as $3,000 monthly.

The German work-study system is a particular boon for midsized companies, which are the ones that take the lion's share of apprentices, because they have found that the training prepares students for their tasks so they can be productive more quickly when they start working full-time. This training also reduces job disappointment and creates a bond between students and their companies.

In other Northern European countries, over the years, many companies shut down their in-house training programs because of low enrollment and to cut costs. But in the past decade, a number of national programs have been initiated and enrollment is on the rise. At the same time, manufacturing companies without their own programs have begun to collaborate with regional technical schools to offer new forms of vocational training. They look to Germany as a model, but then they discover that the German system was created within its own distinct tradition and that the system is not easily copied. Martin Frädrich, director of the Chamber of Commerce in Stuttgart, agreed. "When we explain the system, it is so complicated that many wonder how it can work so well. Even we do." To make such programs successful, you need a true public-private partnership, an institution like the Chamber of Commerce that is close to the business community but not part of the government, and you also need close cooperation with unions. And, very important, the program should not be compulsory— otherwise, in Frädrich's opinion, "Enthusiasm goes away."[18]

In Eindhoven, Brainport Industries is developing just such programs. The company devotes significant attention to training middle management in technical skills, in programs very similar to those we saw at TEC-SMART in the Hudson Tech Valley, such as internships and work-study courses. There is a shortage of internships, however, so thirty companies in the Eindhoven region are working to establish the Brainport Industries College. Its founders—including DAF, Philips, and their suppliers—hope to create a steady stream of skilled welders, metalworkers, and machine makers. We have seen that a physical facility is important to making the brainsharing activity tangible and highly visible. To that end, Brainport Industries plans to construct Brainport Industries Campus on a parcel of land reserved for the purpose by the city. With this campus, Brainport Industries aspires to create an environment where employees from different companies work together seamlessly and utilize shared high-tech facilities.

Their enthusiasm has not gone away; it has only grown.

Funding

Innovation is often associated with small, vibrant start-ups, financed by optimistic venture capitalists and managed by inventor-entrepreneurs, but this is only part of a much larger picture. Innovation is a marathon rather than a sprint, and often the road to developing an exciting, innovative product begins with a government grant issued years (or even decades) before a start-up commercializes the knowledge or technology gained during that basic research and extends long after the start-up phase.

Sharing brainpower, therefore, only works when a whole series of funders smoothly "pass the baton" along the entire course of an idea's development. Even the best ideas will not reach the marketplace without an often massive amount of money invested all along the route. Discontinuity in funding at any stage can doom innovation, and as a result, a range of financing sources—each uniquely suited to the task at hand—must be available to equip researchers with the tools they need to create products that can change the world. National governments currently provide most of the funding for basic advanced research, and private companies are the major funders of applied research, with start-ups usually relying on personal connections (angels, family, friends) for small contributions until they develop their ideas enough to attract capital from larger funds and investors.

Although there are many funding sources, and huge quantities of capital available to be invested, the process is not perfect and needs improvement. Millions of dollars in research are wasted because funders or investors ignore worthy projects, invest too much in unworthy ones, lose interest in projects they have funded, steer them in the wrong direction (through poor board-level decisions about strategy or hiring), or decide to cut their losses before a technology or product is fully developed.

Most important, from our point of view, is that funders and investors need to have a better understanding of the importance of brainsharing. In the United States in particular, investors are so enamored of the lonely hero model—the genius entrepreneur and the go-it-alone company, located in iconic hotspots of innovation—that they can easily overlook promising initiatives that involve complex, multidisciplinary collaborations and that take place in out-of-the-way areas such as the brainbelts we visited on our journey.

Basic and Applied Research

In 1994, the National Science Foundation (NSF) provided a $4.5 million research grant to Stanford University as part of its Digital Libraries Initiative, which sought to develop the tools to find and sort information on the nascent World Wide Web. The grant enabled Sergey Brin and Larry Page, two young graduate students and the eventual cofounders of Google, to develop the search engine that became the basis of the tech giant's incredible success.[19] Early government funding has yielded many other breakthroughs, including the Internet, jet engines, nuclear power, the semiconductor, and GPS.[20] These examples illustrate the enormous potential of funding for basic research, the first stage of R&D and one of its most essential—if less discussed—components.

According to the NSF, "Basic research fuels technological innovations and is critical in fostering the vitality of the US science and technology enterprise and the growth of highly skilled jobs."[21] Basic research aims to investigate and answer broad scientific questions rather than produce a specific end result like a new drug or material. But because its returns are not immediately apparent or directly calculable, basic research is unpopular with private-sector investors, and as a result, governments provide the majority of funding, for which universities and research institutes are the primary recipients. This is also why it's so important that we develop new metrics for the evaluation of innovation performance, including assessments that help us gauge the value of efforts in the earliest stages of research.

In the United States, fundamental research dollars come from not only the NSF and the National Institutes of Health but also the Department of Defense (which alone accounts for over half of total funding for basic research), the National Aeronautics and Space Administration (NASA), and the Department of Energy. The United States spends far more of its R&D budget on basic research than any other country—its $75 billion in fundamental research spending nearly matches the rest of the world's combined $90 billion and far outstrips the European Union's $40 billion and Japan's $18 billion. Interestingly, South Korea spends more money on fundamental research ($11 billion) than China ($10 billion).[22]

In Europe, there is no military industrial complex comparable to that of the United States, the European Union is fragmented, and innovation policies are nationally driven. The European Commission is, however, working to bridge the gaps between the national efforts. The Horizon 2020 initiative, begun in 2013, seeks to stimulate economic growth and employment through innovation. And for the first time, projects will be selected for funding on the basis of their scientific quality rather than to achieve equal distribution of research funds over the member countries of the European Union, as they have been in the past.

Although the innovation scene in Europe has been fragmented, it also has some powerful assets that are unmatched in the United States. Most important is the extensive network of public-private entities—including Fraunhofer in Germany, TNO in the Netherlands, and EMPA in Switzerland—that were founded in the late nineteenth and early twentieth centuries. They are key building blocks in the creation of the smart manufacturing world in which sharing brainpower is so essential.

Another positive trend we saw in Europe is that more state funding and subsidies are linked with requirements that projects be multidisciplinary. In Switzerland, for example, there is the SystemsX.ch initiative aimed at supporting research in systems biology.[23] The research must be carried out by people in a wide range of disciplines, such as biology, physics, chemistry, engineering, mathematics, computer science, and medicine. This unique, federally organized network enables an efficient, interdisciplinary collaboration of more than 1,000 scientists, in almost four hundred research groups, working on approximately two hundred projects.

Unlike basic research, applied research—the second stage of R&D that focuses on specific products, materials, or drugs—receives most of its funding from corporations, particularly those in science-intensive industries such as chemicals, pharmaceuticals, and aerospace. The United States spent $82 billion on applied research in 2011, with businesses providing just over half the funding.[24] Universities, hospitals, corporate research labs, and start-ups conduct the majority of applied research, and their reliance on private-sector financing makes corporate funding and venture capital essential to this stage of R&D, although governments still provide over one-third of funding.

Of the total R&D dollar expenditure in the United States, about 20 percent goes to basic research, 20 percent to applied research, and 60 percent to development. There has been a lot of hand-wringing about growing global competition in R&D spending, but the "old" economies remain preeminent,[25] with a 60 percent share in 2014—31 percent for the United States (nearly double its 16 percent share of the global economy), 19 percent for the European Union, and 10 percent for Japan, compared to China's 18 percent.[26]

This leadership in research has stimulated the rustbelts to reawaken in both the United States and Europe, but obviously the two regions have taken very different approaches to funding. The strongest attributes of research funding in the United States are entrepreneurship, strong support from the military and government agencies, the freewheeling ways of Silicon Valley, investments by university endowments, philanthropy, and the abundance of venture capital.

Start-ups in the United States receive over two-thirds of all global venture capital, compared to only 14 percent in Europe, giving the former a distinct advantage over the rest of the world.[27]

By contrast, Europe's strengths are its Fraunhofer-type institutes, the largesse of the European community in its support of long-term projects like the Factory of the Future or the European Spallation Source, the helping hand offered by science-park incubators, and the subsidization of clean-energy initiatives.

The difference in attitudes toward start-ups in the two regions is particularly striking. In the United States, start-ups have not only caught the popular imagination but are the major driving force in innovation. Entrepreneurs who fail are still looked down on in Europe (although this is gradually changing), whereas American venture capitalists view a record of failing as a badge of honor and proof of prior experience that they want to see before they invest. In Europe, it is the midsized companies that are revered and even coddled.

"What we lack in Germany is a culture of start-ups," Alec Rauschenbusch, a founder of Stuttgart-based venture-capital firm Grazia Equity, told us when we met him in his modern office overlooking Stuttgart. "We have so much car expertise that Tesla could have started here, but we don't really have an ecosystem for young entrepreneurs in manufacturing. Banks don't lend, there is no credit-rating system, and not enough venture capital money."[28] As a result, instead of starting their own business, young engineers in Europe find open doors not only at the Mittelstand companies but in global giants like Bosch, Daimler, and Porsche or the top American firms in Europe like IBM and Hewlett Packard (HP). For them, in-house R&D is still an important model and young engineers are still attracted to the advantages of working in large, stable organizations.

Venture Capital

Venture capital (VC) is financial capital invested in an early stage company, usually one with a cutting-edge technology or business model (hence the concentration of venture capital in high-tech industries like life sciences and IT),[29] in exchange for equity in the company. Companies in which VC firms made investments are responsible for over 20 percent of all US business revenues,[30] and without those investments, many well-known companies that together employ more than one out of eight Americans simply would not exist. Iconic tech companies such as Microsoft, Apple, Amazon, Google, Facebook, and Twitter as well as pioneering life-science companies like Boston Scientific, Intuitive Surgical, Amgen, Genentech, and Gemzyne can all (at least partially) credit venture capital with their enormous success.

All venture capital is invested with the same goal—to buy into a young company with disruptive technology, high profit potential, and a skilled management team—and it has both private and public sources. There are two private sources of venture capital, the first of which is dedicated venture-capital firms, whose sole focus is investing the pooled resources of the backers and funds they manage. The average investment made by a VC firm is about $4 million,[31] and many specialize in specific industries. There are roughly 1,000 venture capital firms in the United States, most of which are clustered in Silicon Valley, the Boston-Cambridge area, and New York City.[32] The second private funding source is the corporate venture-capital arms of large technology firms like Google, Intel, Cisco, Microsoft, and Qualcomm, and life-science companies like Johnson & Johnson, Medtronic, Biogen Idec, GSK, and Roche. Together, these companies have invested $61 billion over the past twenty years, accounting for 10 percent of total VC funding and 17 percent of all investments.[33]

Another source of venture capital comes from the public sector, particularly a little-known breed of government-backed funders that have become crucially important in the United States. One of the boldest, most innovative, and most important is the Defense Advanced Research Projects Agency, the $3 billion venture-capital arm of the Department of Defense created in 1958 in response to Sputnik. Ever since, DARPA's grants and competitions have played an enormous role in the development of critical technologies, including the Internet, self-driving cars, next-generation robots, and all kinds of new materials. The Department of Energy runs the Advanced Research Projects Agency– Energy (ARPA–E), which focuses more on early stage research than on venture capital investments.

Even the Central Intelligence Agency (CIA) has entered the realm of venture capital with In-Q-Tel, the nonprofit VC firm it established in 1999, which over the years has invested in two hundred start-ups (to the tune of $60 million per year) and currently maintains a portfolio of about one hundred ventures with total assets of $219 million.[34] Although In-Q-Tel[35] focuses on data analytics and cyber security, it has found success in other fields as well, most notably with Keyhole, a start-up that developed the satellite mapping software that later became Google Earth (Google acquired the firm in 2004). Oracle, IBM, Lockheed, and others have all bought companies that received early In-Q-Tel funding. Not to be left behind, in 2006 NASA contributed $75 million to a partnership with Red Planet Capital, a California-based VC firm, in order to "attract private sector innovators and investors who typically have not done business with the agency."[36]

Looking ahead, all of these organizations will have to adapt to a model of venture capital funding that has fundamentally transformed in recent years. Together, the widespread push among start-ups toward sharing equipment and services in incubator spaces and the flexibility of quick, low-cost prototyping with 3D printers have dramatically reduced the capital requirements of the newest generation of "makers." "You now only need $50,000 to test an idea rather than $5 million," Kip Frey, a serial entrepreneur and partner at Intersouth Partners, explained during our visit to North Carolina's Research Triangle Park. "As a young entrepreneur, why would you give away majority ownership in your start-up to a venture capital firm when you don't need so much money and there are plenty of like-minded angel investors around?"[37]

Research Through Acquisition

Although research and development are intimately related—which is why they are usually referred to together as "R&D"—they in fact require different resources and approaches in order to be done successfully. Johnson & Johnson, Medtronic, and many other life-science companies now realize that conducting innovative research requires out-of-the-box thinking and a willingness to take risks, for which small, unbureaucratic start-ups are much better suited than big hierarchies. Development, meanwhile, is process oriented and requires stable structure, long-term and substantial financing, and market power—qualities that large corporations have in spades. As a result, acquisitions have become a way of life for big companies looking to stay innovative, as we learned when we visited Minneapolis.

Medtronic, the main player in the Minneapolis medical device brainbelt, provides a good example of how research has moved from claustrophobic corporate silos to fresh innovative start-ups. An undisputed leader in medical device research, Medtronic spends $1.6 billion, or 9 percent of its revenues, on R&D every year—more than three times the percentage of the typical American corporation. For a company that yields over 40 percent of its revenue from products introduced within the previous three years, innovation is a matter of survival, and its in-house R&D program employs 12,000 engineers, scientists, and technicians—about one-fourth of the company's workforce.[38]

However, in an effort to address the low yield on the company's in-house R&D, CEO Omar Ishrak decided to refocus Medtronic's R&D efforts on acquisitions, firing several thousand in-house researchers in the process. Some detractors lament the gradual disappearance of the internal research activity, and others believe that some of the large acquisitions by many life-science companies are mostly for tax reasons, but most recognize its necessity. Norman Dann, a venture capitalist in Minneapolis, minced no words when he told us: "Large organizations tend to be too slow and hierarchical. Researchers get punished for being wrong rather than for being too late. They become silos that can't make decisions." The best R&D, according to Dann, "is done by a small band of researchers without hierarchy who can correct mistakes rapidly and work in a culture that understands that mistakes are unavoidable in research."[39] Therefore, though big companies like Medtronic are still vital in managing product-development tasks like organizing huge clinical trials and building support systems, innovative, flexible start-ups have inherited the torch of next-generation research.

Private Funding

Entrepreneurs usually raise their first round of financing (ranging from $50,000 to $250,000) from family and friends, from seed capital funds like those started by many universities and by former entrepreneurs,[40] or from government-funded programs like Small Business Innovation Research (SBIR). Once these initial investments run out (which can happen quickly), entrepreneurs must then attract outside investors, who look for start-ups with a unique product, an exciting growth story, and a capable management team.[41] Venture capital firms also insist on a clear exit strategy that calls for the firm to end its involvement with the start-up within seven years. Their accountability to their own investors means that they often stay away from early stage investments they see as too risky, small, and time-consuming.

Entrepreneur Kip Frey believes that venture capital has become a less important source of capital at the very early stages of start-ups because the old financing model itself has become outdated and not suited to the world of brain-sharing and smart manufacturing. "Few [VC firms] have really been successful in an industry that, like the record or movie industry, is driven by the few big hits that pay for the many failures," he explained, observing the difficulty for most venture capitalists to impress their limited partners (endowments and pension funds) when five or so firms reap 80 percent of the returns. Moreover, local entrepreneurs now see more value in national firms with global talent networks, in anticipation of the days of scaling up their business.

The financing process for start-ups is changing, and three groups have stepped up to fill this funding gap: angel investors, business incubators, and crowdfunders. Angel investors are wealthy individuals, often entrepreneurs themselves, who invest in others in order to scratch their entrepreneurial itch. More and more start-up entrepreneurs are attracted to angel investors because the arrangement gives them much more flexibility than a typical deal with a venture capital firm would. Angel investing totaled $23 billion in 2012 in the United States[42] and €5.5 billion in Europe, and there are now over 250,000 angel investors in the United States—nearly ten times as many as in Europe.[43]

Incubators provide a safe haven for early start-ups looking to take their next steps by providing them with shared lab and office space, and these arrangements often emerge from local or state initiatives to attract young new entrepreneurs. There are 1,400 business incubators in the United States and 1,000 in Europe (half of them in Germany) that support some 30,000 new companies every year. These two growing sources of financing—angel investors and incubators—have become indispensable in both the United States and Europe, making up as many as one-fourth of all early stage investments[44] and also often staying in for later investment rounds.

Crowdfunding sites such as Kickstarter, Fundable, and Indiegogo are the newest source of early stage capital and have opened up opportunities for everyday people to contribute to R&D like never before. They enable those with interesting or quirky ideas but who lack real business sense and long-term growth strategies—leaving them hopelessly unable to attract traditional venture capital—to realize their dreams. Form1, for example, raised $3 million from 2,000 backers for researchers from the MIT Media Lab to build an affordable home printer for 3D printable clothing.[45] All told, the exploding popularity of angel investors, business incubators, and crowdfunding over the last decade has reinforced the critical role of private capital in the R&D chain.

Recommendations

So, based on our research and analysis of what works—and what doesn't—in brainbelts around the world, we offer the following recommendations for making the financial environment more conducive to the sharing of brainpower for new product innovation:

- *Policy makers should build political consensus for basic research, even with tight budgets.* Not funding basic research is "penny-wise and pound-foolish" because its payoffs for innovation, economic growth, and living standards are so high. For example, every dollar of NASA spending yields about nine dollars in economic activity,[46] and NASA innovations generate about $1 million in revenue for each of its spin-offs.[47] Fortunately, the widespread fears about cutbacks in basic research spending in the wake of the financial crisis largely failed to materialize, but the threat remains. Impatience for tangible results in the form of profitable commercial applications is as alive as it was in the days of Bell Labs. Even if there is no room in school curriculums to study the impact of innovation, political leaders, educators, and the entertainment industry should work together to ensure that starting in high school, students can learn how different daily life would be without the inventions stemming from basic research.

- *Government-funded research should benefit from later financial success.* If the government already demands high interest rates when it bails out a company in a financial crisis or loans money to college students, then it should also benefit financially from supporting applied research. Legal clauses that make the government a modest financial partner in the companies and start-ups to which it provides grants would create a visible link with success stories and allow the profits from these investments to fund future projects. The technology transfer and licensing programs at major research universities have learned this lesson, and the government should, too. Some of these profits could be set aside to help finance work-study programs for job training.

- *Venture capitalists should teach their investors to think longer term and early stage.* There is more to innovation than just software, social media, and the life sciences, which receive the vast majority of venture capital. The industry's maxim is that only one in five investments works out well, but a less skewed investment portfolio would lead to fewer big winners and many more solid performers. As an investment manager, Antoine saw firsthand how a broad diversity of emerging markets stocks helped to mitigate the volatility inherent in making risky investments, and venture capitalists should apply the same lesson by greatly diversifying the range of sectors in which they invest.

Organization and Culture

The main focus of the brainbelts central to our research was always on developing solutions for today's complex technology challenges. But often that also required creating new work arrangements that would facilitate and enable the collaborative, cross-disciplinary relationships that are necessary in brainsharing initiatives. Because these working arrangements may evolve during different stages of a project, and because the players within an initiative often have very different organizational structures, flexibility is key.

It isn't easy for global companies, with their large hierarchies and long-standing working relationships, to achieve the necessary flexibility. Jeffrey Immelt, CEO of GE, for example, wants his company to work in multifunctional teams and to partner with educational institutions. But many of his employees are union members, and Immelt's actions can be at odds with union regulations. Immelt has no desire to do battle with union leadership but seeks rather to convince them that his goal is always to create new jobs, not just eliminate old ones. Accordingly, when opening a new facility or creating a partnership that would create new opportunities, Immelt looks to reduce wage levels where it makes sense and to make less-stringent work rules where it is possible. By using common sense and building trust, Immelt has engineered many deals in the United States that have not only created jobs but also changed how the jobs look. He has also been successful with this approach in France, when GE sought to obtain most of the assets of the French company Alstom in 2014, a deal that was politically fraught and highly contested.

Immelt recognizes that innovation involves more than a technical process—the social and cultural aspects are just as important. He leads the way for other CEOs who seek to create new organizational structures that will accommodate brainsharing and come to terms with unions. This is particularly important in former rustbelt areas where unions played an important role in big-manufacturing activities—such as automaking and steelmaking—but are less canny when it comes to high-technology sectors.

In Europe, the situation is more complicated, because employers and unions are part of the welfare state that democratic governments have built over the past half century. The promise of the system is that people will be assured of a steady job, but the need for flexibility makes that promise harder to keep. The big question for policy makers is how to maintain solidarity with workers while creating more freedom of movement for companies and individual employees. For decades, Europe has engaged in ideological discussions about how society should be organized at the highest level, but now the conversation is much more practical and regionally focused.

There has been progress in this regard. In the wake of the financial crisis, key players in Germany and Holland—including unions, employers, and political authorities—were willing and able to create more flexible working arrangements, albeit temporary ones in some cases. European policy makers still fear, however, that any changes to the welfare state will expose Europe to the "American disease," whose symptoms are enormous income inequality and an increasing percentage of the population living below the poverty line. But doing nothing is not an option in Europe. The challenge for European authorities is to respond constructively to the need for more flexibility while devising a new form for social solidarity.

There is also no option, in Europe or the United States, but to move away from traditional forms of manufacturing toward smart manufacturing. As we discussed in the first chapter, these two approaches to making things look very different.

These characteristics go well beyond issues of technical process and organizational structure: they affect the cultural and social norms. The emphasis on teamwork, creativity, information sharing, and interdisciplinary relationships—all driven by a sharp market focus—will turn traditional hierarchical systems and organizational cultures upside down. But the changes can be made successfully, and universities and hospitals are at the forefront of the shift.

As we've discussed, the emergence of a new model of brainsharing inevitably happens at least in part as the result of large forces, particularly necessity, but leadership is essential to hasten the process and make it more effective. Leaders must learn to manage companies with a higher percentage of professionals on the payroll than ever before. These are people with strong opinions and deep affiliation with their discipline. They respond more to inspiring visions than to the commands of formal authority. The leader must recognize that innovation and collaboration cannot be motivated or evaluated by financial targets alone and must set greater goals by identifying new markets to conquer and new products to create. Efficiency will always be necessary, but effectiveness will be the paramount concern.

It is relatively easy for leaders to try different organizational forms and embrace new ways of thinking when times are good—when the economy is strong, the industry is expanding, and the company is achieving good results. When pressure mounts, however, leaders tend to fall back onto old habits, asserting their power and playing people off against one another. The challenge for leaders facing tough times will be to use brainsharing to find new ways forward, by bringing together the ideas of diverse individuals and groups, who will explore quirky ideas and offer unorthodox approaches. If leaders reject creativity and multidisciplinary collaboration during difficult times, the result can be destructive. But those who succeed in handling situations that are difficult—and even situations that threaten existence—through sharing of brainpower will further strengthen the organization and make it more capable of facing the next challenge.

WE MEET AT THE END

We have come to the end of our journey. It brought us to unlikely places in the United States and Europe that had transformed from rustbelts to brainbelts. This phenomenon surprised us at first, because the vibrancy in the brainbelts had not shown up yet in the statistics. As we discussed in the last chapter, this reveals a deficiency in our metrics that must be remedied so that policy makers have the instruments they need to make smart decisions.

At the start of our journey, we two authors had very different perspectives on what was happening in the brainbelts. Fred saw the primacy of a new process of innovation through the intense sharing of brainpower. Antoine was intrigued by the use of new technologies and the creation of smart new products. In the end, our perspectives merged into a common view: the brainbelt phenomenon involved connecting people in a new process (brainsharing) as well as connecting the digital world of IT, data analytics, and wireless communications with new and old ways of "making things" to create new technologies and products (smart production). The hundreds of people we met and talked with crystallized and inspired our thinking. They helped us shape our conclusions that economies that were not long ago dismissed as being outdated are in fact entering a revolutionary new phase and that the global competitive advantage is shifting from cheap to smart.

For the United States and Europe, this means that many activities that had been outsourced will return to home shores. This is good news. After decades of the cheap-labor advantage, the new competitive edge will derive from a very different kind of economic and industrial trump card. The rising demand for smart products of all kinds will require the sharing of brainpower in development and smart-manufacturing methods in the making. Manufacturing will not so much "return," then, as be reinvented. The new manufacturing will be highly automated, and products will be created to custom specifications, in small batches, and as physically close to the customer as possible. As demand increases for smart products and the new ways of working and manufacturing are adopted, more and more brainbelt areas will emerge. Beyond those discussed in our book, we're already seeing where they are developing, as we mentioned in the Introduction.

The rise of the brainbelts and the spread of automation are sure to have a disruptive effect on the current areas of low-cost manufacturing, particularly China, and it will also have an impact on who will have the best opportunities for employment in the United States and Europe. And that leads us to the burning question people asked us over and over as we were working on this book: what will happen to jobs?

This is an age-old concern. Ever since the Industrial Revolution, fears—sometimes bordering on panic—have caused people to worry about the future for jobs. Over the past few decades, we watched as millions of manufacturing jobs disappeared and we heard about China becoming the manufacturing center of the world. Then, the deep economic crisis of 2008, and robots, added further fuel to the fiery debate. How would people make a living? What jobs would be available in the future? Now we may ask whether the benefits of brainsharing and the smart, new economy will spread beyond the top 1 percent to the middle class or whether income and wealth inequalities will become more exaggerated.

The further hollowing out of the middle class, which is a particular problem in the United States, although it is also happening elsewhere, could not only exacerbate existing social tensions but also slow the growth of consumer demand and undermine efforts to improve the standard of living for all. Although the threat to the well-being of the middle class is partly attributable to the economic crisis of 2008 and, before that, the decline of the power of trade unions, it remains a question whether rustbelts can be revitalized quickly enough—and in enough places—to reverse a decline that has separated winners from losers, based mostly on education and location.

In general, we believe that the concern about the loss of jobs, for the middle class and for the society as a whole, is ill-informed and misguided. It's ill-informed because we are much better at counting the number of lost jobs than the newly created ones. And it's misguided, because it misses the main point. The real concern is not that there will be no jobs, but that there will be a lack of trained workers to fill them. (The worry is also futile, because so many of the "lost" jobs were antiquated and would not have lasted, even without the job exodus to China.) The real concerns should be about slow wage growth and wage inequality and, in the longer run, job training and education inequality.

Not only is the concern about jobs not new, neither is the profound rejuggling of jobs that we are now facing—so usual is it that we could call it "the old normal." Over the centuries, each successive wave of innovation (from the steam engine to the Internet) has led to job losses and made certain skills obsolete, even while each wave has also led to a higher standard of living. Joseph Schumpeter called this "creative destruction." We have seen this time and time again. At the time of the American Revolutionary War, farmers made up 90 percent of the labor force. By 1900, that number had shrunk to 38 percent, and by 2000, it was down to 2 percent,[1] even though far more food is now produced. Over 200,000 elevator operators in Manhattan alone were put out of work by automatic elevators. Typists, telegraph and switchboard operators, milkmen, and bank tellers—the examples of jobs that have been replaced and absorbed in the economy are too numerous to mention. Painful, concentrated job losses from factory closings, financial crisis, and outsourcing understandably make the news, but the more diffuse creation of all kinds of new jobs often goes unnoticed. Economic history is full of examples of how adjustment and resilience are underestimated, and those characteristics are evident again today: they are the catalysts that bring rustbelts back and turn them into brainbelts.

It's easier and more politically advantageous to blame job losses on China, however, than to accept that factories (like farms before them) have become much more efficient and that the jobs they depended on are no longer necessary or relevant. For example, the 94,000 people working in the steel industry in 2012 produced 14 percent more steel than nearly 400,000 workers did in 1980,[2] and a typical GM employee now makes twenty-eight cars per year, four times the seven cars of Detroit's glory years in the 1950s. Painful adjustment, yes. The end of the car and steel industries, no. Moreover, prosperity is a direct result of constantly improving productivity.

In their book *Race Against the Machine*, Erik Brynjolfsson and Andrew McAfee point to a "polarization of labor demand"—meaning that there has been an increase in demand for high-skilled jobs and for low-skilled jobs, and less demand for everything in between—and this has kept payrolls flat for decades and put downward pressure on labor's share of the economy. From our discussions in the United States and Europe, together with studying reams of labor statistics, we agree that "the good news is that this has radically increased the economy's productive capacity." The bad news is that it "does not automatically benefit everyone in a society."[3]

There are plenty of winners, therefore, but not everyone falls into the winning category. That has been as true in the past as it will be in the future. Education has been the key difference. For example, those with a high school education or less (which describes people who held more than half of the manufacturing jobs in 2000) have been the main victims. During the 2000–2012 period, people with a community college degree, occupational degree, or graduate degree gained a higher percentage of manufacturing jobs, and that trend is expected to continue and even accelerate.[4]

We believe that the predictions of millions of further job losses in manufacturing are wildly exaggerated, at least in the United States and Northern Europe, and they are based on looking in the rearview mirror. These losses have been taking place since the 1980s and are largely behind us.[5] There are, in fact, only 740,000 production-line workers (once the heart of manufacturing) left in the United States, a miniscule 6 percent of the total jobs in manufacturing.[6] The future impact of automation in the old economies will instead be felt mostly in service jobs.[7] And not all of those jobs will be low-skill. Data analytics will create many new jobs, but the need for sophisticated pattern recognition will affect many existing ones as well, including those of radiologists, translators, interpreters, spies, and analysts.

Another big difference between the last few decades and the next few will be the shift in demographics. We are still captive to an outdated understanding of demographics that originates in the postwar baby boom. The sudden six-year rise in unemployment induced by the 2008 economic crisis made us lose sight of the fact that more experienced workers in the current generation of baby boomers in the United States began to retire in 2011. Three million more people retired in 2013 than did in 2007. An aging population tends to push the so-called labor-force participation rate down further, whether economic times are good or bad.[8]

Now let's turn to the other side to the story: the many new jobs—both high-skilled and low-skilled—that have been created as a result of innovation. Where are these new jobs? They are to be found not only in advanced manufacturing, the Internet, software, R&D, and bioscience—where they will keep growing—but in the additional jobs these industries create in support and partner industries and businesses. Today, as many as one-tenth of all jobs in the United States belong to the "innovation sector," as many as there are in manufacturing. Not only is the innovation sector itself labor-intensive but, as Berkeley economist Enrico Moretti shows in his book *The New Geography of Jobs*, for each new urban high-tech job, there is a huge multiplier of five additional jobs that are created outside the high-tech sector. Three of these jobs are for professionals such as doctors, lawyers, and yoga instructors, and two of them are for lower-wage nonprofessionals such as waiters and store clerks.[9]

We cannot fight the tide of history as industry and society change. Instead, we should recognize that innovation is what makes us competitive. It is an important motivator in the market economy, a much more important and sustainable one than greed. Remember that Lenin said that capitalists, motivated by the lust for profit, would sell rope to others who would turn around and use it to hang the capitalists.[10]

As we come to recognize the innovation imperative, the concept of innovation will evolve. Although Schumpeter talked about creative destruction and we have become enamored of the idea of revolutionary, game-changing, out-of-the-box, breakthrough innovations, the fact is that much innovation is gradual and incremental. Gradually, then, we will come to think of innovation as a continuous and integrated process of renewal, product updates, and technology evolution—an oxygen that breathes new life and vibrancy into society, organizations, and regions. The process will, however, be harder to see than our current model, which places such value on disruptive and highly visible acts of creative destruction, and therefore it will be harder for some to cope with. Once again, the remedy will be found in education and training, with plenty of attention paid to the cultural and social aspects of an increased focus on innovation.

As organizations and smart manufacturing concentrate in brainbelts and innovation hubs, individuals will need to focus on improving their adaptability. To add value in the new competitive environment, people will have to master a broad set of skills, many of them social. It will be the individual's responsibility to be aware of changing requirements and adapt before their responsibilities and skills are no longer relevant. It will be the employer's responsibility to help their employees acquire the needed skills to make the adaptation. In this way, employees will come to think of their work as a lifelong personal education program rather than just a job.

The skills of the connector, in particular, will become increasingly valuable to companies, and especially to regional initiatives. They will be responsible for the social innovation needed to make the brainsharing approach and the smart-manufacturing methods function well. Working in multidisciplinary relationships redefines competition as between groups rather than between individuals. But groups must also learn from other groups, even as they compete with one another. That will require that connectors help people work to achieve their group's goals while maintaining an attitude of openness and generosity. This is a rare combination of skills and qualities, and there is no doubt that companies will engage in a war for connectors, just as they have engaged in a war for technical talent.

The changing face of the job market will have a huge impact on vocational training, which, as we discovered on our journey, had almost disappeared, especially in the United States. Although there are many local and regional programs to rebuild the vocational training system, a much wider initiative must be undertaken to promote technical education to help young people see that making things can be fun and challenging. Germany provides the best model for the world to follow. Germans have long been known as experts in machine building, and they feel a national pride in making reliable products. Vocational training is a fundamental part of their culture. Although their system is difficult to replicate, other countries can learn from it and adapt it to their own needs.

Europeans, in turn, can learn from the United States, particularly in the way the US financial network supports start-ups and spin-offs and builds on the entrepreneurial spirit. Although venture capital is concentrated in Silicon Valley, Boston-Cambridge, and New York, the US capital market is integrated in such a way that its resources can easily be accessed by regions that need funding. In Europe, the capital markets are more fragmented than in the United States, which means that resources cannot be optimally directed to the regions that need them most, because of various allocation restrictions.

What struck us both during our visits to the brainbelts was the pragmatism, ambition, and the collaborativeness of local and regional politicians, entrepreneurs, and scientists. Collaboration was not a political or business buzzword, but rather a real activity often born, as we have seen, of necessity. Through collaboration, a new mix of market forces and local politics was created. Regional politicians became facilitators and connectors. Their pragmatic approach resulted in the creation of better policies and a longer-term perspective.

Although brainbelt areas will take on many of the challenges that lie ahead, there are some investments and initiatives that must be undertaken by larger authorities, and often on a national level. Everywhere we went, for example, we saw the need for improved infrastructure, especially a nationwide energy grid that can handle the increasing decentralization of electricity production and a Wi-Fi broadband network that can handle the data explosion that the Internet of Things is already causing.

National policy makers must also push forward initiatives that promote the interdisciplinary collaboration that scientists everywhere told us is a must to address the most complex challenges in chips, new materials, and life sciences. The Obama administration took a small step in this direction, with its $50 million investment in the National Additive Manufacturing Innovation Institute (NAMII). The small budget should not be seen as a limitation but rather as an incentive to bring different companies and universities together in joint research programs. In Europe, similar initiatives are centered in the applied research institutes, which smooth collaboration between companies and universities and between disciplines. Joe Gray, of OHSU in

Portland, predicted that, within a decade, "the Nobel Prize will be given to a team instead of to an individual."

The enthusiasm for interdisciplinary collaboration and the sharing of brainpower that we witnessed on our travels was countered by the skepticism of others who fear that scientific freedom will be restricted and that basic research will be endangered. We took these concerns seriously. There will always be a need for basic research that is not required to lead directly or immediately to commercial products. Basic research is still the only path to the discovery and pursuit of new knowledge whose commercial potential is not certain but which may bring tremendous benefits to society in other ways. The Hubble telescope, for example, has generated vast quantities of information and insight about our universe over the years it has been operating in outer space, but it has not directly spawned new industries or revenue streams.

Other people had deeper and more fundamental concerns, particularly about the role of technology, analytics, and the Internet of Things in our society—the well-known issues of privacy and security. In this book, we have described how new technologies can help bring major societal challenges closer to a solution, in a positive way. We have talked about how 3D printing and robots will change production processes dramatically and how sensors and chips, via the wireless Internet, will provide a digital infrastructure that can connect everything.

But the concern we heard was about the price we may pay as technology plays an ever-greater role in our lives. Will we become a servant to a technological monster that takes away jobs and, increasingly, makes important decisions for us? There is no doubt that new technologies will have a major impact on us and on the way we live. That will raise ethical questions and privacy issues, which will generate heated debates among politicians, researchers, companies, and NGOs. Ideally, these discussions will lead to new agreements and understandings that will prevent us from being buried by an avalanche of undesirable or uncontrollable technologies.

That societal discussion may take time to reach actionable decisions, and when necessary, it would be wise for participants to take a pause in the deployment of new technologies and products. A striking example of this was the call by a group of biologists in the spring of 2015 to establish a moratorium on the use of a new genome-editing technique that would alter human DNA in a way that could be inherited.[11] Not enough was known about the possible benefits and risks.

Technology, as the film director Fritz Lang—whose movie *Metropolis* depicted a grim industrial dystopia circa 2027—put it, is in itself soulless. Only human beings can direct the course of technology into positive channels that benefit human society and prevent a divisive, techno-driven world.

One way to do this is to rethink one of the organizing principles that has driven us for the past half century: money. In this period, achieving financial gain has been the primary motivator and key success indicator of human activity, particularly in the United States. The primacy of money has led to the development and use of a technical language and set of metrics that have limited the discussion to an elite, largely composed of technocrats. Financial flows have determined social and political life. Financial growth has become the standard for what is right or wrong, what is valuable and what is not. In 2008, the financial crisis was a wakeup call. Suddenly we had to ask ourselves: is this what we want? Is this how we want to judge ourselves and motivate our children? For more and more people, the answer is no.

So what should the organizing principle be if it is not about money? In the coming decades, two new forces will play a determining role in the relationship between human beings and technology: the Internet of Things and the need for the sharing of brainpower. Those two forces make human beings indispensable, because of our knowledge, expertise, and empathy. The opportunity then is to base our activities around what best realizes our potential as human beings and as a society, not what puts more money in our pockets and portfolios.

But this new understanding of how people and technology should move forward together will not develop on its own. Technology gains soul only when we make the decisions that make that happen. That is why the brainbelt regions are so important. As we developed our understanding of what was happening there, we came to see that a brainbelt is far more than a region or a collection of physical facilities. Rather, it is a metaphor for a way of thinking and acting, a description of the new form of global competitiveness and a technological development with deep social consequences. It would seem that the sharing of brainpower in collaborative teams discourages excessive income inequality and winner-take-all mentality. So, although we acknowledge the concerns regarding privacy, security, and even morality, we believe that the only way to address the critical issues that we face is through the most diligent and rigorous application of multidisciplinary sharing of brainpower.

And that is why we do not say "beware" of the brainbelt but rather offer this "welcome" to a smarter, more collaborative, more effective world.

ACKNOWLEDGMENTS

Both of us—Antoine and Fred—have spent our careers as participants in and observers of the financial sector. Antoine worked as a banker, development banker, and investment manager, witnessing firsthand how the Third World developed faster than anyone expected into emerging markets and how their hard-charging companies became competitive players in the global marketplace. Fred worked as a journalist and followed European monetary developments for more than a decade. He came to recognize how the economic and financial debate was actually a political struggle centering on the question of the principles on which a united Europe would be organized.

Over three decades, we saw a whole new global financial order take shape—and then risk falling apart in the financial crisis that began in 2008. Although the decline of traditional industries was obvious, especially in the United States, we did not buy the notion that manufacturing in the developed world was a thing of the past but instead saw the first signs of a very different trend. Cheap labor was losing ground as a competitive trump card in favor of added value from smart innovation.

This book would not have been possible without the help of many people who encouraged us to write it and helped us in clarifying our thoughts, pointing us in new directions and challenging our ideas. We take full responsibility for the ultimate outcome.

In the book, we talk about the importance of "connectors." It turned out that we had two important connectors on this project. The first was Jan Fred van Wijnen, the editor who originally brought us together. The other was John Butman, who stepped in at a critical moment when our muse had left for vacation and put the book back on track with his consummate editing skill. He also came up with the idea of the final book title after we had gone through and rejected many others. We owe him huge thanks. Peter Osnos of PublicAffairs immediately encouraged us to write this book. We are grateful that our editor, John Mahaney, made sure we stayed focused on the big picture and was both flexible and encouraging when Fred had to stop working on the book for a number of months because of a serious illness. Shena Redmond was our project editor and ensured that nothing went wrong during the final stages. We were lucky that meticulous copy editing was in the skillful hands of Michele Wynn.

Daniel Huffman, Antoine's research assistant, was immensely helpful in preparing background information for our interviews. He also shaped Google's translation of some of Fred's writings into readable English and was on hand for most of the early editing. Cathryn Hunt, Antoine's assistant during the final stages of the book, helped with the huge task of selecting and obtaining the photos in the book.

Other colleagues at Garten Rothkopf—Yuxin Lin and Jonathan Goldstein—also provided helpful research. At an earlier stage, James Gerstenzang helped us lighten and focus the story.

Many friends and colleagues provided helpful comments on various drafts, including David Rothkopf, Claire Casey, Strobe Talbott, Bruce Katz, Mark Muro, John Hauge, Rita Lun, Steven Silver, Carl Peck, Bob Kaiser, Hamilton Loeb, Thees Peereboom, and Rien van Lent, and many of those we interviewed for the book were kind enough to check (and sometimes correct) the accuracy of what we wrote down, learned, and observed. Peter van Agtmael took Antoine's author photo for the back cover and ventured into the cleanroom in Albany.

Antoine is also profoundly grateful for what he learned from his colleagues at the World Bank Group, EMM, and the Strategic Investment Group as well as discussions at Brookings, NPR, and the Peterson Institute for International Economics. Fred feels similar gratitude toward his colleagues at Het Financieele Dagblad and the European financial world.

We traveled around the United States and Europe, researched books and articles, spent numerous hours writing at the computer, and were preoccupied to the point of obsession, none of it designed to make us popular at home. Antoine is grateful to Emily, and Fred to Frances, for (again) putting up with all of this. You deserve better.

NOTES

Introduction: Welcome to the Brainbelt

1. Jeffrey R. Immelt, "The CEO of General Electric on Sparking an American Manufacturing Renewal," *Harvard Business Review* (March 2012).

2. The University of Texas has 48,000 students, including 8,000 engineering students and a strong computer science department supported by grants from the Gates and Dell Foundations. Austin is also home to more than 3,600 biotech firms and nearly 1,000 private scientific R&D firms with over 20,000 employees (www.biospace.com/News/top-12-hot-biopharma-regions-for-growth-and/347389). Texas ranked second in the nation for the number of physicists and life scientists. The Texas Emerging Technology Fund was created by the Texas legislature in 2005 to support R&D and emerging technologies and has distributed over $525 million in grants, half to universities and half to 145 early stage companies (www.ce.org/i3/Move/2015/March-April/Tech-Hub-Austin.aspx). In 2014, the National Science Foundation designated the University of Texas at Austin, Rice University, and Texas A&M as an Entrepreneurial Innovation Node with a $3.75 million grant (news.utexas.edu/2014/08/26/nsf-i-corps-node). Austin has a large and growing gaming and Internet industry.

Chapter 1: Sharing Brainpower and Smart Manufacturing

1. "Intel in Oregon," Intel, at www.intel.com/content/www/us/en/corporate-responsibility/intel-in-oregon.html.

2. See www.qiagen.com for a company overview.

3. See the Toolpoint for Lab Science website, at www.toolpoint.ch.

4. To give just a few examples, people such as William Shockley, who was instrumental in developing the transistor at Bell Labs but moved to California

and whose colleagues went on to found Fairchild Semiconductor (after Sputnik and President Kennedy's announcement of the race to the moon, a natural candidate for NASA funding) and later Intel; Lee de Forest, an early pioneer of the vacuum tube; and William Hewlett and David Packard, Stanford graduates (with their oscilloscope, and later their PC and ink jet printer), who were among the first to move from their garage to the Stanford Industrial Park. They built on earlier strength in the region (often on the basis of defense contracts) in the areas of telegraph, short-wave radio, and very high frequency transmission as well as radar and aerospace.

5. Fred Bakker and Jeroen Molenaar, "Duurzaamheid als drijfveer voor innovatie" (Sustainability as a driver behind innovation), *Het Financieele Dagblad*, May 5, 2012, Amsterdam.

6. See poet-dsm.com.

7. These statements were excerpted from an interview conducted at Rensselaer Polytechnic Institute with President Shirley Ann Jackson and Vice President of Research and Professor of Biology Jonathan Dordick, August 24, 2013.

8. Interview with Lesley Spiegel, June 12, 2014, Zurich.

9. Now in a strategic alliance with Sonoco Alloyd, the sealing-machines unit of Sonoco Products Co., will provide fully automated custom packaging lines and complement Sonoco's Sawyer collaborative robot for machine tensing and circuit board testing (see Zacks.com, August 12, 2015).

10. MIT's Media Lab has made the Cambridge-Boston area one of the main American research centers on robotics, together with the Stanford Research Institute (SRI), Carnegie Mellon, Berkeley, and the University of Pennsylvania. Just as Rethink Robotics focuses "above the belt," another MIT spin-off, Boston Dynamics (now owned by Google), has concentrated its efforts "below the belt" on balance and motion. Backed by the Defense Advanced Research Projects Agency (DARPA), it has developed a number of innovative four-legged robots that can move at high speed. Its Atlas can carry high loads and clear debris. Japan's Schaft, which was also acquired by Google (clearly making robotics one of its future priorities), won the December 2013 DARPA Robotics challenge that ranked the top sixteen humanoid robots for its $2 million prize. Also in Japan, Honda's Asimo looks humanlike and can walk up and down stairs, talk, kick a soccer ball, and bring coffee.

11. Rethink Robotics' closest competitor for second-generation factory robots is Denmark's Universal Robots that sells 800–1,000 single-armed robots per year for about $26,000 each to companies such as Bosch, BMW, and Samsung. Its UR-5 and UR-10 robots cost more and are far less versatile but carry a higher load, are faster (they can move up to one meter per second, or a little over one

yard), more accurate, and have a longer life of nearly twenty years, which makes them even cheaper to operate at only $1 per hour. Data from Casey Nobile, Robotics Business Review, *Perspectives 2013*.

12. There are many sensor-equipped, mobile research robots but, as of now, few factory robots, made by traditional robot makers or start-ups. Leading industrial robot maker Kuka in Germany has a one-armed Light Weight Robot (LWR) that can play Ping-Pong just like TOPIO, developed by Tosy Robotics. ABB's FRIDA (Friendly Robot for Industrial Dual-arm Assembly) was introduced in 2011. Motoman Inc., the American robotic subsidiary of Yaskawa Electric in Japan, is on its fourth generation of dual-arm robots (the SDA series) with payloads up to 44 pounds that can pick out different-colored Lego blocks and assemble tiny electronic components. The Italian Institute of Technology developed the COMAN robot with the ability to walk and balance in rough terrain. Meka Robotics, cofounded by Aaron Edsinger, who worked with Rodney Brooks, makes small robots for research labs. Companies in Japan, the United States, Germany, South Korea, Turkey, Iran, and China are working on better, faster, and more versatile robots. Sources: *Perspectives 2013* and Wikipedia.

13. Based on discussions with Phil Knight at Brookings in Washington, DC, on June 3, 2013, and May 29, 2014. Also discussed in an interview with CEO Eric Sprunk at Nike Headquarters on October 15, 2014.

14. National Institute for Standards and Technology, *Robotics Systems for Smart Manufacturing Programs,* March 20, 2014.

15. The 3D printing process begins with a metal plate, called a substrate, which forms the base to which the first layer of the piece(s) will be attached. Because each layer is only about the thickness of a human hair, the substrate must be extraordinarily flat—within 1/1,000th of an inch—in order to avoid warping (even a slightly inclined surface would produce uneven layers). Plastic printers use nozzles to direct where the next layer of material should go. In metal printers, once a very thin layer of metal powder has been uniformly spread across the substrate, a high-powered laser etches specific areas to bind them to the previous layer. Excess metal particles are removed from the surface (for recycling back into the metal-powder supply) and the process is repeated.

16. Youngstown, once a major steel and transportation hub located halfway between New York City and Chicago, lost 60 percent of its population when the steel industry closed its doors.

17. The combination of congressional Republican resistance and sequestration blocked the requested funds from ever being released. In desperation, the president scraped together $40 million from the budgets of other federal agencies—including the Department of Defense, NASA, and the National Science

Foundation—to kick-start one facility as a pilot project. With unusual speed, the federal government produced a Request for Proposal in only three weeks, which gave university institutes and industries across the country forty-five days to present proposals. In the end, the Ohio tech belt's bid won the coveted contract, and together with Penn State, the first NAMII facility was set up in an old warehouse in Youngstown.

18. Technicians demonstrated for us three distinct types of experimental 3D printers. The first (and best known) is called a fused deposition modeling printer, first developed by Stratasys in the late 1980s, which resembles an ink jet printer that replaces sheets of paper with successive layers of quickly drying materials. Consumers can already purchase simplified versions of these machines for under $500. Second, a powder bed and binder jet (invented at MIT and manufactured by Z Corporation) does not use a nozzle but looks more like a machine that builds sand dunes. Finally, a selective laser-sintering machine (SLM), developed at the University of Texas in Austin under a DARPA grant, fuses different materials together, ranging from plastics to metals, in layers as thin as 30–40 nanometers. Visit to NAMII on June 13, 2013.

19. Charles Hull, cofounder of 3D Systems in the United States, built the first 3D printer in 1984. Although it was primarily used for building prototypes at first, researchers around the world are now in a race to test the process to work at a speed that allows its use in manufacturing with an immense variety of shapes and materials.

20. Marco Annunziata, "Welcome to the Age of the Industrial Internet," TED Talk, December 17, 2013.

21. Travis Hessman, "The Dawn of the Smart Factory," *Industry Week*, February 14, 2013.

22. Ibid.

23. See Chapter 5 on the difficulties the GE energy storage business has experienced with technology as well as demand, despite lofty expectations when it opened.

Chapter 2: Connectors Creating Communities

1. Interview with Alain Kaloyeros, August 22, 2013, in Albany; all Kaloyeros quotes in this chapter are from this interview.

2. After its start in 2004.

3. This involves a lithography method using EUV (extreme ultraviolet) wavelength, but its use in manufacturing has been delayed because R&D has not yet solved the problem of doing this without requiring too much electric power. It

seems that the cost of lithography has become the dominant stumbling block for moving to the next generation of semiconductors.

4. Chelsea Diana, "Angels Open Wallets for SUNY Polytechnic Battery Start-Up," *Albany Business Review*, April 9, 2015.

5. Jackson further says, "We are proud to say that at RPI we like to work on the hard problems, the earliest stage of innovation, fundamental research. Only universities can do this now. That is why only 10 percent of our $100 million research program is supported by industry and 10 percent by New York State but 80 percent by the federal government and the reverse of what you see at the Nanotechnology Center. At RPI, we have had our own partnership with IBM and the State of New York since 2006 to set up the Computational Center for Nanotechnology Innovations for this purpose. We do that with the help of a petascale supercomputer. Petascale computers, among the world's fastest supercomputers, are used in advanced simulations in such diverse fields as climate, fusion science, and quantum chemistry. In fact, we will soon have the most powerful supercomputer of any university that is among the thirty fastest in the world. We are making our own big bet on the use of big data. I am not talking here about crunching massive amounts of data but about using them for insights in very fundamental research. We are good at that here at RPI, where engineering traditionally has been a huge strength." Interview, August 21, 2013.

6. GlobalFoundries is owned largely by Abu Dhabi's Advanced Technology Investment Co. It was created when Advanced Micro Devices (AMD) divested its manufacturing arm in 2009 and GlobalFoundries then acquired Singapore-based Chartered Semiconductor Manufacturing Co. Ltd. in 2010. It is about one-fourth the size of the largest foundry, TSMC in Taiwan. Plant visit and interview with Mike Russo, August 21, 2014.

7. With 300-millimeter wafers of 14–20 nanometers.

8. See www.globalfoundries.com.

9. See www.infineon.com.

10. See www.hightech-startbahn.de.

11. See www.mpg.de/en.

12. See www.fraunhofer.de.

13. See www.helmholtz.de/en/home.

14. See www.leibniz-gemeinschaft.de/en/home.

15. See www.amtc-dresden.com/content/index.php?xmlfile=general.xml.

16. See www.siltronic.com/int/en/home/index.jsp.

17. See www.das-deutschland.de.

18. See www.hap.de.

19. See www.ais-automation.com/de/index.php.

20. See www.deru-reinraum.de/home.

21. Interview with Gitta Haupold, November 13, 2015, Dresden; all Haupold quotes in this chapter are from this interview.

22. See www.infineon.com/cms/de/about-infineon/press/press-releases/2014 /INFXX201404-033.html.

23. See www.silicon-europe.eu/about/silicon-europe.

24. See tu-dresden.de/forschung/epc/contact/ueber_uns/ueber_uns/document _view?set_language=en.

25. Interview with Bettina Vossberg, November 11, 2014, Dresden; all Vossberg quotes in this chapter are from this interview.

26. See www.futuresax.de.

27. See www.dresden-exists.de/index.php?id=30&no_cache=1&tx_queoevents _events%5Baction%5D=teaser&tx_queoevents_events%5Bcontroller%5D=Event &cHash=29da65cc4d2938c0c24e5b13279263e9.

28. See sherpa-dresden.de/index.php?site=team.

29. See www.intelligentcommunity.org.

30. See www.hightechcampus.nl.

31. See www.holstcentre.com.

32. See www.imec.be. In 1982 the Flemish government set up a program in the field of microelectronics with the goal of strengthening the microelectronics industry in Flanders. This program included setting up a laboratory for advanced research in microelectronics (Imec), a semiconductor foundry (former Alcatel Microelectronics, now STMicroelectronics and AMI Semiconductor), and a training program for VLSI design engineers. The latter is now fully integrated into Imec activities. Imec was founded in 1984 as a nonprofit organization. It is supervised by a board of directors, which includes delegates from industry, Flemish universities, and the Flemish government.

33. Companies like Dupont Teijin Films, Solvay, BASF, Bayer, Merck, and Agfa contribute their knowledge of substrates and materials. Equipment suppliers and organic electronic manufacturers such as Orbotech, Coherent, Roth & Rau, ASM, ASML, Singulus Mastering, and Plastic Electronic provide a deep understanding of the production processes and facilities. Integrated device manufacturers like Philips, Panasonic, and Polymer Vision give clear specifications of what market-ready technology and system design should look like. See www.holstcentre.com.

34. See www.philips.nl.

35. See www.asml.com.

36. Interview of Martin van den Brink in *Het Financieele Dagblad*, April 24, 2004.

37. Interview with Hans Duisters, November 11, 2014, Dresden; all Duisters quotes in this chapter are from this interview.

38. See www.sioux.eu.

39. See www.phenom-world.com.

40. See www.mutraxc.com.

41. See www.bom.nl.

42. See www.brainportindustries.com.

Chapter 3: Making a New Movie of an Old Story

1. All Proenza quotes in this chapter are based on interviews in Akron, June 12–13, 2013, and follow-up interview by phone on August 29, 2014.

2. Luis M. Proenza, "The Akron Model: Toward a New Framework for University Entrepreneurship, a Narrative Briefing for the Ewing Marion Kauffman Foundation," July 2011.

3. The Austen Bioinnovation Institute website in Akron, at www.abiaakron .org.

4. Jobs-Ohio, Ohio Polymers & Chemicals at jobsohiowest.com/industries /polymers-chemicals.

5. Ohio State had a $983-million R&D budget in 2014 (up from $609 million in 2005) with $478 million coming from the federal government and $118 million from industry (www.research.osu.edu). The Ohio Third Frontier Program is a $2.1 billion initiative that provides funding to Ohio technology-based industries, universities, and nonprofit research institutions (www.development.ohio.gov). The Wright Center for Photovoltaics Innovation is an example of close collaboration between several universities and major businesses (www.pvic.org at www.oee.osu.edu).

6. See Third Frontier website, at development.ohio.gov/bs_thirdfrontier /background.htm.

7. Akron Polymer Systems website at www.akronpolysys.com.

8. Timken has since split into a producer of specialized steel products and bearings such as mega-bearings of the kind found in wind turbines.

9. Quoted in press release by A. Schulman of July 1, 2010, "A. Schulman Expands Support for Polymer Research at the University of Akron."

10. Karl-Heinz Zum Gahr, *Microstructure and Wear of Materials*, Tribology Series, 10 (Elsevier, 1987), cited in Tribology article in Wikipedia.

11. Interview with Barbara Ewing on June 13, 2013, in Youngstown, Ohio.

12. According to Dennis Barber, executive director, Ohio Polymer Strategy Council, the Ohio Polymer Industry, August 2011.

13. Albert Link, "A Generosity of Spirit: The Early History of the Research Triangle Park," published by the Research Triangle Foundation, 1965, p. 10. Further quotes by Williams Little are also from this source.

14. Ibid., p. 43.

15. *Fortune* magazine, September 1966.

16. See www.visitnc.com/listing/american-tobacco-historic-district-lucky-strike -cigarette.

17. Discussion at dinner in Durham, North Carolina, on April 23, 2014.

18. Interview with Chuck Swoboda at the Cree Factory at the edge of the Research Triangle Park on April 25, 2014.

19. After Georgia Tech, Texas A&M, and Purdue.

20. Interview with Randy Woodson on April 22, 2014, at North Carolina State University, Raleigh.

21. For Eastman Chemical.

22. Interview with Bob Geolas at RTP, April 21, 2014.

23. From Sven Hemlin, Carl Martin Allwood, and Ben R. Martin, eds., *Creative Knowledge Environments: The Influences on Creativity in Research and Innovation* (Northampton, MA: Edward Elgar, 2004).

24. Interview with Mats Lindoff at Ideon, September 3, 2013, Lund.

25. Interview with Richard Mosell at Ideon, September 4, 2013, Lund.

26. Interview with Katarina Noren, September 3, 2013, Lund; all other Noren quotes in this chapter are from this interview.

27. See www.nlr.nl.

28. See www.avantium.com.

29. See static.tue.nl/universiteit/faculteiten/faculteit-biomedische-technol ogie/innoveren-met-biomedische-technologie/spin-offs/qtise.

30. From an interview with *Het Financieele Dagblad*, March 9, 2015. Also see static.tue.nl/universiteit/faculteiten/faculteit-biomedische-technologie/inno veren-met-biomedische-technologie/spin-offs/qtise.

31. See the article about his move to Maastricht at www.maastrichtuni versity.nl/web/Main1/SiteWide/SiteWide11/EersteUniversiteitshoogleraarBeno emdAanUM1.htm.

32. *Het Financieele Dagblad*, October 4, 2014.

33. The board of TenCate supports this step. See Fred Bakker and Tjabel Daling, "Textielfabrikant als Hoogwaardige Nichespeler" (Textile producer that turned into a high-quality niche player), *Het Financieele Dagblad*, November 3, 2012, Amsterdam. In July 2015, the Dutch private equity house Gilde formed a consortium that will buy all outstanding shares from TenCate.

34. In July 2015, the British company GKN bought Fokker Technologies.

35. Interview with Wim Pasteuning, July 2012, Hoofddorp.

Chapter 4: White Coats and Blue Collars

1. He also trained Christiaan Barnard and Norman Shumway, who were part of the team that conducted the first heart transplant, as detailed in G. Wayne Miller, *King of Hearts* (New York: Crown Books, 2010).

2. See en.wikipedia.org/wiki/K%C3%A1roly_Ereky.

3. See en.wikipedia.org/wiki/Molecular_biology.

4. Interview with Bernard Fox, chair of cancer research at Providence Cancer Center, Portland, Oregon, and CEO of the start-up UbiVac on October 17, 2014 in Portland, Oregon.

5. World Health Organization, "Preventing Chronic Diseases: A Vital Investment," WHO Global Report, 2005, cited by a Harvard School of Public Health working paper for the World Economic Forum: "The Global Economic Burden of Non-Communicable Diseases," September 2011 (www.hsph.harvard.edu), and the NCD Alliance, "Addressing Global Inequalities in NCD Prevention and Control for a Healthy Future," October 2012.

6. Telephone interview on November 12, 2014, followed by meeting on May 26, 2015, in Washington, DC. Johnson & Johnson is the world's largest medical device company, with ten major medical device platforms of at least $1 billion each and $27.5 billion in revenues in this area in 2014 (out of a total of $73 billion). That could change in 2015, when Medtronic and Covidien will be combined; together they had $28.2 billion in 2014 medical-device revenues. See *Fierce Medical Devices*, April 6, 2015.

7. Germany's Biotronik, founded in 1963 and headquartered in Berlin, is the only significant European company still producing pacemakers. However, its research-and-production facilities are located in Lake Oswego, Oregon. There is also the Sorin Group in Italy, which is much smaller. A single Chinese company makes pacemakers, but its product is not in the same league in terms of sophistication.

8. Clinical studies on the insulin pump therapy effectiveness were done by Dr. Richard Bergenstal and others of the University of Minnesota and published on July 22, 2010.

9. Interview with Ellie Pidot at Medtronic Headquarters in Minneapolis, Minnesota, on July 29, 2013.

10. Scott Litman and John Stavig, "Is Minnesota Successful in Entrepreneurship?" *Minneapolis Post*, June 17, 2013. These authors cite some success stories, for example, Minneapolis-based Code 42 Software that provides online backup for consumers and enterprises, and raised $52.5 million in 2012; enStratius, a cloud-management software provider that was acquired by Dell in 2013; and Compellent, a rapidly growing provider of highly virtualized storage solutions

with automated data management features for enterprise and cloud-computing environments that was also acquired by Dell for $960 million. Nevertheless, a 2013 report by the Kauffman Foundation shows that Minnesota still has a long way to go in new start-ups (where it ranks only fortieth in the nation), although the ranking for new patents is much better.

11. Now a subsidiary of Boston Scientific Corporation.

12. Covidien (now part of Medtronic after its acquisition in 2014) acquired the start-up that originally brought this to market for $2.6 billion. See Covidien Press release, July 12, 2010.

13. *Het Financieele Dagblad*, August 27, 2012.

14. Interview with Norman Dann in Minneapolis on July 31, 2013.

15. Martin Moylan, "At Medtronic, Efforts by CEO Ishrak Appear to Be Paying Off," Minnesota Public Radio, MPR News, July 22, 2013 (mmoylan@mpr.org).

16. He retired in 2014.

17. Interview with Dale Wahlstrom in Minneapolis on July 30, 2013.

18. Andy Giegerich, "Oregon's Biotech Sector Shows New Signs of Life," *Portland Business Journal*, October 26, 2012.

19. "Battelle/Bio, State Bioscience Jobs, Investment and Innovation, 2014," at www.bio.org/sites/default/files/Battelle-BIO-2014-Industry.pdf.

20. OHSU's campus houses three top-notch hospitals: the OHSU Hospital (a Level 1 trauma center and general hospital), Doernbecher Children's Hospital, and the Portland Veterans Affairs Medical Center.

21. After acquiring local Stimulation Technology, Inc.

22. Kelly also cofounded the Sapient Health Network (now part of WebMD) in 1995 and Learning.com shortly thereafter.

23. Beyond the Intel-OHSU relationship, Mary Stenzel-Poore also came up with the idea of other "co-laboratories," with partners like Pacific Northwest National Lab, a Department of Energy research laboratory; and electronic microscope maker FEI, which was important because researchers need to visualize cancer cells and how they interact. Working with companies like Siemens, OHSU has since pioneered the use of a four-dimensional approach to imaging. Comments in this chapter by Stenzel-Poore come from an interview with her at OHSU, Portland, Oregon, on October 15, 2014.

24. Quotes in this chapter by Joe Gray come from an author interview at OHSU, Portland, Oregon, on October 16, 2014.

25. Pawlowski moved to Micron Technology in July 2014 after thirty-one years at Intel.

26. "Portland OHSU Teams with Intel to Decode the Root Causes of Cancer and Other Complex Diseases," OHSU press release, April 22, 2013.

27. See OHSU start-up companies website, at www.ohsu.edu/xd/research/techtransfer/startups/index.cfm. Typically, the university receives one-third of the license fees for inventions made on its campus, the department that housed the research gets another one-third, and the scientist in charge of the research is entitled to the remaining one-third. Interview with Andrew Watson at OHSU, Portland, Oregon, on October 16, 2014.

28. Some start-ups have been successful enough to move to the big bioscience brainbelts in California, including HD+, Edward Life Sciences, Cepheid Inc., and Organovo. HD+ developed an artificial kidney based on nanotechnology, raised over $60 million in venture capital, and then moved to Silicon Valley. Edwards Life Sciences manufactures and repairs artificial heart valves, helping to treat over 2 million patients. Cepheid Inc., now located in Sunnyvale, California, is a medical diagnostics company well known for its contract with the US Postal Service to test for anthrax. Its 6,000 GeneXpert machines use test kits to detect infectious diseases such as tuberculosis and HIV. Organovo, founded in 2007, designs three-dimensional human tissue and tumor models.

29. Knight is not the first or only philanthropist in this area. Other examples are the $2.5 billion Daniel Ludwig has given for cancer research over the years through the Ludwig Cancer Center and the Gates Foundation's $2.5 billion program to fight HIV and malaria, from which an OHSU researcher received a $25 million grant in September 2014 for work on an HIV vaccine. Microsoft's other founder, Paul Allen, gave $100 million in seed money to the Institute for Brain Science in Seattle for brain mapping.

Besides bolstering OHSU, the Knight gift also had a snowball effect in Oregon. Not to be outdone, the University of Oregon started a $2 billion campaign and Oregon State University finished a $1 billion campaign—not bad, considering there are only thirty-five public universities in the United States (and probably the world) that have raised over $1 billion from philanthropy. According to the Chronicle of Philanthropy, *Facts and Figures*, about 14 percent of all American philanthropy is for health ($1.2 billion in major gifts for 2013 alone, not counting the Knight challenge). Even though the federal government still contributes two-thirds of the massive $70 billion in R&D spending on new drugs, biotechnology, and medical instruments, universities worry about the squeeze left by the federal funding gap, particularly because it comes at a time when drug companies and venture capital have also become hesitant about spending the mega-amounts needed for new drugs ("US Investment in Health Research 2012," *Research America*). According to the Science and Engineering Indicators of the National Science Foundation, health is the largest recipient of non-defense spending (defense spending was $83 billion in FY2011, non-defense spending $61 billion, and health spending $32 billion).

30. Interview with Eric Rosenfeld at his office in Portland, Oregon, on October 15, 2014.

31. Interview with Mario Jenni, June 11, 2014, Zurich; all other Jenni quotes in this chapter are from this interview.

32. See www.cvent.com/rfp/zurich-hotels/technopark-zuerich-foundation /venue-2da8053746c74fdebf46a5c8167fdda7.aspx.

33. Interview with Leo Krummenacher in *Sonntag*, June 7, 2009.

34. In an interview June 7, 2009, with the Swiss magazine *Sonntag 1*, Leo Krummenacher recounted how the complex developed.

35. See www.molecularpartners.com.

36. See www.roche.com.

37. See www.esbatech.com.

38. See www.bsse.ethz.ch.

39. See biosaxony.com.

40. See bio-city-leipzig.de/welcome.

41. See www.biotech-leipzig.de/en/unternehmen/383-technologiegrunderfonds -sachsen-seed-gmbh-und-co-kg.

42. See www.iccas.de/uber-iccas/?lang=en.

43. See www.iccas.de/forschung/?lang=en.

44. See de.wikipedia.org/wiki/Kai_Simons.

45. See www.nature.com/nature/journal/v413/n6853/full/nj6853–04a0.html.

46. See www.mpi-cbg.de.

47. See www.tzdresden.de/bioz-location.html.

48. See www.oncoray.de.

49. See www.crt-dresden.de/about.html.

50. See www.ipfdd.de/mbc.

51. See www.bionection.de/programme/format.

52. See www.biotype.de.

53. See www.qualitype.de, and www.rotop-pharmaka.de/en/our-products.

54. So bold and controversial that it drove the then-CEO to suicide before success became clear.

55. Interview with Harri Posti at the University of Oulu, Finland, on September 6, 2013.

56. See www.bme.oulu.fi.

57. See also Ryuji Kohno, University of Oulu Research Institute, "R&D, Standard, and Regulation of Medical Body Area Network (BAN)," 2013 European Connected Health Alliance Leadership Summit, Oulu, June 12, 2013. The quotation is from an interview with Tuula Palmen on September 6, 2013.

58. "Invest in Finland," *Health Care and Wellbeing News*, April 25, 2013.

59. Based on interviews with Seppo Kopsala in Oulu, September 5–6, 2013, and subsequent e-mail correspondence.

60. Medical device makers have revenues over $1 billion. See "The Medical Device Industry in the United States," *Select USA*, at selectusa.commerce.gov /industry-snapshots/medical-device-industry-united-states. Most medical technology companies can be found in California, Florida, New York, Pennsylvania, Michigan, Massachusetts, Illinois, Minnesota, and Georgia, as well as Washington, Wisconsin, and Texas. See also Yair Holtzman, "The U.S. Medical Device Industry in 2012: Challenges at Home and Abroad," MDDI (Medical Device and Diagnostic Industry), July 17, 2012.

61. Ibid.

62. Statistics for medical technology in Europe are by Eucomed, the association of the European medical devices industries (www.eucomed.be/about-us). See www.eucomed.org/uploads/Modules/Publications/the_emti_in_fig_broch_12 _pages_v09_pbp.pdf.

Chapter 5: A Smarter World

1. Pilita Clark, "Global Carbon Emissions Stall in 2014," *Financial Times*, March 12, 2015.

2. Shale gas—which can be found in abundance in the United States, Mexico, Argentina, Russia, China, and many other countries—has dramatically changed the energy picture because both oil and gas have become abundant rather than scarce and thus have dropped sharply in price, defying previous expectations. Environmental groups and others that oppose shale gas in the United States have cited heavy water use, groundwater pollution, methane emissions, the risk of minor earthquakes caused by hydraulic drilling, and the dangers of transporting shale oil by train, made necessary because of the lack of adequate pipelines. In Europe, political opposition has been far more intense than the pushback in the United States. Opposition has not, however, had much effect on drilling. The increase in shale oil has made the United States far less dependent on foreign oil and gas, and power companies have been able to move away from coal, which is a much dirtier source of carbon-based fuel. Still, shale gas is viewed by many as a "bridge" source of energy, its production justifiable only until alternative sources such as solar become less expensive and more practical for widespread use.

3. "Tesla's New Product Is a Battery for Your Home," *CNN Money*, May 1, 2015.

4. Interview with Prescott Logan and company management on August 22, 2013.

5. Curt Woodward, "After Five Years and $50 Million, 24M Unveils New Design for Lithium-Ion Batteries," *Boston Globe* (BetaBoston), July 22, 2015.

6. MIT News, Fortune.com, Navigant Research, 24M, Quartz.com. For Venkat Viswanathan's quote, see David Chandler, "New Manufacturing Approach Slices Lithium-Ion Battery Costs in Half," *MIT News*, June 23, 2015. Also Katie Fehrenbacher, "This Start-up Is Looking to Revolutionize Lithium-Ion Batteries," *Fortune* magazine, June 22, 2015.

7. See www.shell.com/global/future-energy/inside-energy/inside-energy-stories /could-sun-charged-batteries-power-our-homes.

8. See www.edison-net.dk.

9. On October 14, 2015, Tesla provided a software update to Tesla car owners that was a significant step toward the dream of a self-driving car. It is quite an amazing experience for the driver—after activating the advanced cruise control with a simple double click—to sit in the car on the highway without touching the steering wheel and watch how the car comfortably keeps its lane, smoothly changes lanes to pass other cars, slows and speeds up with the traffic, stops gradually as the car in front stops, reacts fast in an emergency, and even finds a parking spot. The driver must still take the wheel when changing to a different road or when road conditions are poor. It is virtually certain that other carmakers will follow soon.

10. See www.darpa.mil.

11. *New York Times*, interview with Christopher Urmson, May 27, 2014.

12. See www.bloomberg.com.

13. On the Apple Car, see www.MacRumors.com and Daiske Wakabayashi, "Apple Targets Electric-Car Shipping Date for 2019," *Wall Street Journal*, September 21, 2015.

14. See www.micreos.com website and Gina Kolata, "In Good Health? Thank You 100 Trillion Bacteria," *New York Times* (International), June 13, 2012; also "Rising to Meet the Infectious Disease Challenge," *Pharmafocus* (July–August 2015), which cites ESCMID president Murat Akova as saying that "the rapid increase in antimicrobial resistance in Europe and the world is jeopardizing modern health care."

15. See www.themato.nl/gesloten-kas.

16. See www.kubo.nl/en/productconcepten/artikel/ultra-clima-greenhouse-en.

17. Tim Linden, "Houweling's Continues to Pioneer Sustainability Efforts," *Produce News*, August 11, 2015.

18. See www.newscenter.philips.com/main/standard/news/press/2014/2014 0509-philips-and-green-sense-farms-usher-in-new-era-of-indoor-farming .wpd#.VClnuvl_tSo.

19. See www.usa.philips.com/a-w/government/articles-and-solutions/lighting /increasing-food-security-and-reducing-carbon-emissions.html.

20. See www.delaval.com, and www.lely.com.

21. In 2001, Emmo Meijer was the first CTO of DSM, the Dutch health nutrition and materials company. In 2005, he switched to Unilever, the British-Dutch food and personal care company. In 2011, he joined Friesland Campina; he retired mid-2014.

22. Interview with Emmo Meijer, August 2012, Amersfoort; all other Meijer quotes in this chapter are from this interview.

23. See strp.nl/nl.

24. See www.tekes.fi/en/-the Finish Agency that finances innovation.

25. See www.pt-it.pt-dlr.de/de/3069.php.

Chapter 6: Awakening the Beauties

1. "Economists Are Asked by Brussels to Hammer Together a New 'Innovation' Model," *Het Financieele Dagblad*, August 9, 2015.

2. Robert Solow, "We'd Better Watch Out," *New York Times Book Review*, July 12, 1987.

3. Cited in an interview on June 26, 2013, with Alexandra Kwit, a Johns Hopkins graduate student working with high-throughput screening robots as part of a joint NIH-Johns Hopkins project. Ncats.nih.gov is the website of the National Institutes of Health, National Center for Advanced Translational Sciences (NCATS). Francis Collins helped showcase NCATS's high-throughput screening facility with its multi-armed robots that can perform tests of potential drugs in one week—tests that would take a scientist twelve years to do manually.

4. Both speaking at the conference "The Future of Work in the Age of the Machine," held at the National Press Club, Washington, DC, the Hamilton Project and the Brookings Institution, February 19, 2015.

5. Stavey Vanek Smith, "When It Comes to Buying Decisions, Why Feelings Come First," *Planet Money*, National Public Radio, April 17, 2015.

6. Jake Rocheleau, "The 20 Top Coworking Spaces in the United States," *Hongkiat*, at www.hongkiat.com/blog/top-coworking-spaces-usa.

7. Bruce Katz and Julie Wagner, "The Rise of Innovation Districts," Brookings Institution, June 2014.

8. Anthony Carnevale, speech at New Futures, Washington, DC, October 7, 2014, based on his Georgetown University study, "Recovery: Job Growth and Education Requirements Through 2020," February 2014.

9. Deloitte and the Manufacturing Institute, "The Skills Gap in US Manufacturing," October 17, 2011, cited in "Future of the Manufacturing Workforce Report," *Manpower.*

10. William C. Symonds, Robert Schwartz, and Ronald F. Ferguson, "Pathways to Prosperity: Meeting the Challenge of Preparing Young Americans for the Twenty-First Century," Pathways to Prosperity Project, Harvard University Graduate School of Education, 2011.

11. Conference at the Brookings Institution on "Skills and Industry: A New American Model," May 22, 2014, Washington, DC.

12. Visit to TEC-SMART and interview with Penny Hill on August 21, 2014.

13. All David Larkin quotes in this chapter are from a telephone interview on August 25, 2014.

14. Conference at the Brookings Institution on "Skills and Industry" and discussion afterward, May 22, 2014.

15. Interview with Dr. Jan Stefan Roell, CEO of Zwick Roell, at the factory in Ulm, September 9, 2013.

16. Interview with Engelbert Westkämper in Stuttgart, September 9, 2013.

17. National Education Statistics for 2013.

18. Telephone interview with Martin Frädrich on September 24, 2013.

19. The Story of Google is told by David Hart, "On the Origins of Google," August 17, 2004, National Science Foundation, Where Discoveries Begin, at www.nsf.gov/discoveries/disc_summ.

20. Cited in Robert D. Atkinson and Stephen J. Ezell, *Innovation Economics: The Race for Global Advantage* (New Haven: Yale University Press, 2012). See also EY Global, "Venture Capital Insights and Trends 2014."

21. National Science Foundation website, www.nsf.gov/statistics/nsb0803.

22. National Science Foundation, Science and Engineering Indicators 2014 (for the year 2011), Table 4-14 and Table 4-6. Based on PPP (purchasing power parity) data for 2011 from the National Science Foundation, *Science and Engineering Indicators 2014.* Only France spends more of its total R&D on basic research (25 percent), compared with 17–18 percent for the United States and Korea, 12 percent for Japan, and a much lower 5 percent for China.

23. See www.systemsX.ch.

24. National Science Foundation, Science and Engineering Indicators 2014 (for the year 2011). The largest contributor to applied research funding in 2011 was business (53 percent), followed by the federal government (37 percent), nonprofit organizations (5 percent), academia (4 percent), and nonfederal governments (1 percent).

25. Ibid.

26. Battelle Memorial Institute, 2014 *Global R&D Funding Forecast.* Total spending on R&D of $465 billion (est.) in 2014 was far more than the European Union's $313 billion ($188 billion for Germany, France, and the UK), China's $284 billion, Japan's $165 billion, or South Korea's $63 billion. China aspires to be a knowledge economy rather than just a manufacturing base and wants to reach that goal by 2020, with plans to equal R&D spending of the United States by 2022 at $600 billion. China has already surpassed R&D spending of Japan, and its patent applications and scientific publications have grown more rapidly than those in the United States and Europe. However, just as Chinese economic growth has slowed from double digits, the growth of R&D investment has roughly halved from 24 percent in 2007.

27. According to Ernst & Young Global's *Venture Capital Insights and Trends 2014,* in 2013 venture capital raised $33 billion in the United States, $7.4 billion in Europe, and $3.5 billion in China, providing on average $4 million to each company in the United States, $2 million in Europe, and $7 million in China. In the same year, there were 74 VC-backed IPOs in the United States, 15 in Europe, and 15 in China, raising $8.2 billion, $0.6 billion, and $2 billion, respectively.

28. Interview with Alec Rauschenbusch at his office in Stuttgart on September 10, 2013.

29. Ernst & Young Global, *Venture Capital Insights and Trends 2014.*

30. Jeffrey Bussgang, *Mastering the VC Game* (Portfolio, 2010).

31. Ibid.

32. VC firms also briefly flourished in places like Minneapolis and the Research Triangle in North Carolina but pulled back their horns after the dot-com bust and now operate mostly from the West and East Coasts.

33. According to the National Venture Capital Association, venture capital firms (including corporate venture capital) invested $615 billion in 78,000 companies between 1995 and 2014.

34. See Matt Egan, "In-Q-Tel: A Glimpse Inside the CIA's Venture-Capital Arm," FoxBusiness, June 14, 2013.

35. Named after "Q," the MI6 agent who develops all of the high-tech gadgets in the *James Bond* films.

36. Brian Dunbar, "NASA Forms Partnership with Red Planet Capital, Inc.," *NASA,* September 20, 2006, at www.nasa.gov/home/hqnews/2006/sep /HQ_06317_red_capital.html.

37. This Frey quote and others in the chapter come from an interview with Kip Frey in Durham, North Carolina, on April 22, 2014. He retired in 2014. During the 1990s, Frey ran three start-up companies—Ventana Communications Group, Accipiter, and OpenSite Communications—that were each acquired at large multiples of the capital invested in them. He is also an adjunct

professor at the Sanford School of Public Policy at Duke University. See "Kip Allen Frey," Wikipedia, at en.wikipedia.org/wiki/Kip_Allen_Frey.

38. Medtronic, Annual Report 2013.

39. Interview during lunch with Norman Dann at Marriott Hotel in Minneapolis, Minnesota, on July 31, 2013, and follow-up phone call on September 2, 2014.

40. Notable examples include Dave McClure, an early investor in PayPal and Facebook, and Marc Andreessen, who founded Netscape.

41. Typically, VC firms also insist on a clear exit strategy within seven years, as their accountability to their investors means that they often avoid early stage investments because of their risk, limited returns, and time consumption.

42. "Angel investor," Wikipedia at en.wikipedia.org/wiki/Angel_investor.

43. "Statistics Compendium," European Trade Association for Business Angels, Seed Funds, and other Early Stage Market Players, 2014.

44. Ernst & Young Global, Venture Capital Insights and Trends 2014.

45. "Ten Crowdfunding Success Stories to Love," *Entrepreneur*, March 18, 2014.

46. "Economic Impact and Technological Progress of NASA Research and Development Expenditures: Volume 1: Executive Report," *Midwest Research Institute*, 1988.

47. The Tauri Group, "NASA Socio-Economic Impacts," 2013, at www.nasa.gov/sites/default/files/files/SEINSI.pdf.

Conclusion: We Meet at the End

1. Statistics from National Institute of Food and Agriculture, US Department of Agriculture.

2. Marc Levinson, "Job Creation in the Manufacturing Revival," Congressional Research Service report, June 19, 2013.

3. Erik Brynjolfsson and Andrew McAfee, *Race Against the Machine: How the Digital Revolution Is Accelerating Innovation, Driving Productivity, and Irreversibly Transforming Employment and the Economy* (Lexington, MA: Digital Frontier Press, 2011).

4. Levinson, "Job Creation in the Manufacturing Revival."

5. According to robotics analyst Dan Kara, there are only 800,000 manual labor jobs in manufacturing involved in simple, nonskilled tasks with light payloads. See Dan Kara, "Rethink Robotics: Unpacked," *Robotics Business Review*, October 1, 2012.

6. Levinson, "Job Creation in the Manufacturing Revival."

7. It will, however, be threatening to millions of basic manufacturing jobs in emerging economies.

8. Heritage Foundation and Bureau of Labor Statistics. Cited in James Sherk, "Not Looking for Work: Why Labor Force Participation Has Fallen During the Recovery," September 4, 2014, at www.heritage.org/research/reports/2014/09/not-looking-for-work-why-labor-force-participation-has-fallen-during-the-recovery. The labor force participation has come down from 66 percent in 2007 to just below 63 percent.

9. Enrico Moretti, *The New Geography of Jobs* (New York: Mariner Books, 2012).

10. Vladimir Ilyich Lenin, August 11, 1918.

11. "DNA-Editing Leap Brings Call for Ban," *New York Times* (International), March 21–22, 2015.

BIBLIOGRAPHY

Books

Atkinson, Robert D., and Stephen J. Ezell. *Innovation Economics*. New Haven: Yale University Press, 2012.

Barber, Benjamin R. *Mayors Ruled the World: Dysfunctional Nations, Rising Cities*. New Haven: Yale University Press, 2013.

Berger, Suzanne. *Making in America: From Innovation to Market*. Cambridge: MIT Press, 2013.

Blom, Philip. *The Wars Within: Life and Culture in the West, 1918–1938*. London: Atlantic Books, 2014.

Brouwer, Jaap Jan, and Guido van der Zwan. *The Dutch Industrial Landscape: Fifty Inspiring Business Cases*. The Hague: Dutch Government Publication, 2011.

Brynjolfsson, Erik, and Andrew McAfee. *The Second Machine Age*. New York: Norton, 2014.

———. *Wired for Innovation*. Cambridge: MIT Press, 2009.

———, and Andrew McAfee. *Race Against the Machine*. Lexington, KY: Digital Frontier Press, 2011.

Bussgang, Jeffrey. *Mastering the VC Game*. New York: Portfolio, Penguin Group, 2010.

Comfort, Nicholas. *The Slow Death of British Industry: A Sixty-Year Suicide, 1952–2012*. London: Biteback Publishing, 2013.

Cortada, James W. *The Digital Flood: The Diffusion of Information Technology Across the US, Europe, and Asia*. New York: Oxford University Press, 2012.

Dauch, Richard E. *American Drive: How Manufacturing Will Save Our Country*. New York: St. Martin's Press, 2012.

Gertner, Jon. *The Idea Factory*. New York: Penguin Books, 2012.

Gladwell, Malcolm. *The Story of Success*. New York: Little Brown, 2008.

Isaacson, Walter. *The Innovators*. New York: Simon and Schuster, 2014.

Katz, Bruce, and Jennifer Bradley. *The Metropolitan Revolution*. Washington, DC: Brookings, 2013.

Khanna, Parag. *Charting a Course to the Next Renaissance*. New York: Random House, 2011.

Liveries, Andrew N. *Make It in America: The Case for Reinventing the Economy*. Hoboken: John Wiley and Sons, 2011.

Moretti, Enrico. *The New Geography of Jobs*. New York: First Mariner Books, 2013.

Pisano, Gary P., and Willy C. Shih. *Producing Prosperity: Why America Needs a Manufacturing Renaissance*. Boston: Harvard Business Review Press, 2012.

Schmitt, Eric, and Jared Cohen. *The New Digital Age*. New York: Knopf, 2013.

Reports

Battelle Memorial Institute and R&D Magazine. "Global R&D Funding Forecast 2014." December 2013.

Center for American Progress. "Sequestering American Innovation." December 2013.

Council on Competitiveness. "Global Manufacturing Competitiveness Index." Deloitte Study, 2010.

———. "Ignite 1.0: Voice of American CEOs on Manufacturing Competitiveness." 2011.

Greenstone, Michael, and Adam Looney. "A Dozen Economic Facts About Innovation." The Hamilton Project, August 2011.

Information Technology and Innovation Foundation. "Federally Supported Innovations: Twenty-Two Examples of Major Technology Advances That Stem from Federal Research Support." January 2014.

Katz, Bruce, and Julie Wagner. "The Rise of Innovation Districts." Brookings Institution, June 2014.

Labaye, Eric, Svent Smit, Eckart Windhagen, Richard Dobbs, Jan Mischke, and Matt Stone. "A Window of Opportunity for Europe." McKinsey Global Institute, June 2015.

Lebedur, Larry, and Jill Taylor. "Akron, Ohio." Brookings Metropolitan Policy Program, September 2008.

Levinson, Marc, "Job Creation in the Manufacturing Revival." Washington, DC: Congressional Research Service, June 19, 2013, updated July 2, 2015.

Manyika, James, Susan Lund, Byron Auguste, Lenny Mendonca, Tim Welsh, and Sreenivas Ramaswamy. "An Economy That Works: Job Creation and America's Future." McKinsey Global Institute, June 2011.

McKinsey Global Institute. "Disruptive Technologies: Advances That Will Transform Life, Business and the Global Economy." July 2014.

Milken Institute. "Manufacturing 2.0: A More Prosperous California." June 2009.

Muro, Mark, Jonathan Rothwell, Scott Andes, Kenan Fikri, and Siddarth Kulkarni. "America's Advanced Industries: What They Are, Where They Are, and Why They Matter." Washington, DC: Brookings Institution, February 2015.

National Research Council. "Rising to the Challenge, US Innovation Policy for the Global Economy, 2012."

President's Council of Advisors on Science and Technology. "Report to the President on Capturing Domestic Competitive Advantage in Advanced Manufacturing." July 2012.

———. "Report to the President on Ensuring American Leadership in Advanced Manufacturing." June 2011.

Sirkin, Harold, Michael Zinser, and Douglas Hohner. "Made in America, Again: Why Manufacturing Will Return to the US." Chicago: Boston Consulting Group, August 2011.

Török, Reka. "Innovation Landscapes: A Study on Innovation Approaches in Three Selected EU States—Germany, Finland, and the UK." Brussels: European Commission, 2012.

US Department of Commerce. "The Competitiveness and Innovative Capacity of the United States." January 2012.

———. "The Innovative and Entrepreneurial University." 2011.

Articles

Andes, Scott, and Mark Muro. "Don't Blame Robots for Lost Manufacturing Jobs." Brookings Institution, April 29, 2015.

Bakker, Fred. "Biotech Bloeit Rondom Zurich." *Het Financieele Dagblad*, July 4, 2014.

———. "Eindhoven Valley: Hoe een Dorp de Slimste Regio ter Wereld Werd." *Het Financieele Dagblad*, April 6, 2013.

———. "Tweede Leven voor Zweedse Broedplaats." *Het Financieele Dagblad*, July 4, 2014.

———. "De Wederopstanding van de Industrie in de VS." *Het Financieele Dagblad*, May 4, 2013.

Bessen, James. "No, Technology Is Not Going to Destroy the Middle Class." *Washington Post*, October 21, 2013.

"Brainbox Nation." Special Report: America's Competitiveness. *Economist*, March 16, 2013.

Cao, Cong. "Patent Picture Overblown: China May Lead the World in Patents, but They Are Not Necessarily Innovative." *China Daily–Africa Weekly*, March 1–7, 2013.

"Cheer Up." Special Report: America's Competitiveness. *Economist*, March 16, 2013.

Cukierman, Kenneth, and Viktor Mayer-Schoenberger. "The Rise of Big Data." *Foreign Affairs*, May–June 2013.

Fallows, James. "Alan Tonelson: The Insourcing Boom That Isn't." *Atlantic*, December 2012.

Fikri, Kenan, and Mark Muro. "Fifteen Hottest New Advanced Industry Places." Washington, DC: Brookings Institution, June 8, 2015.

Fishman, Charles. "The Insourcing Boom." *Atlantic*, December 2012.

Greenblatt, Drew. "Six Ways Robots Create Jobs." *Inc.com*, January 22, 2013.

Grove, Andy. "How America Can Create Jobs." *Bloomberg Businessweek*, July 1, 2010.

Johnston, Louis. "History Lessons: Understanding the Decline in Manufacturing." *Minnpost*, February 22, 2012.

Luxenberg, Stan. "The R&D Advantage." *Merrill Lynch Advisor*.

McKinsey. "Building the Supply Chain of the Future." *McKinsey Quarterly*, January 21, 2011.

Muro, Mark, and Siddarth Kulkarni. "Yes, Advanced Industries Are Providing Jobs to Americans." the Brookings Institution, February 25, 2015.

Rattner, Steven. "The Myth of Industrial Rebound." *New York Times*, January 26, 2014.

Robert, Edward, and Charles Easley. "Entrepreneurial Impact: The Role of MIT." MIT Sloan School of Management, February 2009.

Senate Budget Committee. "Protecting American Innovation." Available at www.budget.senate.gov.

van Agtmael, Antoine. "The End of the Asian Miracle." *Foreign Policy Magazine*, June 11, 2012.

———. "Good Times Made Bad Habits." *Newsweek*, March 2008.

———, and Fred Bakker. "Made in America. Again." *Foreign Policy Magazine*, March 28, 2014.

Webster, MaryJo. "Could a Robot Do Your Job?" *USA Today*, October 28, 2014.

Yangpeng, Zheng. "High-End Manufacturing Holds the Key." *China Daily–Africa Weekly*, March 1–7, 2013.

INDEX

ANTOINE VAN AGTMAEL is senior adviser at Garten Rothkopf, a public policy advisory firm in Washington, DC. He was the principal founder, CEO, and CIO of Emerging Markets Management LLC; previously he was deputy director of the capital markets department of the International Finance Corporation (IFC), where he coined the term "emerging markets"; and a division chief in the World Bank's borrowing operations. Antoine is the author of *The Emerging Markets Century* (Free Press, 2007) and *Emerging Securities Markets* (Euromoney, 1984). He was an adjunct professor at Georgetown Law Center and taught at the Harvard Institute of Politics. Van Agtmael is a trustee of the Brookings Institution as well as co-chair of its International Advisory Council. He is a board member of Magnum Photos, the Smithsonian's Freer-Sackler Gallery, and the NPR Foundation (where he was the chair and a board member of NPR). He is on the President's Council on International Activities at Yale University and a member of the Council on Foreign Relations. He has an MBA from the New York University Stern School of Business, an MA from Yale University, and an undergraduate degree from the Netherlands School of Economics/Erasmus University. *Photograph by Peter van Agtmael/Magnum*

FRED BAKKER, until his recent retirement, was a journalist specializing in monetary and financial affairs with *Het Financieele Dagblad*, the *"Financial Times* of Holland," serving as deputy editor, editor in chief, and CEO. In addition to his writing and editing duties, he helped expand the company from a newspaper publisher to a multimedia company, developing several websites, a business-news radio channel, and a quarterly business magazine, *FD Outlook,* and he established FD*Intelligence*. *Photograph by Binh Tran*

PublicAffairs is a publishing house founded in 1997. It is a tribute to the standards, values, and flair of three persons who have served as mentors to countless reporters, writers, editors, and book people of all kinds, including me.

I. F. Stone, proprietor of *I. F. Stone's Weekly*, combined a commitment to the First Amendment with entrepreneurial zeal and reporting skill and became one of the great independent journalists in American history. At the age of eighty, Izzy published *The Trial of Socrates*, which was a national bestseller. He wrote the book after he taught himself ancient Greek.

Benjamin C. Bradlee was for nearly thirty years the charismatic editorial leader of *The Washington Post*. It was Ben who gave the *Post* the range and courage to pursue such historic issues as Watergate. He supported his reporters with a tenacity that made them fearless and it is no accident that so many became authors of influential, best-selling books.

Robert L. Bernstein, the chief executive of Random House for more than a quarter century, guided one of the nation's premier publishing houses. Bob was personally responsible for many books of political dissent and argument that challenged tyranny around the globe. He is also the founder and longtime chair of Human Rights Watch, one of the most respected human rights organizations in the world.

. . .

For fifty years, the banner of Public Affairs Press was carried by its owner Morris B. Schnapper, who published Gandhi, Nasser, Toynbee, Truman, and about 1,500 other authors. In 1983, Schnapper was described by *The Washington Post* as "a redoubtable gadfly." His legacy will endure in the books to come.

Peter Osnos, *Founder and Editor-at-Large*